THE CHINESE ECONOMY

WORLD ECONOMIES

A series of concise modern economic histories of the world's most important national economies. Each book explains how a country's economy works, why it has the shape it has, and what distinct challenges it faces. Alongside discussion of familiar indicators of economic growth, the coverage extends to well-being, inequality and corruption, to provide a fresh and more rounded understanding of the wealth of nations.

PUBLISHED

Stephen L. Morgan
THE CHINESE ECONOMY

Matthew Gray
THE ECONOMY OF THE GULF STATES

Matthew McCartney
THE INDIAN ECONOMY

Vera Zamagni
THE ITALIAN ECONOMY

Hiroaki Richard Watanabe
THE JAPANESE ECONOMY

The Chinese Economy

Stephen L. Morgan

agenda
publishing

First edition published in 2021 by Agenda Publishing

Agenda Publishing Limited
The Core
Bath Lane
Newcastle Helix
Newcastle upon Tyne
NE4 5TF

www.agendapub.com

ISBN 978-1-78821-080-5 (hardcover)
ISBN 978-1-78821-081-2 (paperback)

British Library Cataloguing-in-Publication Data
A catalogue record for this book is available from the British Library

Typeset by Patty Rennie

Printed and bound in the UK by
CPI Group (UK) Ltd, Croydon, CR0 4YY

Contents

Acknowledgements

No book is done alone. We build on the work of others who are for the most part listed in the bibliography, although some will escape citation because of memory or space, so my apologies in advance for omissions. My thanks to the invitation from Agenda Publishing to submit a proposal for their World Economies series, and the patience of Andrew Lockett and Steven Gerrard when my university role and Chinese politics got in the way of me delivering. I liked that Agenda did not want a conventional book on the Chinese economy, but one that was in my thinking an economic history of the reform period and the future; a story about China's re-emergence as a global economic and political power, combining economic history, an analysis of the economy as well as government and business, and topics including inequalities, urbanization, consumption, energy, the environment, science and technology, and the quest for innovation. And with an eye to the future; history is ultimately a story about the future, not the past; history is focused on how the past has shaped the present in which we as historical actors ourselves will make tomorrow.

Writing this book has been a journey back to my youth and interest in Asia as an Australian growing up during the Indochina wars, which led me to study Southeast Asia, China, and the Chinese and Indonesian languages. I have been a first-hand observer of economic reform in China from a month-long visit in 1981 as a journalist, subsequent stays as a graduate student and journalist in the 1980s and 1990s, and most recently as a part of the senior management team of the University of Nottingham's Ningbo Campus, south of Shanghai. Along the way I have met many Chinese whose life and experiences have been shared with me. They go unrecorded here for obvious reasons in these increasingly fraught times in China, but not without my gratitude.

Among those I want to thank specifically, firstly, the research assistance of Rachel Song, who worked hard to respond to the requests and probing from me as we pulled together the data that underpins Chapters 3–6. It was a pleasure to work again with Annelieke Vries who drew front map of China's provinces and the map of the mega-city regions. I am grateful for colleagues and friends who have shared their input at different times or read chapters or the book in full: Kerry Brown, Cong Cao, Markus Eberhart, John Evans, Tracey Fallon, Lauren Johnson, Martin Lockett, Debin Ma, Yasmin Morgan, Gregory Moore, David O'Brien, Thomas Rawski, Xiaoling Zhang and Minghai Zhou. A theme running through the book is the relationship between innovation, political culture and economic growth, which has been presented in keynotes, lectures, seminars and conference papers between 2016 and 2019. I thank participants at the International Conference on Institutional Economics at Xiamen University, the Asian Historical Economics Conference at the University of Hong Kong, the joint All UC Economic History Group and Asian Pacific Economic and Business History Conference at the Californian Institute of Technology, the Jiangnan Research Group Conference at UNNC and the Nottingham University Business School (China) Annual Research Conference at UNNC. The usual disclaimer applies to errors.

Completing a book on the Chinese economy in 2020 has been a huge challenge. China and the world economy were thrown into chaos by the coronavirus pandemic that emerged in central China in late 2019, wreaked havoc in China in the early months of 2020 and pushed the world into the worst recession since the end of the Second World War. At the end of the year China was well on the way to recovery, notwithstanding recurring breakouts of the virus, while the rest of the world struggled with a devastating third wave of infection just as the newly developed vaccines, which bring hope for a return to normality, were being rolled out. The final chapter all too briefly summarises 2020 and its consequences from the too close vantage point of mid-January 2021 and tries to put in perspective the implications for China. Of the one thing we can be sure is that the effects of the pandemic will reverberate for years to come, not only for China but for all countries, changing economies, polities and international relations.

Lastly, I am as always in debt to Indah who has accompanied me on our sojourns in space and time between Australia, Britain, Indonesia, China, Hong Kong and Taiwan, and our girls Yasmin and Zara who wonderfully adjusted to moving from Australia to Britain and then China where they both completed their high school years. And the support of our son Roby who made his way into adulthood as we headed off to Britain with his sisters.

STEPHEN L. MORGAN

Note on Romanization, pronunciation and currency

The *pinyin* system of transliteration (Romanization) adopted by the PRC is used throughout with some exceptions for individuals who might be better known by another form, such as Chiang Kai-shek instead of Jiang Jieshi, and organizations that retain non-pinyin spelling, such as Peking University or Tsinghua University.

Pronunciation is difficult for some sounds in Mandarin Chinese because there is no direct counterpart in English, which is the reason Romanization is an imperfect match. The "zh" as in the name Zhang or Zhou is an unaspirated "ch" much like a soft "j" for Joe in English. The "x" as in the name Xi Jinping is pronounced a bit like "sh" as in she. In the Wade–Giles Romanization, Xi becomes Hsi. The "q" is pronounced like an aspirated "ch". The Chinese family name precedes the given name, as in Li Keqiang, but where a Chinese author publishes in English the given name may appear in front of the family name, Keqiang Li.

The PRC currency unit is known as the people's money, *renminbi* (RMB) and the unit is the yuan (¥). In mid-2020, one US dollar bought about 7 yuan. Conversion of the yuan to US dollar equivalent between 1980 and 2020 is at the average reference exchange rate for the year in question based on the rate reported in the *China Statistical Yearbook*.

Tables and figures

FIGURES

Abbreviations

ABC	Agricultural Bank of China
ACFIC	All China Federation of Industry and Commerce
ACFTU	All China Federation of Trade Unions
AFC	Asian Financial Crisis, 1997–98
AMC	asset management company
ASEAN	Association of Southeast Asian Nations
BoC	Bank of China
BoCom	Bank of Communications
BRI	Belt and Road Initiative, also known as One Belt, One Road (OBOR)
CC	Central Committee (CPC)
CCB	China Construction Bank
CDB	China Development Bank
CDIC	Central Discipline Inspection Commission of the CPC
CFB	Chinese family business
CJV	contractual joint venture
CPC	Communist Party of China
CPPCC	Chinese People's Political Consultative Conference
CSY	Chinese Statistical Yearbook
EJV	equity joint venture
FDI	foreign direct investment
GDP	gross domestic product
GFC	Global Financial Crisis, 2008–09
GNI	gross national income

ICBC	Industrial and Commercial Bank of China
IMF	International Monetary Fund
LGFV	local government finance vehicle
MNE	multinational enterprise
MofCom	Ministry of Commerce
MOST	Ministry of Science and Technology
NPC	National People's Congress
NIE	newly industrialized economy
NRC	National Resources Commission
NSB	National Statistical Bureau (formerly known as the State Statistical Bureau)
OCP	one-child policy (1980–2016)
OECD	Organization of Economic Cooperation and Development
OFDI	outward (overseas) foreign direct investment
PBOC	People's Bank of China
PC	People's Congress, local level NPCs
PLA	People's Liberation Army
POE	private-owned enterprise
PPCC	People's Political Consultative Conference, local level CPPCCs
NPL	non-performing loans
NSB	National Statistical Bureau
PRC	People's Republic of China
R&D	research and development
S&T	science and technology
SASAC	State-owned Assets Supervision and Administration Commission
SC	Standing Committee
SGN	Shaanxi-Gansu-Ningxia Border Region
SME	small- and medium-sized enterprise
SOE	state-owned enterprise
TFR	total fertility rate
TVE	township and village enterprise
WFOE	wholly foreign owned enterprise
WHO	World Health Organization
WTO	World Trade Organization
WIPO	World Intellectual Property Organization

Map of China

Note: The insert shows the nine-dash line, a contested maritime zone in the South China Sea over which China claims sovereignty. Several countries in Southeast Asia also claim parts of these waters. In 2016, a tribunal under the United Nations Convention of the Law of the Sea concluded that China's maritime claim had no lawful effect. The publisher does not take a view on the merits of any jurisdictional claim.

1

Introduction: past and present

When I first went to China at the start of the 1980s it was a very poor country, poorer than much of the rest of Asia. Everyone was dressed in drab blues and greens, food and most consumer products – to the extent there were any – were rationed, and the traffic of the cities comprised throngs of many thousands of bicycles. The World Bank development indicators placed China in the late 1970s among the poorest countries in the world with a per capita income about the average for Sub-Saharan Africa.

Poor as China was, this was also an exciting time. The "Gang of Four", which was led by Mao Zedong's wife Jiang Qing and blamed for the excesses of the Cultural Revolution had been put on trial, and China was embarking on economic reforms. Markets were reviving, China was re-engaging with the world, minds were reopening, and the Chinese people were beginning to experience a new world of economic and personal freedoms they had not known for decades. At Nanjing University where I studied between 1982 and 1985, for example, all sorts of "salons" (*shalong*) sprouted up to debate western philosophies and theories, and the departments of sociology and psychology among others were restarted. Young Chinese were again going abroad in search of knowledge to serve China.

Fast forward 40 years and we arrive in a very different China, one with an upper-middle-income economy, which has a large urban middle class who can afford overseas holidays, modern cities and infrastructure, and whose political leaders are aggressively wanting to stamp China's vision on the future of the world economy and the system of global governance. The personal freedoms that had blossomed in the first three decades of reform after 1978 have been curtailed increasingly after 2008–09. The Communist Party of China (CPC) under General Secretary Xi Jinping has reasserted the authority of the party in all areas of life, preoccupied as it is with "stability maintenance" (*weiwen*) and its survival. Since 2011 the internal security budget has even exceeded that of defence, such is the party's fear of internal dissent (Shambaugh 2016: 63).

China's success in overcoming the worse of its past poverty and backwardness was announced to the world in 2010 when it overtook Japan to become the world's second-largest economy after the United States; measured in terms of purchasing power parity (PPP), which account for the differences in what money will buy in each country, China was the world's largest economy.[1] In the same year China also graduated into the ranks of the upper-middle-income group of countries. Both events signalled the huge progress that China had made since the late 1970s. The transformation was unparalleled. No country has sustained for so long such high economic growth, let alone one as big as China that accounts for one-fifth of the world's population. This chapter will first outline the contours of the economic and social change over the past four decades and summarize each chapter, and in the second half explore the long-run historical change from 1500 to *c*.1870 when China began to tackle the challenge it confronted from the economic and military might of an industrializing Europe.

CATCHING-UP

Between 1978 and the 2010s, market-oriented economic reforms and opening to the outside world unleashed latent capacity in many sectors, incentivized farmers and others, raised incomes and diminished poverty on a huge scale, and wrought huge institutional change. Deng

Xiaoping, the early reform period leader of the CPC who steered China out of the autarkic poverty of the planned economy, declared that getting rich was glorious. It was fine to enrich oneself and family. Many did, and some became fabulously wealthy. The rising tide of economic liberalization raised livelihoods of all Chinese. The phenomenal transformation however spawned a rapid increase in inequality from the mid-1980s. The unbridled economic growth and the all-consuming focus on GDP spawned an increase in air pollution that made some cities nearly unliveable at times, polluted waterways and poisoned agricultural land.

China's model for economic renewal was based on the experience of the "miracle" Newly Industrialized Economies (NIEs) of Asia – Taiwan, South Korea, Hong Kong and Singapore – that had built export-oriented manufacturing economies (Chowdhury & Islam 1993; World Bank 1993). The NIEs showed how the import of advanced technologies that China so desperately needed to revitalize the economy could be funded through manufactured exports. Foreign direct investment (FDI) would be encouraged, and contrary to the experience of Japan, China welcomed foreign firms. The inflow of FDI, technology and management know-how turned China into the factory to the world (*The Economist* 2010a). In the process, China radically changed the cost of manufactured products globally. Prices for consumer products fell in real terms, from simple manufactures such as textiles and toys to automobiles, computers, mobile phones and telecommunication equipment.

China was a major beneficiary of the openness of the global economy in the closing decades of the twentieth century (Naughton 2018). Consumer demand in advanced economies and global competition among firms transformed supply chains. Labour-intensive manufacturing after the 1970s was shifted increasingly from Western advanced economies to East Asia and developing economies, with each in turn taking on roles that befitted their combination of technological competencies and costs. Japan's automotive and electronic firms pioneered production networks in Asia in the 1980s, but American firms were not far behind (Hatch & Yamamura 1996). China became the final assembler of choice for many multinational enterprises and their supply-chain partners who set up shop in China. Core technologies, design and marketing remained at home, while production of intermediate and final products was outsourced to countries such as China.

Economic reforms reconfigured China's state-owned enterprises (SOEs). Their restructuring from the mid-1990s turned the largest central SOEs into global giants as they went offshore in search of resources, technologies and brands. They listed on the stock markets of Hong Kong, New York and elsewhere. Some soon were among the largest firms in the Fortune Global 500 list. Many smaller provincial and municipal SOEs were sold off or closed. In parallel the private sector re-emerged. At first, in the 1980s and 1990s, private firms hid under the "red hat", masquerading as collective or community-owned enterprises (Dickson 2008). As the economy and society liberalized, their position changed from one tolerated by the party-state to one encouraged as agents of growth. During the 2000s and 2010s, private firms were not only the most efficient in the economy, but also accounted for the lion's share of employment and output.

Despite the importance of the private sector, the largest state firms are privileged in their access to state-controlled resources (Lardy 2014, 2019; Yang & Morgan 2011). Since the mid-2010s reform of the state sector has ground nearly to a halt. Still, China has narrowed the gap with the world's advanced economies and continued to grow at a high rate for such a large country, above 6 per cent (to 2019), according to official statistics. The impact of the coronavirus pandemic in 2020 reduced GDP growth to 1–2 per cent, while the rest of the world went into recession. The income and technology gap with advanced economies in the long term will narrow further provided innovation can sustain growth in industry and services, but undoubtedly at a diminishing rate. Sustaining growth is a huge challenge, one that is discussed in several chapters and addressed in detail in Chapter 6.

Phenomenal as the changes to Chinese business, economy and society may appear, China has some way to go to become a rich and strong country (*fuqiang guo*). Certainly, it has been very successful in catching up. No country historically has sustained such a high level of economic growth for as many years as has China. The scale of the change – reduced poverty, improved livelihoods, modernized transport and urban infra-structure, and technological advancement – is impressive yet difficult to grasp. But the distance between China and the advanced economies of the world is greater than many imagine, both in and outside of China. Fig-ure 1.1 shows China's trajectory from a low-income economy in 1980 to an upper-middle-income economy in the 2010s. In 1980, China had per capita income of $220 compared with Japan's $8,810, West Germany's $11,730 and the United States' $10,630.[2] More than 80 per cent of the pop-ulation lived on or below the then poverty line. In 2019, only 0.4 per cent of the population was officially estimated to live in poverty (NSB 2020b).

Figure 1.1   China's path to an upper-middle-income economy

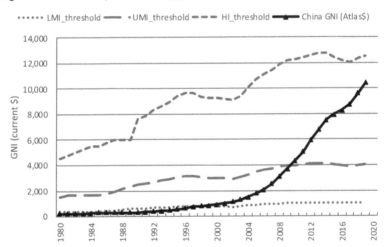

Notes: LMI = lower-middle-income threshold (countries below are poor); UMI = upper-middle-income threshold; HI = high-income threshold (rich, advanced economies). The money values are in current dollars and the measure is gross national income (GNI = GDP + net foreign income). World Bank Atlas GNI$ uses three years of exchange rates to smooth the GNI$ compared to exchange rate conversion for each year.

Source: World Bank, *World Development Indicators* (WDI), 1980–2016; https://data.worldbank.org/data-catalog/world-development-indicators; 2011–19 revised using WDI, July 2020 update.

Just how far has China come in transforming into a modern economy? Displacing Japan as number two is a good place to start to assess China relative to advanced economies. Modern economic development transforms the economy and society, including the structure of output (GDP), from predominantly agriculture to manufacturing and services; the structure of employment, from working in fields to working in factories and offices; and the place of residence, from villages and towns to cities and urban agglomerations. China entered the reform period with an unusual economy for a poor developing country thanks to Soviet-style industrialization of the 1950–70s. It had a large industry sector, dominated by heavy industry, accounting for almost half of GDP, while agriculture counted for 28 per cent and services just 22 per cent (CSY 2019: table 3.2). Industry is still today above 40 per cent of GDP, similar to Japan during its post-1950s high growth phase. In agriculture, China's share of GDP has fallen to about 7 per cent and the share of employment has shrunk from about 70 per cent to below 30 per cent, around the level Japan reached in 1960. Rapid service sector growth led it to eclipse industry's share of GDP in 2012 to account today for more than half of GDP and 45 per cent of all employment, which again is similar to the level of Japan in the 1960s (CSY 2019: tables 3.2, 4.2; Minami 1986, 1994).

These comparative measures of the structure of the economy suggest China is roughly where Japan was at the peak of its high-growth phase between 1960 and 1973, although per capita income and the technological level is relatively lower for China. Demographically there is another uncomfortable comparison. From the 1970s to 2010 China enjoyed a demographic dividend, as did Japan after the Second World War, but increasingly like Japan it faces the challenge of how to sustain economic growth with both a shrinking and ageing workforce, and one with a level of education similar to that of Japan in 1960 (see Table 5.4).

THE FRAMEWORK OF THE BOOK

My approach to China is informed by institutional economic history, with borrowings from political science and sociology. Political and economic institutions set the "rules of the game" (North 1990), the constraints that shape what is possible for the ways individuals and firms engage in economic exchange. Institutions structure incentives for individuals and ultimately shape how societies evolve over time. For many economic historians, institutions explain to a large extent the differences in economic growth and performance among countries far more than cultural traits or geographical endowments (Acemoglu & Johnson 2011).

In China, recurring periods of growth in the past have occurred in the presence of severe weaknesses in formal institutions. Property rights and personal security were often fragile. The imperial state could easily lay claim to assets, although in practice this was infrequent. In China today, the party-state exercises far-reaching authority over individuals and firms, whatever the constitution or formal laws might claim, and whether they are state or private owned. Institutions are undeveloped and even mediocre. From a comparative perspective it is difficult to account for China's success. Allen (2011: 144) suggested the appropriate question "is not 'why have China's mediocre market institutions performed better than central planning?', but rather 'why have its mediocre institutions worked as well as they have?'."

Part of the answer might lie in legacies of China's planned economy that underpinned early growth in the countryside. Another part lies in the role of informal institutions, which are the interpersonal networks of social relationships that form the fabric of Chinese business and social life. These have enabled the circumvention of the many constraints and penalties on individuals and firms that would otherwise arise from predatory state actions. But the reliance on social networks comes at a steep price, including pervasive uncertainty in economics and politics, inefficiency in factor use that inhibit innovation, big inequalities in the distribution of the benefits of recent economic growth and widespread corruption.

Approaching China is difficult. First, the scale is overwhelming. Continental in size, with 1.4 billion people, diversity within China cannot be ignored, but often is. Macro-level national data alone are inadequate to understand the country's economic and social development. Where practical, I will discuss the provincial and regional differences. Depending on from where you view China, the country has characteristics that range from an advanced economy to those of a very poor one. A short car journey from the bustling modern cities of Beijing, Shanghai and others in East China into the countryside might take you back two or more decades to a time of far lower levels of development.

Second, history matters in ways it seldom does for other countries. Of course, as many economists have rediscovered since the Global Financial Crisis (GFC) in 2008–09, history always matters for making sense of economic and financial change. For China and its party leaders, however, history infuses everything. Xi Jinping is fixated on realizing his two "centennial goals". The first goal is for China to become a moderately well-off society (*xiaokang shehui*) by 2021, the centenary of the founding of the CPC. The second is to make China a rich and strong country (*fuqiang guo*) by 2049, the centenary of the founding of the People's Republic of China (PRC). This "rejuvenation" (*fuxing*) of the nation would finally redress historical wrongs and reclaim China's place in human affairs as the dominant global economy. Only then will China have thrown off the "humiliations" inflicted on it by imperial powers between the First Opium War (1839–42) and the founding of the PRC in 1949.

Third, party politics is central to understanding contemporary China. The party-state's primary focus is survival. Regime preservation will always trump economic or social policy, whatever their merits. For three decades from 1980 it seemed as if the party-state had retreated as China transitioned from a planned economy to a market-oriented economy and global trading giant. Indeed, the state did step away from the administrative direction of the economy and allowed markets to operate increasingly – China grew out of the planned economy (Naughton 1996). Individuals have freedom to choose where to live, to work and to travel depending on their means that were unknown to the earlier generations of the PRC. Yet, overall party-state intervention in the economy is pervasive and its surveillance of everyday life has been empowered by new technologies.

Finally, a recurring theme in my analysis will be the challenge of innovation. How will China foster innovation for it to grow and to realize the 2049 centennial goal? The challenges are many and deep. Despite pumping money into education and research, narrowing the gap with the advanced economies is still a distant dream. The glistening cities of the eastern seaboard and the high-speed trains, road infrastructure and telecommunications that connect them, masks the low level of average human capital. Education on average is not to the level required. Moreover, party-state institutional constraints on a marketplace of ideas stifle the flow of information and the top-down direction of research does not bode well for making China a clever and innovative advanced economy.

OUTLINE OF CHAPTERS

The second half of this chapter takes us back into the Ming Dynasty (1368–1644) and the voyages of discovery when Europe found a maritime route to East Asia through to 1860s–70s when the Qing Dynasty (1644–1911) had been brought to the brink of collapse. Asia in 1500 accounted for two-thirds of world GDP; China and India produced a quarter each (Maddison 2001). Deep changes in Europe from the 1500s to the 1700s in institutions, science and the application of useful knowledge would forge a new type of economy, the Industrial Revolution, which by the 1800s had led to an increasing gap between China and the modernizing economies of northern Europe that has become known as the "Great Divergence" (Pomeranz 2000; Mokyr 2002, 2017; Vries 2015).

Chapter 2 explores the "long twentieth century" between the 1860s and the 2010s when China struggled to find a pathway to modern growth only to be undone time and time again. The mid-nineteenth century rebellions motivated modernization based on state sponsored ventures. China's defeat in the First Sino-Japanese War (1894–95) heralded a new phase of development where the private sector and foreign firms would drive growth. Shanghai and other cities boomed with factories. The Second Sino-Japanese War (1937–45) and the ensuing Civil War (1946–49) between the Nationalist and the Communist forces put growth on hold. Important legacies from the period, however, in state planning and state-run firms would influence subsequent decades.

In 1949, the PRC was founded. From 1953 to 1978 a Soviet-style planned economy was implemented, emphasizing heavy industry, extraction of agricultural surplus and compressed consumption. Political and economic chaos during the Great Leap Forward (1958–60), famine (1959–61) and the Cultural Revolution (1967–76) by the late 1970s left the Chinese people impoverished and the country falling further behind. In late 1978, China launched a programme of economic reform and opening to the world (*gaige kaifang*), which would transform it into a market-oriented and modern upper-middle-income economy.

The focus of Chapter 3 is the contemporary economy. It will present a scorecard of the China economy up to 2018, the fortieth anniversary of the policies to reform and open, including noting regional diversity, the differences between and within provinces. As already mentioned, in China we can find all levels of development: high-income cities in eastern China, many provinces with a middle-income status, and poor inland provinces that are mostly low-income economies. The diversity and disparities are a major challenge for state policy and development goals.

Diversity in contemporary China is similarly evident in government and business, the focus of Chapter 4. The structure and role of the party-state will be examined for the way it influences business, including corruption. The rest of the chapter is on business, beginning with a discussion of business culture and social networks. Next, the chapter will examine the re-emergence of the private sector and the restructuring of state-sector firms. By the 1990s, the private sector had become the mainstay of employment and economic growth. The state-owned sector was overhauled in the late 1990s and since the 2000s giant firms have been publicly listed, which catapulted some into the ranks of the world's largest companies. China is now second only to the United States in the number of firms ranked on the Fortune Global 500 list.

Chapter 5 focuses on inequality, health and welfare. Over the past four decades China went from one of the most equal societies in Asia to one of the most unequal. Big disparities exist in income, in access to education and in provision of healthcare within cities and between regions, between rural and urban populations, and between the 56 ethnic groups that comprise the Chinese nation. The national legislature, the National People's Congress, has dozens of US-dollar billionaires among its delegates. Yet overwhelmingly, the Chinese on average have experienced real gains. They are richer, taller and increasingly fatter; economic transformation has brought about an escape from poverty and chronic hunger and a lifestyle transition that gives China a morbidity and mortality profile similar to developed countries.

By the 2000s questions were being raised about the sustainability of China's economic modernization. Many cities were enshrouded in pollution, waterways were full of effluent, and farmland in places was poisoned with contaminants. Energy use and greenhouse gas emissions soared along with economic growth and domestic consumption. Chapter 6 will explore urbanization, consumerism, energy and the environment, and the prospects for fostering innovation. China is home to some of the world's largest urban agglomerations and over the next 20 years another 200 million people will move into cities where none have existed in the past. By that time more than one billion Chinese will be city dwellers compared with only 172 million in 1978.

The second half of Chapter 6 examines innovation, which is required to address the many challenges China faces if it is to sustain economic growth in ways that will deliver a higher living standard for all and make China wealthy and strong. This section will bring together threads from the previous chapters that have flagged challenges for sustaining future growth and fostering innovation. Three sets of constraints are identified. The first are demographic centred on the shrinking workforce and the ageing population. The second are related to state approaches to fostering research and science and the comparatively underdevelopment of human capital. The third are constraints inherent in the party-state and the country's political economy.

Before we turn to the present and recent past, we need to step back in time to grasp how China's re-emergence as a major economy in the late twentieth century is situated in the history of global capitalism, and the eclipse of China and other parts of Asia for several centuries after 1500. The "rise of the West" and the "decline" of China symbolized in the "humiliation" of the First Opium War are deeply ingrained in the psyche of the Chinese, which makes the recent reversal of past misfortune and impoverishment a source of great pride.

FALLING BEHIND, 1500–1860S

The voyages of discovery in the late fifteenth century ushered in the modern phase of globalization. Searching for a maritime route to "Cathay" (China) and the "Spice Islands" (modern day Indonesia), Christopher Columbus crossed the Atlantic to the Americas in 1492 and Vasco da Gama rounded the Cape of Good Hope to reach India in 1498. China and India in 1500 were the world's largest economies, of about equal size, and combined they equalled half of the estimated global GDP; in 1820, China counted for 32 per cent of global GDP, while India had slipped to 12 per cent (Maddison 2001, 2007, 2010). That was about to change.

The industrial revolution in England stimulated modern economic growth, the sustained increase in per capita income and the escape from the Malthusian world that had previously characterized human history. As the nineteenth century unfolded, an aggressive Europe with growing military might and hungry for resources and markets pushed into China. China's share of world GDP fell to 17 per cent by 1870 and just 4.5 per cent in 1950. India was 4.2 per cent the same year. From the mid-twentieth century to the late 1970s, China's share of world GDP barely increased.

The Ming–Qing period to the nineteenth century was largely one of economic expansion, if not per capita growth. Commerce and trade flourished, and a vibrant urban culture emerged. The population increased from about 70 million in 1400 to about 430 million in 1850. Brandt, Ma and Rawski (2014: 53) argue population growth occurred without an obvious decline in the standard of living: "The capacity of the Ming–Qing system to ward off diminishing returns rested on progressive intensification of agricultural rhythms, growing household and regional specialization, expanded transport systems and deepening markets for commodities, as well as the land and labor that produced them". Recent GDP estimates show to the contrary that per capita income fell precipitously during the eighteenth century to about 60 per cent of the 1700 level by 1800 (Broadberry *et al.* 2018).[3]

Of course, the tempo of economic development varied over such a long sweep of time. The interregnums between the change of dynasties were periods of civil war. Millions perished in fighting, famines and natural calamities at these times. Economic growth was muted at best for the first half of the Ming Dynasty (1368–1644) to 1500. The first Ming emperor Hongwu (*r.*1368–96) promoted an autarkic vision of village self-sufficiency, which shrank the market economy that had sustained prosperity since the eleventh century (von Glahn 2016; Liu 2015). Commutation of labour service to silver tax payment in the 1480s allowed more efficient use of labour. As a result, agricultural output rose, regional specialization resumed, and marketing of cotton, silk and porcelain revived long-distance trade. Commercialization propelled the growth of market towns, which multiplied throughout the more developed regions and into the nineteenth century (von Glahn 2016; Elvin 1973; Skinner 1977).

The major constraint on the Ming economy was a shortage of bronze coinage and silver. New discovery of silver in Japan in the 1530s led to large exports to China until Japan's seclusion policies in the 1630s. The Portuguese arrived in China in 1522 and bought porcelain with silver from the New World. Soon the Spanish followed. Their founding of Manila in 1571 inaugurated a direct trans-Pacific galleon trade in American silver, which was exchanged for silks, porcelain and other goods. As von Glahn (2016: 308) points out, the inflow of silver "after 1570 was a crucial catalyst for the explosive commercial growth of the late Ming period".[4] China was importing 115 tonnes or more in the first half of the seventeenth century. Half came from Japan and the rest from Mexico and Peru.

In addition to silver, New World foods – peanuts, potatoes and maize – were to have lasting beneficial effects. Sweet potatoes, for example, could be cultivated on poor land unsuitable for grain and their short growing period and high yield made them a famine reserve that helped to reduce social unrest during the Qing dynasty (Jia 2013). Commercial and urban growth brought not only prosperity, but also economic volatility, social conflict and political strife. To the North, the Manchu tribes were consolidating into a new state. Increased taxes for defence depressed the Ming economy. Peasant rebels seized Beijing in 1644, which was the pretext for the Manchu to intervene, conquer China and establish the Qing dynasty.

Economic recovery proved elusive for the new dynasty. Cold weather until the 1690s stalled agricultural recovery, reduced incomes and curtailed the demand for textiles and other goods. Silver inflows had dwindled in the 1640s and prices plummeted. The Manchu policies to consolidate rule worsened the economic malaise, such as the blockade of the Ming loyalist Zheng Chenggong (also known as Koxinga) in Taiwan. The Qing banned foreign trade and relocated inland the southeastern coastal population.

Only with the Qing capture of Taiwan in 1683 did recovery begin, silver inflow resume and the Qing state begin to expand money supply even more through the minting of bronze coinage, the medium of exchange in local markets. The period from the later part of the reign of the emperor Kangxi (r.1662–1722), his son Yongle (r.1723–35), grandson Qianlong (r.1736–95) and into the early Jiaqing reign (r.1796–1820) is lauded as an "age of prosperity" (shengshi). Long-distance trade revived, markets became highly integrated, the money supply expanded, prices steadily rose, and an unprecedented population boom occurred. Although scholarly estimates vary, the population grew from 140–150 million in 1700, equivalent to the Ming peak in the early 1600s, to around 340 million by 1800, and reached 410–430 million by the 1840s–50s (Brandt *et al.* 2014; Elliot 2009; von Glahn 2016; Broadberry *et al.* 2018). The period was one of relative peace, if we exclude the wars the emperor Qianlong waged around China's periphery. Qianlong extended Chinese rule to its farthest limits with the incorporation of Xinjiang ("new territories") in wars against the Dzungar (1755–59) and other campaigns, although the forays into Burma (1767–71) and Vietnam (1786–89) were disasters (Elliot 2009: 86–106; Purdue 2005; Millward 1998).

Growth and maturation of the domestic market in the eighteenth century is the singular most striking facet of the Qing economy. Interregional long-distance trade produced a high degree of market integration, which was comparable to the advanced parts of Europe around the middle of the eighteenth century (Shiue & Keller 2007; Bernhofen *et al.* 2015). Huge volumes of grain were shipped down the Yangzi River to the grain deficit lower Yangzi delta. From there, grain was sent north to Beijing as tribute for the Imperial Household and for private sale, and south to Fujian and Guangdong. Manufactured products from the lower Yangzi region were exchanged for rice from the middle and upper Yangzi. Soybean cake from Manchuria went south to fertilize the cotton and rice fields of the lower Yangzi. The predominantly private economy was made possible by institutional innovations such as lineage trusts, which pooled family resources; native-place merchant networks, which lowered transaction costs over distance; and new instruments for credit and exchange. Vibrant as this commerce was, large parts of rural China were bypassed. Only a small fraction of agricultural output entered into long-distance trade. But the scale of long-distance trade dwarfed that of Europe such as the Baltic wheat trade or European trade with Asia at the time.[5]

Big increases in population and agricultural output occurred in the middle and upper Yangzi River provinces (Hunan, Hubei and Sichuan), the Central Plains and the southern Fujian, Guangdong and Guangxi provinces. Even as early as the 1740s officials began to worry about population growth outstripping food production, driving up grain prices and inflicting environmental damage (Kishimoto 2010: 120–23). By 1800, migration and population growth had filled up the middle and upper Yangzi regions. Many had moved into uplands, often engaged in slash and burn cultivation of maize and sweet potatoes, which also led to conflicts with the upland non-Han Chinese people.

Ecological damage was huge. Deforestation incurred vast losses of topsoil from erosion, which silted waterways far afield. In the lowlands, riverbanks and lake edges were converted into fields and no longer the buffer for flood waters, which worsened with larger runoffs from deforested upland areas (von Glahn 2016: 321–2, 328–9, 363). Population growth in Sichuan, for instance, reduced the grain surplus available for sale and stimulated local handcraft industries. Increasing self-sufficiency in the periphery had an import substitution effect, which reversed the impetus for market integration and reduced the demand for lower Yangzi manufactures (von Glahn 2016: 372–3). The water transport network, which was so vital for the shipping of low-value bulk grain, was impaired by silting as a consequence of upland erosion and worsening maintenance because of the insufficient fiscal capacity of the state.

The last decade of the eighteenth century sharpened the dilemma. Earlier prosperity had masked the lack of innovation. The intensification of farming had increased output to about keep pace with population growth. The millenarian White Lotus Rebellion (1796–1804) was the beginning of the domestic crises which would bring down the Qing dynasty a century later. Breaking out in the uplands of central-west China where in-migration had outstripped resources resulting in economic hardship, it spread widely through central China. Repeated military setbacks from the late eighteenth century exposed the weakness of the Qing armies and the incapacity of the state to defend its territory and address economic development.

The Jiaqing emperor shored up the dynasty in the early years of the nineteenth century, but he was unable to enhance the state's fiscal capacity. By the 1810s the economy was on the slide again and accelerated from the 1820s, which increased disaffection and social strife. Foreign pressure to open China exacerbated domestic woes, which came to a head in the First Opium War. The Treaty of Nanjing (1842) with Britain forced China to open five treaty ports to trade and cede Hong Kong Island. The Second Opium War (1856–60) opened more ports, including those inland. Emerging in the late 1840s, the Christian-inspired Taiping movement broke out in open revolt in 1851 and between 1853 and 1864 controlled much of the China heartland. Their defeat left Nanjing, Suzhou and Hangzhou in ruins. Other mid-century rebellions further weakened the Qing state: the Nian Rebellion (1854–73) in the Yellow River provinces and the Miao Rebellion (1854–73) in the Southwest (von Glahn 2016: 362, 365–9, 373–4).

In the wake of the Second Opium War, the Qing dynasty sought to modernize China, focused at first on arsenals and shipbuilding. Western technologies and expertise were imported. Despite progress, these efforts were too little too late, which was brought home when Japan defeated China in the First Sino-Japanese War, 1894–95. The war was most remarkable for the Treaty of Shimonoseki, which allowed Japan and in turn other foreign powers to establish manufacturing firms in China. China finally began on a pathway to modern economic development.

THE GREAT DIVERGENCE DEBATE

China has been the dominant global economy over the past two millenniums for all but the past few centuries. For much of world history, China was the largest agricultural producer, the largest manufacturer and home to the world's most populous cities. Population growth has powerfully shaped economic growth in China. The absolute size, growth rate and fertility of the population influence household and government decisions. That China before the twentieth century avoided a Malthusian crisis in the absence of significant technical change owes much to the intensification of farming as well as the gains from specialization and the division of labour that markets allowed.

Although by the sixteenth century Europe was beginning to catch up and overtake China in military and other technologies, China had invented many technologies often centuries before these were used widely elsewhere.[6] The historian of Chinese science Joseph Needham captured the dilemma we face in making sense of why China lost its lead:

Why did modern science, the mathematisation of hypotheses about Nature, with all its implications for advanced technology, take its meteoric rise only in the West at the time of Galileo? … Why was it that between the second century B.C. and the sixteenth century A.D. East Asia culture was much more efficient than the European West in applying human knowledge of Nature to useful purposes? (Needham 1969: 16)

Needham's question is often rephrased: why did an industrial revolution (capitalism) not emerge in China given its precociousness in the application of useful knowledge to transforming nature in the service of humans?

China's science and technology, and its commercial markets, would seem to have laid the basis for modern capitalism to emerge. Indeed, there is an older literature in Chinese that discusses the "sprouts of capitalism" (*zibenzhuyi de mengya*) or incipient capitalism (Xu & Wu 2007 [1985]). The older literature in European languages on the topic, however, blames China's tradition and culture – Confucianism and perennial corruption in the bureaucracy – as the impediment to indigenous innovation or new ideas from the West. Another strand points to the adverse land–labour ratio that encouraged labour-absorbing rather than labour-saving (augmenting) practices, coupled with negligible technical change and even less interest in promoting technical change (Jones 1982; Landes 1969, 1998; Elvin 1973). All of these were important factors that played a role in inhibiting the emergence of modern economic growth in China, but they are often mono-dimensional and ignore other elements at play.

An assessment of China around 1800 needs to conclude China was far from a failure compared with Europe. Development from 1500 along a different path had, however, opened a gap in its technological and economic capability. Markets were remarkably free in China. Shiue and Keller (2007: 1190) claimed "as late as 1780, [grain] markets in China were comparable to most of those in Western Europe". However, these markets were soon to become far less integrated (Bernhofen *et al.* 2015). Domestic trade volumes far surpassed long-distance trade anywhere else in the world. Market networks were dense and supported extensive urbanization, yet overall urbanization was 7 per cent or less (Rozman 1974; Skinner 1977).[7]

Kenneth Pomeranz, whose *The Great Divergence* (2000) drew together a body of revisionist literature on comparative world economic history, asserted that "western European land, labor and product markets, even as late as 1789, were on the whole probably *further* from perfect competition ... than those in most of China" (Pomeranz 2000: 17). For him, there were "surprising resemblances" between the advanced parts of Europe and those of China and East Eurasia. They shared similar sophisticated agriculture, commerce and non-mechanized industry, but all faced Malthusian constraints on energy, food and fibre for human livelihoods. Cheap energy from coal and land-extensive products from the colonies, Pomeranz argued, allowed northern Europe new economic possibilities. It was able to escape from the constraints of a Smithian economy based on division of labour and specialization for market exchange to another, a Schumpeterian one of intensive growth using mineral energy which applied technologies that had come from innovation over the previous two centuries.

Missing from this argument are two crucial elements. First, Pomeranz had assembled vast amounts of data to support his contentions, but these were fragmentary. The available data were inadequate to assess long-run change with statistical rigour. Estimates for the common comparator of economies, per capita GDP, were not available to him. Second, the role of institutions in promoting (or inhibiting) economic growth figured only loosely in his story, yet economic, political and social institutions set the bounds of possibilities at any moment in time. Differences in institutions matter more for the differences in economic development between countries than geography or culture, although a recent literature that links culture back to institutions and the motivations of humans makes for a more subtle and compelling argument than institutions alone in explaining modern economic growth.[8]

A lasting contribution of Pomeranz's thesis was to motivate the search for data to test the validity of his claims and to compare the historical processes of economic growth in Asia and Europe. These studies have vastly expanded our knowledge of national accounts before 1900, agriculture output and technologies, real wages and the standard of living, and human capital broadly. Li Bozhong questioned past narratives that China's agricultural productivity and incomes were stagnant. Despite shrinking farm size in the Lower Yangzi delta, he claimed productivity increases in the core of this advanced region and women's sideline employment in home-based textiles raised incomes 18 per cent in the eighteenth century.[9]

Based on Li's data, Allen (2009) showed that lower Yangzi farm productivity was high by 1600 and remained so in 1800, comparable to the level of England. Li and van Zanden (2012) compared the advanced counties of the lower Yangzi in 1820 with the Netherlands. Both areas had a similar geography and level of urbanization and commercialization, but the lower Yangzi had more employed in industry and fewer in finance. They found that Dutch per capita income was 86 per cent higher in PPP terms; the lower Yangzi per capita GDP of $988 (1990 dollars) was about 83 per cent of Western Europe overall.

Income, wages and other measures for the standard of living were low for China; Adam Smith had noted the cheapness of labour.[10] Real wages in Beijing, Suzhou and Guangzhou were far below those of London and Amsterdam during the eighteenth and nineteenth centuries. Allen *et al.* (2011) shows the average building worker in China could barely keep himself let alone a family, although the efficacy of wage data to assess the standard of living in China at the time can be questioned. Very few Chinese were employed for wages alone, unlike in Europe or in England in particular, and most Chinese relied on farming directly for food and income.

Human capital levels varied widely, but literacy in the lower Yangzi might have been as high as 40 per cent of males in the 1800s, which was about the level needed to enable modern economic development (Naquin & Raswki 1987). Adult human stature, which is a net measure of nutrition from birth to maturity and is correlated with per capita incomes in low-income societies, was comparable to southern Europe in the early nineteenth century (Baten *et al.* 2010; Morgan 2009). Average stature was static or even declining over the course of the century until after the 1880s when it rose especially in the lower Yangzi region, the most economically open area of China. In contrast, average height in England and the Netherlands increased rapidly from the 1850s and also from the late-nineteenth century in Taiwan and Japan (Morgan 2004a; Morgan & Liu 2008; Ma 2008; Baten *et al.* 2010). Numeracy, however, was surprisingly high in China for such a poor country (Baten *et al.* 2010).

A focus of the research on the Great Divergence has been the construction of national accounts to estimate long-run change in per capita income. Past estimates for England and parts of Europe from the twelfth century have improved over time and are quite robust but often estimates for the rest of the world are little more than guestimates.[11] New estimates for China (Broadberry *et al.* 2018) show there was a long-run decline in per capita GDP from $997 in the Song dynasty (1990 dollars) to $600 in 1850 (see Table 1.1). In the eleventh century, China's per capita income was 20–40 per cent higher than England, but by 1450 it had fallen behind England and the Netherlands. In 1850, per capita income was about 20 per cent of Britain, although in the lower Yangzi region income was 60 per cent higher than the China average but still below the European periphery. There was also a "little divergence" in Asia with Japan pulling ahead of China in the nineteenth century (Bassino *et al.* 2019; Francks 2016; Sng & Moriguchi 2014).

Much as we know more about the size of China's economy in the past, explanations for China falling behind remain controversial. Institutions are a part of the story. Recent research has focused on the capacity and actions of the Qing state: the sheer size of the empire made it difficult to govern (Sng 2014; Sng & Moriguchi 2014). Emperor Kangxi's 1713 freeze on land tax, which accounted for nearly 80 per cent of state revenue, strained the fiscal capacity of the state to provide public goods for a growing population. China was a low-tax regime compared with Western Europe (von Glahn 2016) and the state bureaucracy tiny with about

Table 1.1 Per capita income levels in Europe and Asia, 1090–1850 (1990 International $)

	GB	NL	Italy	Japan	China	India
1020					997	
1090	723				862	
1280	651			531		
1348	745	674	1,327			
1400	1,045	958	1,570		991	
1450	1,011	1,102	1,657	548	970	
1500	1,068	1,141	1,408		852	
1600	1,077	1,825	1,224	667	859	682
1650	1,055	1,671	1,372			638
1700	1,563	1,849	1,344	676	1,089	622
1750	1,710	1,877	1,466		749	573
1800	2,080	1,974	1,327	828	654	569
1850	2,997	2,397	1,306	904	600	556

Note: The abrupt reversal in per capita income for 1700 is an artifact of new higher estimates for cultivated land and in turn higher agricultural output than had previously been estimated.

Source: Broadberry *et al.* (2018: table 8).

25,000 officials, which was a fraction of the many who passed the imperial examinations that made them eligible to serve the state (Elliot 2009).

The imperial examination system, so often admired by eighteenth-century Europeans, has also been blamed for China's falling behind. Confucian education emphasized the mastery of the Confucian canon, with a focus on literary formalism to the neglect of empirical experimental knowledge (Lin 1995; Elvin 1973; Elman 2000; Mokyr 2017). This criticism is not entirely valid, however. While many elite Chinese disdained manual activities that engaged thinkers of the Enlightenment in Europe

(Mokyr 2017), there was a deep interest in the European science, even if the Jesuits confused the story by rejecting the ideas of Copernicus and Galileo, which had revolutionized scientific thinking but challenged Christian orthodoxy about the cosmos (Elman 2005). For example, some officials were ardent in their study and application of engineering to control flooding: the "Chinese state contributed to generating and diffusing innovations, for example in hydraulics, which may have compensated for limited private-sector dynamism" (Brandt *et al.* 2014: 60).

However, I would argue contra Brandt and coauthors that it was not the private sector that failed, but the state; further, it did not so much fail, but rather deliberately muzzled innovative capacity. On the one hand, the state feared social unrest and dislocation from technical and economic change that came with new ideas. This was one of the reasons for nineteenth-century opposition to the self-strengthening modernization movement. On the other hand, however, there was more at stake. New ideas were potentially incompatible with Confucian ideas of kingship and could challenge the legitimacy of the regime. This in my view was the more fundamental reason behind the failed impetus to innovate in the Qing dynasty.

From the early Qing period, neo-Confucian thought based on the twelfth century interpretation by Zhu Xi of the Confucian canon, which was the legitimizing ideology of the imperial state, had become increasingly ossified and past revering in its focus. Compliance with past interpretations was the test of correctness of thinking among officials and the literati elite. The imperial examination, which served to perpetuate and preserve the legitimacy of the state reinforced this conservative turn (Wu 1999; Elliot 2009; Mokyr 2017). The Confucian elite and serving officials were not simply averse to new knowledge, or merely inclined to literary pursuits and rent seeking from official posts. As mentioned above, some pursued studies of hydraulic engineering and astronomy. These were acceptable investigations because such knowledge could help to ensure the legitimacy of the dynasty.

Other forms of knowledge or views of the world, however, were perceived as a threat that could weaken accepted Confucian orthodoxy and were thus inimical to the legitimacy of the dynasty. Qianlong was zealous in his support for a narrow, past-revering view of acceptable interpretations of the Confucian classics (Elliot 2009; Koyama & Xue 2018). A "coercion bias", the ability of those in power – the emperor, the imperial bureaucracy and the Confucian elite – to suppress innovation and persecute heterodox views made the state an obstacle to innovation in Qing China (Mokyr 2017). The unified Chinese empire allowed no escape from persecution as did Europe's fragmentary and competitive state system. European thinkers and religious nonconformists could flee to a more congenial dominion. That was not possible in China. Weakness in fiscal and administrative capacity further undermined the Qing state's ability to deliver change. That is obvious, but the state's coercive strength to stifle a marketplace for ideas and crush alternative voices, which it did with a vengeance, was, I would argue, decisive in stunting innovation and change in the Qing period.

Taking stock of the institutional comparisons between Qing China and contemporary China, Brandt and coauthors (2014) noted four continuities: (1) the persistence of authoritarian politics and elite patronage; (2) particularistic assignment of officials and local–central government tension; (3) decentralization and local experimentation in economic policy; and (4) a focus on education in interest of the state. There were also four discontinuities: (1) the Communist state has a vision that embraces the future; (2) elite recruitment is more open; (3) state capacity is enabled by unprecedented resources; and (4) political leaders have an outward view of the world. These discontinuities were vital to China's recent economic success. However, the continuity of authoritarianism that has pivoted politics and policy backward into a past-revering worldview focused on the successes of the party as articulated by Xi Jinping, in contradiction to a future-orientation that strives for a rejuvenated China, might undo the efforts to foster innovative capabilities and sustain China's growth into the mid-twenty-first century. Chapter 6 will come back to this topic of innovation and politics.

From the 1500s to the mid-1800s, the Chinese economy declined in its relative share of world output, eclipsed by an expanding Europe. This great divergence for China has only in the past 40 years been reversed. Brave if not desperate economic reform from the late 1970s transformed China from a poor and inconsequential economy into the world's second largest. We begin the story of China's re-emergence as an economic superpower with a survey of the quest for modernity and industrialization from the second half of the nineteenth century to the early twenty-first century, the focus of the next chapter.

2

China's "long" twentieth century

The latter half of the nineteenth century to the second decade of the twenty-first century for China were turbulent decades of crises and wars, economic growth and contraction, and finally an extraordinary few decades of transformation of the economy and society. The calamities of the mid-nineteenth century brought a new reckoning about China's future that set the country on the long road to modern economic development. External defeat and internal insurrection had bloodied the Qing dynasty. Britain's victory in the Second Opium War had disposed of the belief that the foreigners had got lucky in the First Opium War less than two decades earlier.[1] British military technology was superior to anything China had, while the domestic rebellions had laid waste large parts of the China heartland, robbed the administration of vital revenue, and exposed the inadequacies of the state to maintain internal security. Confronted with these near-death experiences, prominent court and provincial leaders initiated a modernization programme, despite opposition from conservative officials and outright hostility from most of the Confucian elite.

China's "long" twentieth century, the focus of this chapter, began with these "self-strengthening" (*ziqiang*) modernization initiatives in the 1860s and 1870s. New state institutions were created and the state sponsored arsenals and firms in shipping, textiles and mining. These fared little better than Japan's state-sponsored firms around the same time. In hindsight, the steps were too small, too few and too limited in scope. Their failings were exposed in the crushing defeat a modernizing Japan dealt China in 1894. The treaty that concluded the brief war with Japan allowed foreigners to establish manufacturing enterprises in China. Between 1895 and 1937, foreign capital and the private sector drove Chinese economic development. Shanghai and a few other places became vibrant centres of modern industry, commerce and urban culture. That economic growth was snuffed out in 1937 when Japan launched a full-scale invasion.

China during 1937–45 was characterized by multiple economies: the Japanese controlled the cities of east and central China, the Nationalists controlled southwest and west China, and in the interstices of the rural spaces between and the remote northwest provinces, the Communists held sway. The rampant inflation and civil war following Japan's defeat in 1945 was brought to an end by the Communist victory over the Nationalists in 1949. The Nationalists retreated to Taiwan where they would nurse their wounds and pride, and at the urging of the United States and with its military protection in the 1950s embarked on a journey to become one of East Asia's "miracle" economies.

On 1 October 1949 atop the Gate of Heavenly Peace (Tiananmen), the entrance to the imperial palace in Beijing, the Communist leader Mao Zedong inaugurated the People's Republic of China (PRC). China had "stood up" and thrown off a century of humiliation, he declared. The early years of Mao's "New China" were those of consolidation of economic, political and social control. Early dreams of many Chinese for a new beginning would soon dissipate as the party, growing confident in its control over China, shifted from a mixed economy to an increasingly "socialized" one.

From 1953 to 1978, a Soviet-style planned economy was implemented. Heavy industry was emphasized, consumption suppressed, and extraction in the countryside ramped up. The political and economic chaos of the Great Leap Forward (1958–60), the ensuring famine (1959–61), and the Cultural Revolution (1966–76) impoverished the Chinese. By the late 1970s, the country was floundering. China launched a programme of economic reform and opening to the world. From the 1980s to the 2010s economic growth lifted China out of poverty, transformed it into a manufacturing and trading superpower, and impelled it upward to become an upper-middle-income country.

One of the persistent themes that run through this narrative of economic development is the tension between the Chinese state and merchants, or private business more generally, and in particular the role of markets in the Chinese polity. This persists to the present day in the vacillations in policy between strengthening state actors or allowing greater freedom for markets and private actors. Politics and political institutions have always set the boundaries of the possible for the economy. The Chinese view of economics – the East Asian view for that matter – is statist; the state and its priorities are privileged. This contrasts sharply with the Western idea of economics derived from the Greek word for the management of estates and households, and consumer sovereignty in modern economics. Instead, the Chinese view emphasizes regulation and social order rather than the household, a conceptualization which is implicit in the modern Chinese term for economics, *jingji*, a nineteenth century Japanese-coined contraction of the classic Chinese statecraft idea of *jingshi jimin* (to regulate the world in order that the people are succored).[2] Over the centuries the test of any economic initiative was overwhelmingly political, focused on the contribution of the economy to the preservation of the current regime and the maintenance of the social order that underpinned the legitimacy of the state, of which sustaining the livelihood of the people was crucial.

Surveying the past century and a half of efforts to develop a modern economy in China the impression is a sense of many promising pathways not taken, starts that were shunted aside or quashed by political events. Still, the achievements that can be quantified from the early twentieth century point to quite surprisingly strong growth. Table 2.1 shows that industrial output between 1912 and 1949 on average grew faster than in Japan, India or the former Soviet Union. Growth was strong during the planned economy; the type of growth, however, did little to improve the standard of living of the Chinese – unlike the growth that has taken place since 1978.

Table 2.1 Comparative growth of industrial output of China and selected others, 1912–2008

	China	Japan	India	USSR/Russia
1912–36	8.0	6.7	3.4	4.8
1912–49	4.1	2.5	3.9	3.9
1912–52	6.2	4.0	n.a.	4.8
1952–65	12.3	14.3	8.2	6.4
1965–78	10.2	8.2	4.3	3.8
1978–95	11.6	2.8	6.8	n.a.
1995–2008	13.8	0.7	7.8	3.1
1952–2008	11.9	6.1	6.8	n.a.
1912–2008	9.5	5.2	5.5	n.a.

Source: Brandt *et al.* (2017: table 1).

THE SELF-STRENGTHENING MOVEMENT, 1860S–94

China's defeat in military engagements with Britain between 1856 and 1860, and the Treaty of Tianjin (1858) and Convention of Beijing (1860) wrought a rethink at the Qing court even before it had quashed the mid-century rebellions. Prince Gong, the xenophobic younger brother of the Xianfeng Emperor (r.1851–61) pivoted 180 degrees. Left in Beijing in 1859–60 to negotiate with the British and French while his brother and court fled the invading armies, which burned the Summer Palace, he begrudgingly came to admire British power. Further, he was convinced China had no alternative but to learn to live with the West. China needed to "self-strengthen" (*ziqiang*).[3]

The first step was changing how the Qing state handled foreigners who it had consented to treat as equals in the 1860 convention. Prince Gong set up the Zongli Yamen in March 1861, the forerunner of the Ministry of Foreign Affairs. The Zongli Yamen not only handled relations with the foreign powers whose diplomats were now allowed to reside in Beijing, but also promoted modern schools, Western science, industry and communications. Attached to it was also the Inspectorate-General of Customs and the language school, the Tongwenguan, which became the first state-sponsored Western school in China.

The first phase of the self-strengthening movement from 1861 to 1872 stressed the adoption of Western arms, science and the training of technical and diplomatic personnel. Promotion of military industries was central. These were "official run" (*guanban*) and relied on foreign advisors, such as the Jiangnan Arsenal in Shanghai established by Zeng Guofan and Li Hongzhang, the Nanjing (Jingling) Arsenal established by Li Hongzhang and the Fuzhou Dockyards established by Zuo Zongtang. Materials were imported. There was little coordination between them, and poor leadership and corruption resulted in guns and ships that were inferior to Western equivalents but produced at greater expense.[4]

The second phase from 1872 to 1885 reflected increasing recognition that wealth was the source of power. Better transportation, industries and enterprises were needed. "China's chronic weakness stems from poverty", Li Hongzhang declared in 1876 (cited in Hsu 1990: 284). More attention was paid to civil enterprises, which were known as "official-supervised merchant-run" (*guandu shangban*) undertakings (Feuerwerker 1958). The model for these enterprises was the Imperial Salt Administration, which had long contracted to merchants the production and distribution of salt, an imperial monopoly. Many of these were to have lasting influence, including the China Merchants' Steam Navigation Company, the Kaiping Coal Mines, the Shanghai Cotton Cloth Mill, and the Imperial Telegraph Administration. Funds came from merchant shareholders, but officials or private individuals managed the undertakings. Li, who sponsored most of these endeavours, became the unrivalled leader of the self-strengthening movement and as the governor-general of Zhili (1870–95), the province surrounding Beijing, waged an unceasing ideological battle with court opponents.

During the third phase from 1885 to 1895 the focus remained on building up the army and navy, including the establishment of the Board of Admiralty in 1885 and the Beiyang (Northern) Fleet in 1888. Enriching the nation through light industry also won favour. Two new types of organizations emerged, "joint official-merchant enterprises" (*guanshang heban*) and private enterprises (*shangban*). Neither succeeded at the time. The joint official-merchant Guizhou Ironworks (1891) and Hubei Textile Co (1894), for example, foundered on the opposition of officials to private control, who forced out the merchants. Private merchants were unable in general to raise the capital required for modern enterprises, but in practice institutional uncertainties were too big to gain the confidence of investors without an implicit state backing to a venture. Chinese investors were willing to back modern enterprises, which was evident in the stake they took in foreign-run ventures, but they did not trust the state to protect their interests from the predatory actions of officials (Hsu 1990; Feuerwerker 1958).

Were the self-strengthening enterprises successful? Many failed, but some played vital roles in subsequent economic development. The China Merchants' Steam Navigation Co has survived to the present day and is one of China's large state-owned enterprises.[5] We can explore their success by asking five questions. First, was the attitude of the government supportive, or not? Hardly. Overwhelming conservative opposition of the court and others frustrated many initiatives, despite the influence of officials such as Li Hongzhang. So, the answer would seemingly appear a no. Second, was modern managerial expertise available to tap? Apart from those who had worked for foreign firms, such as Tang Tingshu, the former comprador of Jardine Matheson & Co who was involved in China Merchants and the Kaiping Coal Mine, competencies were in short supply. Third, were there incentives for the brightest Chinese youth to switch from the imperial examinations to commerce or industry as a pathway to fame and fortune? No. Fourth, was there access to capital and technology? Poor capital markets constrained opportunities to fund innovation. The fifth question is focused on how to forge backward and forward linkages in the economy. Ventures like the Hanyang Ironworks, for example. were islands of modernity with undeveloped linkages backward to suppliers or forward to buyers, which lessened its potential to spur development. China Merchants was a partial exception to this generally negative assessment.

Established in 1872 to take on the foreign shipping of coal along the China coast, China Merchants stimulated the development of modern coal mining at the Kaiping coal mines (1877) near Tangshan. Transporting the coal to the nearest port in turn led to the creation of the Imperial Chinese Railways (1886). Although only 410 kilometres (255 miles) of line was built by 1894, it became the foundation of the country's modern railway system.[6] Local iron-working and related industries developed around the Tianjin-Tangshan region, which became a centre for machinery, tools and the metal industry in Republican China (Hershatter 1986).

Throughout the three and half decades from 1860 debate waxed and waned about the scope and focus of the modernization programme: How much reform? What kind of reform? Who would share the costs and the benefits? The modernization projects were predicated on more state intervention than in the past. Tax revenues were insufficient to support the required level of state investment, at least in the early phase, as were management and technological competencies to run the projects. But ideology mattered most. Debates in official and literati circles exposed the lack of consensus among officials and elites.

The pro-development faction championed military strengthening and later economic growth to fend off foreign incursion. Many at the Qing court and Confucian conservatives in the provinces, however, feared the projects would undermine social values and destabilize China. Should railways be allowed, opponents argued, unemployment of traditional transport workers would lead to social strife that could imperil survival of the dynasty and permit even deeper foreign penetration of China (Huenemann 1984:

37–42). These debates were framed in terms of a dichotomy between *ti* (essence, principle or spirit) and *yong* (function, practice).

The reforming official Zhang Zhidong had phrased the concept "Chinese learning for basic principles, Western learning for practical use" (*zhongxue wei ti, xixue wei yong*) (cited in Hsu 1990: 377). The question for many was whether China could take on Western technologies (the *yong*) without undermining its civilizational values and norms (the *ti*). Conservatives feared that Western ideas would ultimately supplant Confucian orthodoxy and institutions. A striking parallel played out a century later in the 1980s when the factions in the Communist Party debated the pros and cons of China's post-Mao opening. Deng Xiaoping convinced colleagues that China could cope with whatever Western social maladies may come in along with the advanced technologies of the capitalist West.

Qing elites were finally shocked into realizing the inadequacy of even their limited modernization when Japan defeated the Chinese navy in September 1894 and land forces occupied Dalian in Liaoning and Weihaiwei in Shandong. The war was over Japan's role in Korea, which had long been a tributary state of China. Defeat in the First Sino-Japanese War galvanized the rise of Chinese nationalism, motivated a raft of central and provincial reforms and allowed Chinese and foreign private capital to develop modern industry.

EARLY MODERN INDUSTRY AND COMMERCE, 1895–1937

The 1895 Treaty of Shimonoseki that concluded the war was another humiliating deal. China agreed to recognize the independence of Korea, pay Japan an indemnity of 200 million taels, and cede Taiwan and the Liaoning peninsula.[7] Secession of Liaoning was soon reversed by the intervention of Russia, France and Germany. The Taiwan population resisted for a while, declaring a short-lived independent republic. Most far-reaching for development was the granting of Japanese nationals the right to set up factories, which extended to all foreigners under the terms of the most favourite nation clause of the First Opium War. The treaty led to a scramble for concessions among the imperial powers. China was sliced like a melon, each imperial power claimed rights in specific regions and forced the Qing government to agree long leases over ports or proposed railway corridors.

Among the Qing elite the idea of constitutional reform gathered support. Conservative and moderate reformers pursued a Confucian renaissance that joined education and industry. Radical reformers such as Kang Youwei and Liang Qichao sought to remake imperial institutions, creating a constitutional monarchy. For 103 days in 1898 they had the ear of Emperor Guangxu (r.1875–1908). Dozens of decrees were issued to reform education, government, industry and international relations before the movement was crushed by the Emperor Dowager Cixi, who imprisoned the emperor for the remainder of his life.

Despite the setback to reforms, the Qing dynasty carried out many of these reforms in the early 1900s, which included the end of the examination system and introduction of modern schools, and the creation of modern ministries for commerce, industry and foreign relations. Meanwhile, nationalist revolutionary groups mounted local uprisings. These culminated in the uprising at Wuhan in October 1911 that finally brought down the last imperial dynasty of China.[8]

Republican China between 1912 and 1949 was a period of instability and war, but also one of vibrant cultural, economic, political and social change. The 1910s to the 1930s might have led to modern economic development had political conditions been more favourable. The modern sector grew strongly, new social classes emerged, Western managerial knowledge was embraced, agriculture became increasingly commercialized and incomes grew, at least in the more developed regions of China. During the later years of the Nanjing decade (1928–37) a developmental-type state began to emerge, which favoured planning and public ownership.[9] Economic planning increased during the Second Sino-Japanese War (1937–45) and persisted across the 1949–50 divide. State planning and the communist factory management system in China after 1949 were not a simple transfer of Soviet planning (Kirby 1990; Morgan 2006).

Development of the modern sector in China during the first four decades of the twentieth century was a story about the Chinese private sector. The fiscal weakness of the state before 1937 hampered economic growth, much as it had for the Qing administration. Tax collection was no more than 5–7 per cent of the value of total production, while the public sector accounted for 3 per cent of sales of large enterprises in the 1930s (Rawski 1989: 31–2.). Foreign participation stimulated economic growth and structural change, rather than obstructed, as an older literature once argued. Chinese entrepreneurs had often gained experience, knowledge and capital through working for foreign enterprises. Growth of the modern industrial sector was impressive. Chang (1969: 71, 83–5) estimates average industrial value-added increased 9.4 per cent a year between 1912 and 1936, and an even higher 10.9 per cent for consumer goods (textiles and yarn), 17.7 per cent for ferrous metals and 18.4 per cent for electric power.[10] Rawski's slightly lower estimates confirm the dynamism. The average growth rate for industry was above that of Japan, Britain and the Soviet Union, while the growth rate for factory output was only slightly below Japan's 8.8 per cent during the interwar period (Rawski 1989: 69–70).

The modern mechanized factory sector was three quarters Chinese owned. It was most successful producing consumer products from agricultural inputs, such as cotton textiles, wheat flour, cigarettes, matches and rubber goods. The sector was a very small part of the overall economy. It accounted for 2.2 per cent of GDP and 0.4 per cent of the workforce in 1933, compared with Japan in 1936 where factory output was 25.9 per cent of GDP and employed 17.7 per cent of the workforce. China's level of factory output was one-quarter of that in Japan at the time of the First Sino-Japanese War in 1894 (Rawski 1989: 71). Regional segmentation was acute with two-thirds of modern industrial output coming from the lower Yangzi River region's Jiangsu province (including Shanghai) and Manchuria in the northeast. Factory output of the Lower Yangzi region counted for 10 per cent of the economy in 1933 compared with the national average of 2.2 per cent.

Although industrial development did not generate major structural change, some of the industries were large. Cotton textile production was 76 per cent of Japan's output, equal to the combined production of Britain and Germany, and only the United States and India surpassed China and Japan in output (Rawski 1989: 74–6). Moreover, modern industrial-produced cotton yarn was supplied to the handcraft industries, which far from being destroyed by the factory sector or foreign imports as is often argued, expanded compared with the nineteenth century, including in rural areas where none had previously existed (Rawski 1989: 76–8). Domestic consumption of yarn and cloth more than doubled between 1871/80 and 1934/36 and textiles and the combined value of factory and handcraft output nearly tripled (Rawski 1989: 93–7). The increasing consumption points to rising incomes. This was particularly so in the lower Yangzi region where the average height of adults, a measure of net nutrition that is correlated with income, increased between the 1880s and 1930s (Morgan 2004a; Ma 2008).

All developing countries face shortages of capital to finance growth. The fiscal capacity of the state in Qing and Republican China was inadequate to promote modernization even when there was the will. Limits on money supply, credit and financial services constrained the growth of new industries and expansion of old. However, Rawski (1989: 120) argue the transformation of China's monetary system from the 1900s to the 1930s "brought unprecedented economic integration" of the economy. A modern banking system emerged, which was increasingly able to support growth. For example, the founder of the Shanghai Commercial and Savings Bank, Chen Guangfu, pioneered savings accounts for the ordinary public and supported industry-related economic research (Morgan 2004b, 2006).

Financial innovation even extended to the countryside. Commercialization of agriculture, which was a feature of the period, depended on new sources of finance to enable farmers to shift from subsistence farming to commercial cropping, such as growing cotton for sale to Shanghai factories. The growth of modern banking stimulated China's foreign and domestic trade through lowering the cost of financing interregional commodity exchange. Rawski writes that of all sectors only the monetary and financial sectors "experienced a thorough transformation of structure and function down to the village and household level prior to the Pacific War" (Rawski 1989: 179–80).

Better financing of economic exchange in turn required better communications and transport to move information, commodities, products and people if a more integrated economy was to emerge. Qing China had belatedly and reluctantly allowed development of railways and telegraphs. New forms of transport and communications accelerated economic growth in every sector after 1895. Railways and motorized vessels contracted economic space, and telegraphs and telephones expanded information networks. Railway route length expanded from 410 km in 1895 to 9,624 km in 1912, which increased to 21,720 km by 1937 (Huenemann 1984: 76–7, 251–7; Jin & Xu 1986: 596–613). The major north-south railways, the 1905-completed Beijing to Hankou (Wuhan) line and the 1912-completed Tianjin to Pukou line opposite Nanjing on the Yangzi River, reoriented domestic commodity flows. Transport of bulk goods had been mostly west to east along the rivers before the railways. Northern China was poorly served by navigable rivers compared with the south.

Farmers used the railways to find new urban markets for their produce while urban manufacturers could better source inputs and sell their products. Cotton growers in Hebei, Shanxi and Shaanxi and handicraft artisans across the north and eastern provinces benefited. Farm gate prices for farmers rose 200 per cent between 1900 and 1936 while those they paid rose 117 per cent (Rawski 1989: 182, 188, 226). Output of commercial crops (cotton, tobacco, soybean and peanuts) and fruit, vegetable and animal production for the market all increased, as did market-oriented grain production upon which cash-crop farmers relied for food. Farm productivity rose quickest in areas alongside railways. Travel time was slashed. The Beijing-Hankou line cut the time between the two cities from 50 days to two. Steamships and railways combined to shorten the journey from Chengdu in Sichuan via Hankou to Beijing from 80 days to 10 days. The southern extension of the Beijing-Hankou line to Guangzhou (Canton) in 1936 reduced travel time between Beijing and Guangzhou from 90 days to 3.3 days (it still took 2.5 days in 1982, but just 9.5 hours on the high-speed trains of today).

Steamships similarly transformed river and coastal movement of goods and passengers. Agriculture and manufactured goods were the largest category of shipments. Freight volume for modern shipping and railways expanded about 7–8 per cent a year from 1910 to 1936. Non-mechanized transport remained not only important but also expanded. Many provinces, however, were untouched by railways until the 1950s and many waterways were inaccessible to modern vessels. Traditional transport accounted for three-quarters of the value added in transport and communications in 1933. A 1920s study reckoned sailing craft carried 45 per cent of freight compared with 32 per cent for motorized vessels and 23 per cent for rail. The Maritime Customs Service in Shanghai in 1933 reported clearing 18,115 vessels for which freight was reported and another 61,401 non-mechanized junks for which the cargo was not recorded. Business for traditional transport lost to the mechanized sector was outweighed by new demand arising from growth in domestic trade (Rawski 1989: 194, 196–7, 205, 207).

Land transport, which was costly compared with rail and shipping, was also transformed. Road building in the 1930s grew 16 per cent a year, which was twice the rate of the PRC between 1950 and 1979. The railway spurred the development of feeder roads, many built by merchants, along which plied an increasing number of private trucking and bus operators moving goods and passengers from villages and towns to the railhead (Rawski 1989: 213–4). Total haulage of goods in the modern and traditional sectors tripled between 1895 and 1936, a growth rate of about 3 per cent a year, which was ahead of population growth, and which suggests rising disposable income too. "In transport, as in finance", writes Rawski, "… the impact of innovation spread far beyond the cities that anchored China's prewar networks for the transfer of commodities, passengers and information" (Rawski 1989: 234).

Figure 2.1 Modern communications embraced by business

Note: Left panel, in the speech bubble a "modern" businessman tells a "traditional" merchant he missed the business because he could not be reached by telephone. The horizontal text below tells readers "if you want a thriving and prosperous business, please then install a telephone". Right panel, tells readers "Telephone: save time, money and worry. The more you use it the greater its value".

Source: Shanghai Telephony Co. advertisement in the *Dongfang Zazhi* (Eastern Miscellany), *c*.1930.

Lastly, the telegraph and telephone introduced a new information age to China, which business embraced. In 1935, less than one-fifth of the 2.1 million telegrams sent were by government officials, the remainder were mostly sent by businesses transmitting orders and market information. As early as 1912, 42 per cent of telephone subscribers were businesses (Rawski 1989: 217). In 1921, the founder of the largest Chinese-owned firm in the leading cotton textile sector, Rong Zongjing, insisted on their new headquarters in Shanghai being sited in a location with telephone access. He required all his plant managers to telephone him daily for instructions, while he used the telegraph to converse with purchasing agents in cotton growing districts (Cochran 2000: 124–6). An advertisement in the popular magazine *Dongfang Zazhi* (*Eastern Miscellany*) captures the effect of the telephone. A Western-suited businessman tells an old-style gown-dressed merchant, "You don't have a telephone, so I was unable to find you – the business went to another" (see Figure 2.1). Other advertisements for telephones emphasized the savings in money and time for business and the stay-at-home socialite wife.

Not only was business, communications and transport transformed before the Pacific War, but culture, politics and society too. New social classes emerged between the 1910s and 1930s, and a new consciousness of what it was to be Chinese and modern (*modan*, in the mandarin of the day), at least in the cities. The adoption of vernacular Chinese in writing in the 1910s profoundly changed publishing, which in turn promoted a new cultural awareness. Activists in the New Culture Movement championed democracy and science and criticized Chinese tradition and Confucianism. Newspapers, magazines, novels and films brought novel ideas to a wider audience than in the past, reaching out into the countryside. Writers, students, urban workers, businessmen and women demanded their voice be heard. Anarchism, communism, feminism, liberalism and many other "isms" stirred debates and movements, including the founding of the CPC in July 1921. Associations and societies proliferated, not least those serving business, management and professionals. Scientific management, industrial rationalization and cost accounting were the big business topics of the day (Morgan 2006).

The vibrant display advertising in newspapers and magazines such as *Dongfang zazhi* captured the spirit of the times, changing fashion and a new commercial culture (see Figure 2.2): Kodak roll film, Ford cars, Bayer painkillers, Eveready batteries, Colgate toothpaste and Palmolive soap, and new-fangled devices like telephones (Cochran 1999; Morgan 2009b). Advertisers even engaged in aggressive ambush targeting, such as an Eveready torch advertisement that stressed the safety of a battery torch over a kerosene lamp, one trademarked SOCONY, Standard Oil, the distributor of kerosene in China.

Figure 2.2 Consumer culture and modern advertising in the 1920s and 30s

Notes: Top left, Eveready Flashlight, "be prepared against the dangers of the night"; top right, Kodak "roll film to keep the memories of your precious"; bottom left, Bayer, "give me aspirin for back pain, not these medicines"; bottom right, Ford, "springtime's most comfortable car".

Source: *Dongfang zazhi* (Eastern Miscellany), *c*.1930 (top left and top right); *Gongshang banyuekan* (Industry and Commerce Fortnightly), *c*.1930 (bottom left and right).

Private-owned Chinese companies were innovating at home and even going abroad. Shanghai banker Chen Guangfu supported the American-trained economist He Lian, who headed the Nankai University Economics Institute in Tianjin, to develop price indices for China as a way to track the value of the collateral on bank loans to his industrial clients. Tycoon Liu Hongsheng not only used his fortunes from shipping and marketing coal to build a cement industry and later China's largest match company, which also fostered the modern chemical industry, but by the mid-1930s he had captured the global market in albumen used as a fixer for textile dyes. Many bankers, industrialists and officials were tied by complex social networks based on native place, education and membership of associations or government boards. For example, the Shanghai industrialist Mu Ouchu, who translated Fredrick W. Taylor's *Principles of Scientific Management*, launched a cotton exchange and established a textile technical college, was a government minister in the 1930s, a confidant of Kong Xiangxi, an influential official in the Nationalist government and the brother-in-law of the Nationalist leader Chiang Kai-shek (Cochrane 2000; Chan 2006; Morgan 2004b, 2006).

China in the 1930s was an economy on its way to catching up with the world. Small as the newly industrialized sector might have been, a base was being built for a modern economy. However, Japanese aggression in the 1930s was to postpone for decades China's march to modernity. In September 1931, Japan annexed the northeast provinces that comprised Manchuria, renamed them Manchukuo, and attacked Shanghai in early 1932, resulting in a heavy loss of Chinese lives and industry before withdrawing. Thereafter, Japan increasingly destabilized northern China until launching a full-scale invasion in 1937. Japan's militarism along with the world depression of the early 1930s, led many Chinese economists and officials to lose confidence in the ability of the market not only to support the economic development of China, but also its very survival in such times. Private sector weakness in basic and heavy industries encouraged a turn towards economic planning and renewed state involvement in the economy in order to strengthen China's defensive capabilities. This shift in thinking would set the die for state intervention in the economy for nearly half a century.

CHINA'S ECONOMY AT WAR, 1938–49

War and revolution are hardly times for economic growth. At least of the conventional kind. It motivates growth and a surprising amount of innovation devoted to survival, to conquest or the avoidance of defeat, but usually not of the kind to raise prosperity and welfare. The Second Sino-Japanese War (1937–45) and subsequent civil war destroyed much of the country's modern economy. Industrial capacity at the end of this period in 1949, according to Riskin, was only 56 per cent of its pre-war peak, but a recent study of twentieth-century industrialization in China shows there was significant rebuilding of capacity if not output after 1945, which laid the foundation for development of the early PRC (Riskin 1987: 33; Brandt *et al.* 2017).[11]

On 7 July 1937, Japan staged the "Marco Polo Bridge Incident" on the outskirts of Beijing (then called Beiping) as a pretext to move its northeast armies into the region.[12] In late July, the Nationalists evacuated Beijing, Tianjin fell two days later, Shanghai was besieged in mid-August and fell three months later with the loss of 250,000 Chinese troops, and in December 1937, Nanjing fell and a vicious onslaught on the civilian population ensued that became the "Rape of Nanjing". Wuhan in central China held out through the spring and summer of 1938. It was in ruins by October. The Nationalist leader Chiang Kai-shek soon after arrived in Chongqing (Chungking), the gritty city on the banks of the upper Yangzi River in Sichuan, which would become his wartime capital in southwest China.

China at war comprised three broad economic regions.[13] Many officials, intellectuals, students and workers made the arduous trek to the Nationalist China base area in southwest China. About 42,000 skilled and semi-skilled workers moved to Sichuan and Yunnan and at least as many university students who would become the next generation of engineers and scientists (Kirby 1992: 190). But most Chinese stayed put in the cities and on farms and lived under Japanese "puppet" regimes. Others, sympathetic to the Communist movement or simply opposed to Chiang Kai-shek, journeyed to northwest China to join the Communist forces at Yan'an in Shaanxi, the capital of the Shaanxi-Gansu-Ningxia Border (SGN) Region. Each region implemented distinct economies, with their own currencies, fiscal regimes and other economic institutions.

Despite the many years since the end of the war, documentary materials are limited for the writing of an economic history of occupied and Communist-controlled areas. We know more about what Westerners called "Free China", the 14 interior provinces the Nationalists ruled from Chongqing, than the rest. This area comprised half of China's population and 60 per cent of rice production but had little modern industry or transport. The railways did not reach Sichuan and Yunnan until the 1950s. Electricity output was about 4 per cent of China's total and at the peak wartime industrial output was about 12 per cent of pre-war output in China proper, with most from the increase in public-owned enterprises. Nationalist China was isolated from the world, without sea links; the road from Indochina was cut in 1938 and from Burma in 1942, which left only the airlift over the Himalayan mountains from India (Kirby 1992: 189–92, 197).

Not only was Free China ill-equipped with modern industry to supply wartime needs, the government lost revenue from customs, salt taxes and factory taxes in Japanese-occupied areas. Revenue declined 63 per cent and expenditure rose 33 per cent. The deficit was made up by printing money, which fuelled inflation. The Nationalists ramped up economic planning and controls, raised taxes and extended state monopolies. Management of the economy came under the Ministry of Economic Affairs, with the National Resources Commission (NRC) at its core. In 1937, the NRC had 23 industrial and mining enterprises under its control; in 1942 it controlled 40 per cent of industry and was one of the largest government bureaucracies. By 1944, the NRC ran 103 enterprises, employed 12,000 staff and a workforce of 160,000, excluding miners. Power generation capacity in Free China had increased seven-fold by 1944 to 49,000 kilowatts, yet that was equal to just 7.6 per cent of occupied China and 8.2 per cent of Manchuria (Kirby 1992: 191–3).

Economic data are unreliable for occupied China.[14] During the first two years of war Shanghai lost more than half of its industries and nearby Nanjing and Wuxi lost up to 80 per cent (Kirby 1992: 185). China's modern textile sector had "almost completely disintegrated" (Chang 1969: 62). Partial protection of industry from imports between the outbreak of war in Europe in September 1939 to Pearl Harbor in December 1941 revived the economy, but thereafter declined. Inflation surged. By 1943, prices were rising faster in Shanghai than in Chongqing and the decline in electrical consumption points to industrial output running about 40 per cent of the 1936 level. Chinese-owned plants had almost all ceased and Japanese ones operated at a quarter of capacity (Kirby 1992: 204). Private sector consumer goods manufacturing in Shanghai "suffered catastrophic reductions" of about 90 per cent in utilization of capacity between 1936 and 1945 (Brandt *et al.* 2017).

Communist-controlled China comprised the base area governments in northwest China and tenuous guerrilla areas in competition with Japanese and Nationalists forces. The SGN Communist base area with its wartime capital at Yan'an was a barren and sparsely populated region of about 1.4 million people.[15] Mao Zedong and a few thousand followers, the remnants of the Long March from Jiangxi, had arrived there in 1935. Land reform was put on hold and the market used to achieve a similar redistributive effect. Rents on land were reduced and a graded land tax made it uneconomic for richer landlords to keep large holdings (Spence 2013: 410). The economy was a mix of public ownership and for the most part private-owned farms and household enterprises.

Subsidies from the Nationalists during the early part of the Anti-Japanese United Front and extensive trade with Nationalist-controlled areas allowed economic consolidation of the SGN. Increasing clashes with the Nationalists and a blockade from 1939 nearly brought down the base area economy. Cut off from the Nationalist currency, the SGN government began to print money to finance imports, which increased inflation. In 1943–44 inflation was five times that of Chongqing. Loss of revenue forced the Communists to impose local taxes. The burden fell on middle-ranking peasants – the poorest one-fifth were exempt – at a level similar to that of provincial governments in the early 1930s but supposedly more equitable. A production drive was also launched, which was successful in raising grain output 40 per cent above the 1937 level and developing cotton growing and textile manufacturing.

When Japan surrendered in August 1945 after the bombing of Hiroshima and Nagasaki there was a mad scramble among the Nationalist and Communist forces to accept the surrender of Japan in China and take possession of their arms and resources. The Communist forces with their "liberated areas" in north and central China were better positioned than the Nationalists in Chongqing. Chiang asked the Americans to airlift his troops to the north. The Soviet Union entered Manchuria in August. They turned over seized arms to the Communists but left in May 1946 taking with them half of the surviving capital stock of Japanese plants in the northeast. The postwar truce between the Nationalists and the Communists collapsed in early 1946, with Chiang's armies suffering losses in Manchuria. In the second half of 1946 the Nationalists regained the upper hand, but military miscalculations led to successive defeats throughout 1947. During 1948 the Nationalists lost control of Manchuria and parts of north China. By early 1949 a rout was imminent. Communist forces pushed south, crossed the Yangzi River in April 1949 and occupied Nanjing. The Nationalist government retreated to Guangzhou, then to Chongqing in October and finally to Taiwan in December, ending the Nationalists rule on the mainland (Hsu 1990: 619–44; Spence 2013: 433–59).

Military failure was not the ultimate cause of the Nationalist defeat. The regime was economically and morally bankrupt by the late 1940s. Failure to implement economic and social reforms after 1928 were important factors, as was the neglect of agrarian poverty. In the cities economic distress and rampant corruption had weakened the legitimacy of the Nationalist state. The deficit financing of the Nationalist Government was exacerbated by wartime spending that was paid for by printing money. Inflation led to hyperinflation. Notes in circulation rose from ¥1.3 billion in January 1937, to ¥15.8 billion in 1941, ¥1,032 billion in 1945 and ¥24,558,999 billion by the end of 1948. The Shanghai wholesale price index in August 1948 was 4.7 million times that of early 1937. Between August 1948 and April 1949, the Shanghai price index rose 135,742 times (Hsu 1990: 612–3, 640–1; Riskin 1987: 33). Urban livelihoods were shattered, and savings wiped out. A sack of rice that sold for ¥6.7 million in early June 1948 was ¥63 million by August; in summer 1937 it had cost ¥12 (Spence 2013: 449).

The legacy of the wartime inflation instilled a deep fear of the consequences of inflation in the future leaders of the PRC. Rapid increases in prices in the 1980s, for example, worried them deeply. The corrosive effect of hyperinflation on the Nationalist regime and on life in the Japanese-occupied areas were seared into the collective memories of the Chinese. Wartime inflation had also affected the CPC's legitimacy in the base areas they controlled. Inflation was worse in Yan'an than in Chongqing after 1940. It curtailed social reform, and at times forced a reversal in Communist policies and the raising of taxes on farmers and others under their authority in some of the poorest parts of China (Van Slyke 1986: 684–5).

Another legacy bequeathed to post-1949 economic development was economic planning and the commitment to state-owned enterprises, which was shared by the Nationalists and the Communists. From the 1930s the state-owned enterprise system and its work unit (*danwei*) began to form. These would dominate institutionally the post-1949 urban industrial sector in China (Bian 2005; Yeh 1995). The war economy, according to Kirby (1992: 198), gave the government "opportunities for economic planning on a scale never before attempted in China".

Looking back at these turbulent years, we can identify three contributions to the economy of the PRC and Taiwan. First, the foundation was laid for the public owned enterprise monopoly in the PRC and the state corporations of Taiwan. Second, economic planning anticipated the

PRC planned economy and the state developmentalism of Taiwan. Third, and importantly, the development of human capital. Most of those who worked for the NRC and its enterprises remained in the PRC after 1949 and staffed the early planning agencies, while those who left for Taiwan were among the leaders of its economic "miracle" between the 1950s and 1970s (Kirby 1990; 1992: 192–3, 198–202, 204–205; Bian 2005; Brandt *et al.* 2017).[16]

One final but by no means trivial consequence of the Sino-Japanese War and its aftermath was the victory of the Communist forces over the Nationalists. Had it not been for the war, the CPC-led forces were unlikely to have become so large or to have gained the territory, the followers and the military capabilities which enabled victory in the civil war. The eight years of brutal conflict with Japan had indeed profoundly changed modern China.

SQUEEZING CHINA INTO "THE PLAN", 1950–78

Mao Zedong's armies won the civil war of 1946–49 and the new Communist state set about to control the hyperinflation that had undermined materially and morally the Nationalist state. China between 1950 and 1978 was a great experiment. The Communist leader Mao Zedong envisioned a new generation of socialist men and women who would create a "New China", a socialist utopia.[17] But it would come at great human and social cost. Rapid rural collectivization after the mid-1950s and the Great Leap Forward (1958–60) would collapse into famine (1959–61) in which millions of people perished. Despite developmental heroics such as putting a satellite into orbit, testing nuclear weapons and building a heavy industry sector, China progressively fell behind the world in technology and productivity growth slowed in industry and agriculture.

The early years 1950–52 were focused on establishing control. By March 1950, inflation had been reigned in, although prices lifted briefly after the outbreak of the Korean War. Agriculture and industry policies were shaped by Mao's theory of the "New Democratic Revolution", a transition stage to socialism that allowed for the persistence of the private sector in a mixed economy. This doctrine provided political space to create new economic institutions before eliminating the power of landlords and industrialists. Control over urban industry was made easier to the extent that 35 per cent of modern industry was state-owned in 1949, run by the NRC. The problem was how to run them when managerial and technical competencies were scarce among Communist personnel and the loyalty of the former Nationalist staff uncertain. Skilled workers and others were promoted, and a Soviet-style factory director system put in place. Private sector industrial and commercial enterprises, which made and distributed consumer goods, was another matter. The new state needed to revive and sustain them while it consolidated control. State purchases during the Korean War expanded the private sector briefly before the state forced private firms to merge into joint state–private firms or to cede control to the state.[18]

In the countryside, a land-to-the-tiller reform was implemented between 1950 and 1952. The ostensible reason for land reform was to unleash rural productivity, but the larger political objective was the elimination of opposition to Communist rule from the rural elite that had exercised authority over peasants. Redistribution of land improved the conditions of the poorer peasantry; they doubled their share of cropped land. Middle-ranking peasants held onto slightly smaller plots on average and rich peasants lost a lot, but on average cultivated twice the area of poor peasants. Equality was never the aim: "The chief significance of land reform therefore was in creating the political and social conditions for change in the direction planned by Mao and the party – towards a collectivized and ultimately industrialized agriculture" (Riskin 1987: 50). By late 1952, Mao was ready to launch the "socialization" of the economy, the implementation of economic planning and eventually the collectivization of the distributed peasant plots. The power of the urban industrial and commercial elites had been quashed and that of landlords brutally so.

There are two common interpretative frameworks for the planned economy period. One is focused on the politics of economic strategy, the swings of the political pendulum to the left or the right, between prioritizing planning or leaning to markets, and the degree of centralization, which polarized the debates inside the party. The other is to carve up the period into chronological markers defined by the five-year plans, shown in Table 2.2. Abrupt twists and turns in the economic policy are best interpreted as a consequence of tinkering with the model of development, between emphasizing central direction or allowing greater decentralization and local control over development, which would allow for experimentation and departures from the strictures of the party and Beijing planners that were more fitted to local conditions.

Table 2.2 Economic plans and their main characteristics, 1953–80

Plan	Period	Characteristics
First	1953–57	Experimentation with Soviet-style plan. Large industrial projects begun. Transformation of ownership. Start of collectivization in the countryside
Second	1958–62	Aborted as the "vision" of the Great Leap Forward takes hold. Accelerated industrialization crashes in widespread hunger and economic dislocation, 1959–62.
Interlude	1963–65	Recentralized control over industry and a partial return to markets enable recovery.
Third	1966–70	Despite the political chaos of the Cultural Revolution, growth was not so nearly disrupted as during the GLF.
Fourth	1971–75	Recovery from the Cultural Revolution and early articulation of the "Four Modernizations".
Fifth	1976–80	Plan emphasized the "Four Modernizations". Realization of just how far China had fallen behind.

The first five-year plan 1953–57 eliminated the private sector in commerce and industry, developed large state industries, and gradually collectivized the rural economy. Outputs rose through to 1958, but not fast enough for Mao. The Soviet-style central planning emphasized investment in producer industries over light industry, agriculture or services.

Set targets were mostly exceeded – modern industry grew 20 per cent, agriculture 4.5 per cent and grain production 3.7 per cent (Riskin 1987: 58, table 4.2). In addition, industry was shifted from coastal cities to inland provinces, a much-needed strategy if modern development was to be more diffused across China's regions. This would be the hallmark of the "Third Front" industrialization of the 1960s (Naughton 1988).

The planned economy required the subordination or elimination of economic activity outside of the control of the state. Modern industry, handicraft industries and retail commerce went through a radical social-ist transformation. Socialist or state-owned industry increased from 35 per cent in 1949 to 56 per cent in 1952 and to 67.5 per cent by 1956; pri-vate industry shrank from 63 per cent to 39 per cent in 1952 and by 1956 had disappeared; and a new category of state-capitalist (state-run) firms emerged that comprised 32.5 per cent of industrial firms in 1956 (Riskin 1987: 96). The handicraft industry before 1949 was the largest employer of non-agricultural workers and accounted for the largest share of industry output. They were converted into co-operatives. Between 1952 and 1956, the handicraft workforce in co-operatives increased from just 3.1 per cent to 91.7 per cent (Riskin 1987: 99). Retail was similarly transformed. Pri-vate traders' share of retail sales declined from 85 per cent in 1950 to 2.7 per cent in 1956, with state-owned and state-capitalist stores accounting for 65.7 per cent and 31.6 per cent of sales respectively (Riskin 1987: 99). By 1957, the non-state competitors in all sectors had been socialized. Their suppression allowed planners to control inputs exclusively for the development of state projects and restrict consumer goods available for purchase, suppressing domestic consumption for more than two decades.

Rural China did not escape the planners. Industrialization required not only agricultural inputs directly, but also farm produce to feed and clothe the industrial workforce and to barter with the Soviet Union in exchange for technology (Riskin 1987; Lardy 1992). Farm output did not grow as fast as desired and increased rural consumption reduced the amount available to planners. Land reform had also not solved the problem of land scarcity. The parcels were too small to sustain rural families. The poorest farmers also had insufficient skills or capital to raise productivity and the more capable richer peasants were unwilling to lend to them.

An initial step to remedy this situation was to form mutual aid teams (MAT), the ad hoc banding together of families to support one another with the heavy labour demands of planting and harvesting. This was typical of past communal practices. Post-land reform collectivization began slowly enough, but party cadres pressed families into permanent MATs. Very quickly these morphed into agricultural production collectives (APCs). By 1956, gradualism gave way to party exuberance as a " socialist high tide" swept through rural China, pushing families from elementary APCs into advanced APCs, which were converted into communes by late 1958, the first year of the Great Leap Forward (Table 2.3). The commune became the basic economic and political unit of rural China for the next 25 years.

Table 2.3 Steps from private farming to collectivized agriculture, 1952–58 (% share)

	1952	1953	1954	1955	1956	Aug 1958	Dec 1958
MATs, voluntary	30	39	32	–	–	–	–
MATs, permanent	10	11	26	–	–	–	–
Elementary APCs	0.1	0.1	11	59	9	–	–
Advanced APCs	–	–	–	4	88	70	–
Rural Communes	–	–	–	–	–	30	99

Notes: MAT = mutual aid teams; APC = agricultural producer cooperatives.
Source: Riskin (1987: 86, adapted from table 5.1).

The Great Leap Forward (GLF) threw to the wind the second five-year plan. The GLF embodied Mao's vision of turning China into a socialist superpower and transforming its people. He envisaged China would overtake Britain in 15 years in iron and steel when it then produced about

5 million tonnes of steel compared with Britain's 40 million tonnes (Riskin 1987: 125). Mao wanted to eliminate what he saw as the contradictions between city and country, between industry and agriculture, and between manual and intellectual labour, which was captured in the slogan "walking on two legs", a sort of technological dualism. Industry would be transplanted to the countryside to serve farmers.

The drive to increase steel output, symbolic of the political mobilization, saw iron and scrap thrown into thousands of small backyard furnaces. Most of the output was unusable. Industrial production surged initially, but soon crashed. Agricultural output rose a little, the 1958 summer harvest being the largest on record, which led to absurd exaggeration by rural leaders eager to demonstrate their political commitments to Mao's vision. Grain output was reported to be 375 million tonnes, twice the output of the previous year. The false impression of bounty led to an increase in state procurement and a neglect of the autumn harvest. Millions of farmers were deployed on off-farm projects, building dams, canals and rural infrastructure, leaving insufficient labour to harvest crops or prepare for the next season.[19] In 1961, China surprised the world by re-entering the international grain markets to purchase 5.6 million tonnes of wheat; by 1965, agricultural imports accounted for 47 per cent of all imports (Riskin 1987: 157). The purchases signaled something was terribly amiss in the PRC.

The outcome of the GLF was a monumental disaster. Industrial and agricultural output collapsed, and famine gripped the countryside. Industry would recover quite quickly, but not so grain output, which in per capita levels did not exceed 1958 until after 1978 (Riskin 1987: 134–5). The famine lasted into 1961, with a mid-range estimate of 30 million excess deaths (Banister 1987). China had a net population loss during these years, the national birth rate fell from 34 per 1,000 population in 1957 to 18 per 1,000 in 1961 and death rate rose 2.5 times to 25.4 per 1,000 (see Figure 2.3). Local level data point to 1960 being the worse year. In the hardest hit provinces of China, the crude death rate exceeded the national level by many multiples. In 1960, Sichuan recorded 54 deaths per

1,000 population and Anhui 69; Henan reached 40, but one of its counties recorded more than 130 deaths per 1,000.[20]

Figure 2.3 Births, death and population change during the Great Leap Forward famine

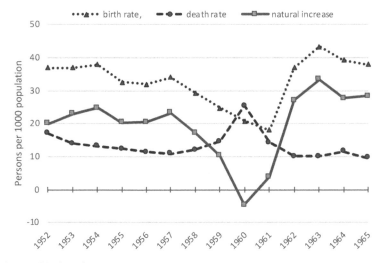

Source: CSY (1985).

The mortality crisis was overwhelmingly a rural phenomenon; urban residents employed in modern industry were shielded from the worse. Table 2.4 shows the large decline in available grain for rural areas because of increased procurement, which led to a big fall in food energy. Many children who survived infancy during these years were on average shorter than siblings born either side of the famine. Party narratives emphasize three years of poor weather, but whatever nature's tempest the consequences were primarily the doing of human actors, an outcome of ideological visions winning over economic logic regardless of the concrete needs of China at the time.

A distorted population structure was a lasting legacy of the GLF. But some positive achievements can be cleaned from the record. The downsized communes became the vehicle for delivery of rural education, health and industrialization in the 1960s and 1970s. Small-scale rural industry facilitated technical change and the infrastructure built through labour teams was important for the rural successes after 1978. During the economic recovery of 1962–64 there was a partial return to rural markets overseen by Deng Xiaoping and Liu Shaoqi. Private plots were allowed. Large projects were canceled. Millions who had fled to the cities during the GLF went back to the villages. For a brief moment the party had learned the enormous error of shifting rural labour to non-agricultural projects without concern for the seasonal cycles of labour demand in cropping.

Table 2.4 Great Leap Forward food and nutrition crisis, 1957–64

	Average per capita consumption (kg/per)		Daily food energy (kcal/per)**	Total grain output (mil tonnes)	State procurement of grain as % of output*	
	urban	rural			total	net
1957	203	204	2167	195	24.6	17.4
1958	198	201	2170	200	29.4	20.9
1959	187	183	1820	170	39.7	28.0
1960	164	156	1535	144	35.6	21.5
1961	159	154	1651	148	27.4	17.5
1962	165	161	1761	160	23.8	16.1
1963	165	160	1864	170	25.9	17.0
1964	182	178	2026	188	25.3	17.0

Notes: * Net procurement is after redistribution to meet grain deficits in specific areas.

** Ash (2006: Table 3) based on agricultural statistics for the period released in 1989, estimated daily food energy for 1959, 1960 and 1961 at 1,688, 1,587 and 1,644 Kcal, and revised down total grain output for 1961 and 1962 to 137 million tonnes and 154 million tonnes respectively.

Source: Riskin (1987: 128, 137).

From 1965 China again lurched to the left, rolling back the post-GLF reforms that Mao had attacked through the "Socialist Education

Movement" (1962–65), which aimed to cleanse politics, the economy, organizations and ideology. Mao launched the "Great Proletarian Cultural Revolution" (1966–76), putting "politics in command" with "better red than expert" triumphant over everything, undermining education, industry and the social fabric. At its root was a rift in the party between the vision of egalitarian utopianism and the bureaucratic realities of developing a very poor country. The political phase lasted from late 1965 to early 1969. From the summer of 1966 to the autumn of 1967 China was convulsed by the violence. The Red Guards, tens of thousands of high school and university students, rallied to Mao's call to attack "capitalist roaders" in the party, government and society, and tear down the "four olds" (*si jiu*): old ideas, old culture, old customs and old habits.[21]

Surprisingly, the Cultural Revolution had slight impact on economic output. There was moderately high growth between 1965 and 1975: output increased 6.5 per cent, per capita income rose 4.1 per cent, and the gross value of industrial output rose 10.4 per cent. Grain output grew 3.7 per cent, but the population increased 2.4 per cent a year, which reduced per capita grain output to about 1.1 per cent a year (Riskin 1987: 185). The policies of the period emphasized self-reliance and egalitarianism. In agriculture, the slogan "take grain as the leading sector" (*yi liang wei gang*) emphasized self-sufficiency, including in areas unsuitable for growing food grain. In industry, self-reliance renewed inland industrialization, the "Third Front", which promoted the building of factories in the interior far from their customers or suppliers out of fear of an attack from the United States or the Soviet Union (Naughton 1988). These gargantuan efforts produced successes – the attainment of nuclear capability and the launching of a satellite – but overall industry began to stagnate, and productivity went into reverse, much as was the case in agriculture.

After Mao's death in September 1976, the leaders of the Cultural Revolution were arrested, and China edged towards reform. The Four Modernizations (agriculture, industry, science and technology, and defence), which was conceived in the early 1970s, was written into the party constitution at the Eleventh Party Congress in 1977. An ambitious ten-year plan was unveiled in March 1978. Investment was skewed to industry still, despite more allocated to agriculture. By this time, however, the economy was in a sorry state. A senior economist, Xue Muqiao, lamented: "The national economy has come to the brink of collapse" (cited in Gewirtz 2017: 33). Per capita grain consumption for most years between 1959 and 1978 was below the 1958 level. Agriculture produced insufficient grain, edible oil, sugar and cotton, while industrial output per unit of capital was only 74 per cent of the 1957 level (Riskin 1987: 264–5). China in 1978 spent one-fifth of its meagre foreign exchange earnings to import food (Riskin 1987: 321). Poor farmers in Sichuan and Anhui abandoned collective agriculture, organizing into family-run farms where they agreed with the commune to deliver a fixed output. The December 1978 Third Plenum meeting of the CPC Central Committee agreed to make agriculture the top priority, followed by light industry, to meet consumer demands and produce exports. A new era of economic reform had begun.

One of the biggest departures of the reforms was to re-engage with the global economy. Of course, Mao's China was not entirely isolated. In the 1950s China had aligned with the Soviet bloc. There was no alternative after the outbreak of the Korean War and the United States-imposed embargo on trade. The break with the Soviet Union in 1960 forced a partial reorientation towards the West, although China accounted for less than 1 per cent of world international trade in the 1960s–70s. For planners, foreign trade was unimportant, its purpose to export unplanned surpluses and import scarce capital goods and materials. Trade was managed through a handful of state-run trading companies, the currency was overvalued to cheapen imports, and access to foreign exchange was tightly controlled. There was in effect an airlock that separated the domestic economy from the international (Lardy 1992; Naughton 2018). International trade was simply a balancing mechanism for state planners.

ECONOMIC REFORM AND OPENING, 1979–2010S

Few at the time could have imagined the "great transformation" of China that the economic reforms and opening to the outside world in the late 1970s would bring (Brandt & Rawski 2008). From a poor, impoverished and backward country to the world's second-largest economy is a wonderful story of transformed lives but one that is increasingly obscured by dimming memory and latter-day Chinese leaders. No one knew where China was going. There was no reform plan as such. All anyone knew at the time was that China needed change. This hesitant ad hoc approach to reform was captured in the phrase the Communist leader of reform Deng Xiaoping used to describe the early initiatives, "crossing the river by grasping stones" (*mo shitou guo he*).[22] China stumbled forward with surprising success.

Deng's phrase says much about his practicality, and the danger of the times, as does the other pithy phrase coined a decade and half earlier in trying to lift China out of the GLF disaster: "it doesn't matter whether the cat is black or white, if it catches mice it is a good cat" (*buguan heimao baimao, zhua laoshu jiushi hao mao*). Success was his measure of the correctness of policy. Or as Deng would instruct in the 1980s, "seek truth from facts" (*shishi qiushi*), a classical aphorism that Mao used too. One of those truths was that the Chinese living standard needed to rise or the party would have failed in its promise to deliver a new China in 1949. Deng was comfortable that reform would make some rich: "wealth is glorious" (*zhifu guangrong*), he said, if that was the price to resuscitate China. This section will map the phases, policies and gyrations of the reforms to the 2010s, leaving detailed analysis of the economy to Chapter 3. Economic reform broadly comprised rural reform, trade and investment, and industry. The milestones for the period are summarized in Table 2.5.

Reforms changed the structure and institutions of the economy. Structural change was marked in the shift of labour from agriculture to industries and services, the emergence of a manufacturing export economy, and the makeover of the urban and transport infrastructure.

Table 2.5 Milestones in reform and opening, 1977–2020

Period	Summary of milestones and characteristics
1977–81	Early rural reform; December 1978 the CCP formally approves reform; tentative opening to foreign investors and creation of special economic zones (SEZs)
1982–84	Consolidation of rural reforms; rural communes dismantled; township and village enterprises (TVEs) and private retail markets expand; foreign direct investments (FDI) slowly take root; 1984 SEZ-like rules extended to 14 major coastal cities.
1985–88	Early reform of state-owned enterprises (SOEs); rural markets adjusted, and farmers allowed to settle in townships to run non-farm businesses; FDI-linked manufacturing exports grow rapidly; "dual-track price system" introduced.
1989–91	Economic and political retrenchment after the Tiananmen Incident, 4 June 1989.
1992–95	The "southern tour" of Deng Xiaoping restarts reform; new laws on intellectual property, tax and FDI rules spur investment; recognition of serious issues facing SOEs; new company law; private sector grows strongly.
1994–96	Fiscal reform enables the central government to regain control over central and provincial budgets.
1996–2001	SOE reforms lay off millions of state workers; reforms of the financial system recentralized fiscal control; the Asian Financial Crisis 1997–98 hits FDI inflow; China agrees terms to enter the World Trade Organization (WTO); joins December 2001.
2002–07	Adjustment to post-WTO environment; inward FDI rebounds strongly; outward FDI of Chinese firms encouraged; large state firms brought under control of the State-Owned Assets Supervision & Administration Commission. New statist policies introduced to foster technological and industrial innovation.
2008–12	Global Financial Crisis 2007–09 hits economic growth; a big stimulus package for massive urban and transport infrastructure projects; rebalancing of economy stalls.
2012–17	Party Secretary-general Xi Jinping begins shift in economic, political and social direction; anti-corruption campaign; 2013 Xi announces the Belt and Road Initiative.
Post-2018	Economic growth slows to 6 percent; rise in economic and political tension with the USA; global pandemic in 2020 produces big contraction in GDP.

Institutional change transformed China from a "command economy", where planners administratively allocated resources, to an economy where the market largely determined prices and allocation of resources, despite a continued state role. Markets and party control were rationalized in the oxymoron "socialist market economy" to describe the new order.

Return to private farming

Between 1979 and 1984, the collective economy was dismantled, rural and later urban markets were revived, and non-farm businesses mushroomed. A primary failure of Maoist development was that collectivization had disincentivized and impoverished farmers, who after meeting state procurement demands were barely left enough to feed their families. Restrictions on private plots cut household by-production of pigs, poultry, eggs and vegetables; the curtailment of rural markets closed off opportunities for income outside of the commune; and the procurement, marketing and planning policies extracted rural surplus for China's industrialization. Rice was the main wage good for urban workers; its price directly affected the cost of industry, so planners accordingly sought to keep it low.

The "price scissor" was especially penalizing for farmers, with the compulsory delivery of farm produce at low fixed prices combined with high prices for industrial inputs like fertilizer.[23] This was nothing less than a tax on farmers to pay for industrialization. The promotion of grain self-sufficiency distorted cropping patterns and regional specialization, which in turn reduced incomes in locations unsuitable for growing grain. This was apparent by the late 1970s in the crises of personal consumption and the growing outlay of foreign exchange to import food and cotton. About 100 million peasants in 1978–80 had an average per capita grain ration of only 150kg, equivalent to a daily intake of 1,500 calories (Riskin 1987: 261–2).

Early reforms raised agricultural output through reorganizing cropping and increasing prices. What became known as the household responsibility system (HRS) evolved through three steps: contracting output to the group (*baochan daozu*), contracting output to the household (*baochan daohu*) and contracting everything to the household (*baogan daohu*). The group responsibility system was barely a break from the commune as the production team was still under unified collective control. Contracting production to the household turned over land to farmers to manage, with farm capital and distribution under the collective. The more radical contracting of everything gave households control of production and distribution, which turned households into tenant farmers with the state (village party committee) as the landlord. Farmers could choose what to grow and how, and output above the contracted quota was retained and sold. By 1984, 98 per cent of rural households had moved to this version of the HRS. Private household-run farming had returned to China.

Besides these institutional changes, the state procurement price was raised for the first time in 20 years. The price of grain increased on average 21 per cent and cotton 17 per cent, and the increase for delivery of produce above the quota was 42 per cent and 30 per cent respectively. Farmers responded enthusiastically to these price signals. The average annual growth of grain doubled to 4.8 per cent a year and cotton increased from 1.0 to 17.7 per cent. Incomes rose in the countryside and the rural–urban gap narrowed from 2.9 in 1977–78 to an all-time low of 2.3 in 1984–85 (CSY 1990: 290). Success, however, had unintended effects. The fiscal burden for the state increased quickly because higher agricultural prices raised urban food prices and increased the outlay on subsidies for urban workers. State procurement payments soared to buy above-quota output. In addition, the short land leases at the time had detrimental effects on the soil as farmers, uncertain about policy, maximized output without regard for the future sustainability of the land.

Many rural households used their new-found incomes to rebuild the family home. They also began to specialize, moving into agricultural sidelines, food processing or off-farm activities, setting up individual businesses (*getihu*) or partnering with neighbours in joint household businesses (*liantihu*). These businesses would form the basis of the non-farm private sector in the countryside. The former commune and brigade industries, which were particularly well developed in Jiangsu and some other parts of China, were renamed township and village enterprises (*xiangzhen qiye*), many of which later became private firms (see Chapter 4).

Further institutional change was needed to allow these new rural organizations to grow. The State Council in January 1984 extended land-use leases to 15 years. The next January in response to the "over production" of grain, the state abolished its 30-year monopoly on the procurement and sale of grain along with the above-quota price. In response to the latter, farmers unsurprisingly switched out of grain and output fell. Rural residents who were self-sufficient in grain were allowed to settle in rural towns to run businesses, a policy expressed as "leave the soil, but not the countryside" (*li tu, bu li xiang*). This was the first step towards dismantling the household registration (*hukou*) system, which had classified the population as rural or urban and which had contained internal migration since the 1950s. A person with a rural *hukou* was until the change assumed to be a grain producer and self-sufficient in food, while an urban *hukou* resident was dependent on the state for their grain through wages and rations issued by their work unit (Morgan 1994).

In the 1990s and the 2000s agriculture faced different challenges (Huang *et al.* 2008; Naughton 2018: 279–306). Chinese farm prices had caught up to world levels, but not necessarily agricultural productivity. Land remained state owned. While leases were lengthened to encourage investment, village officials would sometimes arbitrarily reallocate leases. Rural inhabitants were reluctant to give up their rights to land to enable consolidation because of the lack of pensions and aged care (see Chapter 5). Entry into the WTO in 2001 increased competition for farmers in low-value cropping, while the state has played a tricky game to sustain relative self-sufficiency in food grain without overly subsidizing farmers. Rising incomes has increased the demand for meat, poultry, fish, vegetables and fruit, which opened up new opportunities for farmers able to adapt to the new food supply chains to feed the rapidly growing cities. Urban consumers, meanwhile, worry about food quality and safety as a consequence of polluted waterways and farmland (see Chapter 6).

Opening to the outside world

China's break with an autarkic economic strategy brought the country back into the global economy. The most radical change was inviting foreign direct investment (FDI) to shift the economy to export-oriented manufacturing. Foreign capital brought badly needed technologies through the vehicle of joint ventures between Chinese and multinational enterprises (see Chapter 3). But as would become apparent, more important than capital inflow was the transfer of managerial knowledge and processes that enabled China to build the manufacturing capability it now possesses. The "opening to the outside" (*duiwai kaifang*) hung on three hinges: (1) exchange rate reform – letting the exchange rate slowly devalue to make exports more competitive; (2) decentralization of trade management – devolving foreign trade from central state trading agencies to provincial and city government trading companies and finally to individual firms; and (3) foreign investment – initially limited to special economic zones (SEZs), but eventually extended countrywide.

Both the value of foreign trade and its structure changed profoundly. Exports and imports combined increased from 9.7 per cent of GDP in 1978 to peak at 64.2 per cent in 2006 (see Chapter 3). China rose from the thirtieth largest trading country in 1979 to become the world's largest in the 2010s. The composition of trade shifted quickly, with exports of manufactured goods overtaking exports of primary products in the mid-1980s. Simple manufactured exports became increasingly complex and of higher quality, although the value-added in China was small. Many of the intermediate components in these products, their design and the underpinning intellectual property originated outside of China. China earns only a fraction of the market price of many "Made in China" products. In the 2010s, the value added earned by China from the electronics and IT products that it exported averaged 15 per cent, and much less for products like the Apple iPhone, with the lion's share of the value captured by the foreign firms which own the designs, technologies and brands, and control the marketing and after sales service (Taylor 2016: 57, 60).

On the import side, the increasing domestic demand for oil coupled with earnings from manufactured exports led China to cut oil exports, which had earlier funded the imports of capital equipment and food. It became increasingly a major importer of raw materials and energy – iron ore, alumina, coking coal, natural gas and petroleum as well as land-extensive primary goods such as wheat, soybeans, feed grain and meat. Energy accounted for half of all primary imports in the 2010s and food (including animal feed) another quarter (CSY various years).

FDI was central to China's shift to export-oriented manufacturing. Inflow began slowly, picking up pace through the 1980s, to plateau between 1989 and 1991 after the Tiananmen Square Incident in 1989.[24] It increased again following Deng's "Southern Tour" in 1992, which emphasized China would stay the course on market reform and rose rapidly until the 1997–98 Asian Financial Crisis (AFC). Although the lack of capital account convertibility of the Chinese yuan shielded China from the AFC, the crisis produced a sharp drop in FDI as the investment of ethnic Chinese from Southeast Asia contracted. Asian firms remained the main source of FDI after 2000, although PRC offshore vehicles domiciled in tax havens increased (see Chapter 3). Hong Kong alone accounted for about 60 per cent of FDI in the mid-1980s and the NIEs 67 per cent in the mid-1990s, while the largest Western source of FDI was the United States (CSY 1987, 1997).[25] Most of these Asian firms were supply chain partners of Western firms.

FDI surged after China joined the WTO in 2001. Western firms eagerly entered previously restricted domestic sectors in retail and other services. Taiwan electronics assemblers shifted to China a huge part of their operations, such as Foxconn, one of Apple's assemblers. PRC firms were also encouraged to go abroad (*zou chuqu*) and their overseas FDI soared after the 2008–09 Global Financial Crisis (GFC). An undervalued currency in the 2000s fuelled manufactured export growth, which led to a build-up in foreign exchange reserves from about $400 billion in 2003 to more than $3.7 trillion by the time of the GFC.

Institutionally the favoured vehicles for FDI were the SEZs at the start of reform and the equity joint ventures (EJV) between Chinese and foreign firms. China's most successful SEZ was Shenzhen, the Guangdong province market town abutting the border with Hong Kong, which by 2018 had become a city of 12.5 million and home to a thriving ecosystem of start-ups in technology. From the mid-1980s the government gradually approved FDI throughout China and became more relaxed about wholly foreign owned enterprises (WFOEs), which by the 2000s was the dominant form of FDI.

Many foreign firms in EJVs deployed their second-best technology in China to counter government pressure to transfer technology to their Chinese partners in exchange for state approval. The EJVs in the automobile industry is an example where this policy backfired, inhibiting development of local designed and branded vehicles. In contrast, the earth moving construction equipment sector was free of these government mandates. This allowed a mix of Chinese-owned EJVs and WFOEs to compete for sales in different market segments, which has led to some Chinese firms through partnerships and in competition with foreign firms upgrading and innovating to become world leaders in the sector (Brandt & Thun 2016).

Opening to the outside world was a huge success. China rode the wave of globalization for three decades from the 1980s to become the factory to the world. Foreign exchange earnings supported investment in transport and urban infrastructure. Managerial know-how and technology were transferred and absorbed. Yet, the party-state was not satisfied with the accomplished technical change. This has stimulated industrial policies, such as "Made in China 2025", which led increasingly to disputes between China and Western countries in the late 2010s. China also seeks to project itself as a global leader. The Belt and Road Initiative (BRI) launched in 2013 is an example of China's dream to create a new world order in its own image. The BRI envisages modern trade and communications corridors (belts) across Eurasia, from China through Central Asia to Europe, along with a network of ports (the new maritime silk roads) linking East, Southeast and South Asia with Africa and Europe.

Transforming industry

China's re-emergence as an economic power was founded on several far-reaching transformations. First, the movement of labour out of the countryside from agriculture to industry. Millions of rural migrants flowed across China to the SEZs and the cities of eastern China to work in factories manufacturing for export or in building urban and transport infrastructure. Reallocation of labour from agriculture accounted for about half of GDP growth in the first decade of reform, but less than one-tenth in later years (Brandt *et al.* 2008: 690, 696–7). In 1978, 70 per cent of employment was in the primary sector, barely 10 percentage points lower than 1957, while the primary sector share of GDP had shrunk to 28 per cent. By 2019, primary sector employment had fallen to 25 per cent and its share of GDP to about 7 per cent, while in services employment had increased 3.5-fold to 47 per cent and GDP to 54 per cent (CSY 2020: tables 3.2 and 4.2).

Second, the institutional foundation of industry and organization of enterprises were transformed. No longer was China populated with only state-owned or collective-owned work units, but with firms of various ownership: foreign-invested firms, private-run firms, and shareholding firms publicly listed on the newly created stock exchanges in Shenzhen and Shanghai after 1990. Nominally private firms would displace state firms as the major employer and largest contributors to GDP, becoming the engine of economic growth (Lardy 2014, 2019).

From the 1950s to 1984 state firms were administrative units that served state production plans. They were not firms in the common meaning of the word. They produced goods based on central or local state plans and provided cradle to grave welfare benefits for employees (the iron rice bowl, *tie fanwan*). Outputs were administratively determined; meeting plan targets was the performance goal and profit/loss were irrelevant. Control was exercised vertically from the central government and horizontally by local authorities (Tang & Ward 2005: 65–7). Between 1984 and 1993, China introduced a managerial contracting system to devolve authority to managers, who became responsible for profit and loss. Work units were turned into companies and joined into large enterprise groups (*qiye jituan*). The central state became more a regulator, but the local state was increasingly interventionist with an eye to jobs and profits. Introduction of a dual-track price system, with plan and market prices for the same commodity, allowed a transition to market prices, which Barry Naughton (1995) described as "growing out of the plan". The dual-track pricing system, according to Gewirtz (2017: 125), "would become a defining – and controversial – feature of China's reforms". Much as the party-state might have stepped aside from day-to-day management of the firm, the party retained control over the career path for those in the largest SOEs (see Chapter 4).

None of the changes in industry has been more profound than the emergence of private firms. They were illegal until the 1988 constitutional amendment "permitted" private firms to "complement" the socialist economy. Entrepreneurs time and again pushed the boundaries of the possible, generating employment and growth, which pushed the state to post-facto recognize in law the change in a process Nee and Opper (2012) called "capitalism from below". In 1980, SOEs accounted for 80 per cent of urban employment and the rest were collective owned. By 2018, SOEs employed only 13.2 per cent of urban workers and private firms employed 56.2 per cent (CSY 2019: table 4.1). Consistently private firms outperform SOEs, their average return on assets at least twice the state sector (Lardy 2014, 2019).

The Chinese Company Law of 1994 radically changed the legal environment. All firms whatever their ownership would abide by a common regulatory code. It brought a modern corporate model to China. Limited liability and shareholding firms were allowed. SOEs were only one of many types of firms. State firms were "corporatized" (*qiyehua*) through partial listing on the stock exchanges in Shanghai and Shenzhen, or on overseas exchanges in Hong Kong, New York, Sydney and elsewhere. These listed vehicles are the public face of China's giant SOEs, many of which are among the largest firms in the world. Party Secretary Jiang Zemin declared in October 1997 that the stock holding form of company was not only suitable for capitalist countries, but also for a socialist market economy like China.[26]

Premier Zhu Rongji between 1997 and 1999 restructured SOEs to raise efficiency, which left tens of millions of state workers unemployed and on low state stipends. Growth rates plateaued during these years, but Zhu's radical market policies had rescued the state banks from non-performing loans (NPLs) that threatened the finance system while the increased role of the market and increased competition raised profitability and the return on SOE assets. The NPLs held by the banks were stuffed into asset management companies to recycle. In 2003, the State-Owned Asset Supervision and Administration Commission (SASAC) was established as giant state holding company to take charge of the then 183 largest non-financial central-run enterprises. These firms are joined in political and business networks at the core of the party-state enterprise complex (Lin & Milhaupt 2013; Leutert 2016; Li 2016; Lin 2017).

From the mid-term of General Secretary Hu Jintao (2002–12), China began to drift away from Zhu's market-oriented reform to more statist industrial polices. This was conspicuous in the 2006 and 2007 science and technology policies to foster indigenous innovation (see Chapter 6). State construction, transport and telecommunications firms benefited hugely from the GFC stimulus package. Despite Xi Jinping declaring support for further market reforms early in his tenure, a much-vaunted package of market reforms for SOEs announced in 2013 has seen no progress. To the contrary, private investment has contracted and state investment increased, despite the decline in SOE performance since 2010 (Kroeber 2016; Lardy 2019).

Institutional reform and investment in human capital have driven economic growth since 1978, and incentivized Chinese to respond to opportunities in the countryside and later in the cities. Growth came from the combination of high human capital and relatively low wages that produced the export-generated earnings, which enabled the phenomenal infrastructure investment since the 2000s. China's remarkable period of economic reform from the late 1970s has come to an end. Party General

Secretary Xi Jinping made that clear in his speech to the October 2017 Party Congress when he declared that China had entered a "New Era" (*xin shidai*). Far from a simple rhetorical flourish, Xi's "New Era" captured the sense of change, even reversal, that has emerged since he became party leader in 2012 (Shambaugh 2016; Economy 2018; Minzner 2018). Party control in all spheres of life has strengthened. Space for contrarian ideas in society, politics or economics has shrunk. Reiterations of the party-state's commitments to further reform only underscore the lack of genuine reform of the state and financial sector. Or at least reform in the style of the recent past. Yet, there is reform of a different kind. This is intensely political, a return to the types of political rhetoric and control from before the 1980s, with exhortations to study and adhere to Xi's thought in the "New Era" and shore up the party's control over China, the Chinese people and even those overseas with whom the PRC engages.[27] For many this looks like a new personality cult is emerging in China, not seen since the worse days of the Cultural Revolution.

CONCLUSION

Forty years after China began its transition to a market-oriented economy another political and economic transition is underway. The "New Era" of Xi Jinping has closed the door on reform and opening that Deng Xiaoping had initiated. The rhetoric out of Beijing remains committed to reform, but the substance and more important the will is not there. State enterprises are favoured increasingly, as they have often been over the past 150 years, and the CPC lauds them as pivotal to China's "socialist market economy". The private sector is in retreat and the state sector is back (Lardy 2019), although it had not ever gone away. Vested interests in state entities and ideological blinkers in the party conspire to block change. They fear change that gives sway to private interests and innovation beyond the oversight of the state would put at risk CPC rule. Change will not happen voluntarily.

Since the second half of the nineteenth century, all too frequently crises with devastating human cost have preceded fundamental change in state policies and directions required to unleash the potential for China to move forward. It took the mid-nineteenth-century crises to motivate the Qing state to begin modernizing; the defeat by Japan in 1894 to allow private and foreign capital a greater role in modernization; the 1930s world recession and Japanese aggression to again turn the focus to state-sponsored development; and stagnation in the 1970s to allow a renewed role for markets. Only at times of crises after 1950 – the economic collapse of the GLF and the stagnation of the mid-1970s – has the party turned to markets to incentivize the Chinese and lift outputs. Begrudgingly so, since the party has remained wedded to the centrality of the state sector in the economy, whatever its failings.

Rising prosperity since 2000 and the increase in the financial resources has allowed the state sector to make a comeback compared with the late twentieth century, one which might put at risk the fruits of recent decades: "As China navigates the fourth decade of a transition that produced results beyond anyone's wildest dreams, the strategy of placing state owned firms at the core of the nation's development plans, a constant feature of economic policy making dating from the Chiang Kai-shek administration of the 1930s, emerges yet again as an obstacle to achievement of ambitious economic goals" (Brandt *et al.* 2017). Those goals depend on innovation and political change to raise productivity, which will be explored in Chapter 6. Meanwhile, the next chapter will take stock of the current state of the economy.

3

Measuring the Chinese economy

China's great transformation has created a huge middle-income, urbanized and sophisticated economy unrecognizable from 40 years ago. The especially rapid structural change after the 2001 accession to the World Trade Organization was pushed further by the massive stimulus investment to ward off the feared negative effects of the Global Financial Crisis, 2008–09. This chapter will take stock of the state of the Chinese economy, looking at not only the national aggregates for production, population and labour, finance and public spending, and international trade and investment, but also the diversity of economic change and growth across China's provinces. Achievements are impressive, but mask challenges for sustaining future growth in the context of an older population and shrinking workforce.

The world's number two economy after the United States and foremost manufacturing exporter is a challenge to describe. No country has sustained such high levels of economic growth for as long as China; no country has seen as many people lifted out of poverty in a generation; and no country has developed a vibrant market-based economy that seeks to become an innovative leader without throwing off the shackles of authoritarianism, least of all a former planned economy. Scale is a major challenge in measuring the current state of the economy. Many provinces are the equivalent in size of large national economies.

Diversity is the other challenge. The modernity of the eastern cities is a world away from the relative underdevelopment of the interior. Within China we find economies that are advanced, middle income and low income. As Jane Jacobs (1984) once observed, national economies are a convenient fiction. What matters are the cities and the urban conurbations that drive regional growth within different parts of a country. This chapter will therefore where feasible go beneath the national aggregates to look at the sub-national variations, the differences between and within provinces that make the Chinese economy so complex.

During 2018–19 celebrations of the fortieth anniversary of policies to reform and open up to the world (*gaige kaifang*) and the seventieth anniversary of the PRC's founding there was a lot of drum beating of the success achieved over the previous four decades. These have been remarkable, although they are far from all due to the far-sighted leadership of the CPC, as claimed so frequently these days. The primary focus of the chapter is on the years after 2000 when deep institutional changes allowed China to shift up a gear in its quest to become a rich and powerful country, but the chapter is also intended as a scorecard summary for the period 1979–2019. Since 2012 the China economy has tracked downward. Slower growth is not all that surprising. After several decades of high annual growth in GDP, moving to a 4–6 per cent range and even a 2–4 per cent range over the next decade is only to parallel the experiences of other East Asian high-growth economies that have preceded China. Scale, however, makes the difficulties of managing this economic shift a policy challenge for the party-state and a big political challenge.

ECONOMIC GROWTH

For three decades from late 1978 China's GDP grew on average nearly 10 per cent a year. No other modernizing economy over the past century has sustained these levels of growth for as long as China. There were big fluctuations in growth rates – as shown in Figure 3.1 – but China did not experience in real terms periods of negative growth. Contractions were short lived.[1] They were traumatic for those affected, such as for rural migrants in 1989–90 and employees of SOEs in the late 1990s. Both were policy-induced contractions. Yet the economy sustained surprising momentum, and only rarely grew at rates below 7–8 per cent a year, and some years at double-digit rates. Per capita GDP – and real personal incomes – have grown on average about 1–2 percentage points below the headline GDP growth rate.

China's re-emergence began with rural sector reforms that unleashed growth, raised rural output and incomes, and laid the basis for extending market incentives to the urban-centred and moribund state economy in the mid-1980s (see Chapter 2). Important as these changes were for the many Chinese who lived and still live in the countryside, the driver of economic growth from the mid-1980s was manufacturing and later services. Between 1981 and 1984, agriculture contributed between one-third and up to half GDP growth (Huang *et al.* 2008). Secondary industry was the main contributor to GDP growth from the mid-1980s until the early 2010s. Services have grown strongly since the early 2000s and in recent years have accounted for about 60 per cent of the reported growth in GDP (CSY 2020: table 3.8).

High growth in China has fuelled growth of the global economy, especially after China joined the WTO in 2001. This was captured in the phrase once used to describe China as the "workshop *to* the world". China has been a major beneficiary of the global economy. The open international economic order, the declining costs of transport and communications, and the increasing degree of globalization from the 1970s to the 2010s allowed China to insert itself into global supply chains (Timmer *et al.* 2014). China benefited with rising incomes and modernization of its manufacturing, technology and urban infrastructure; the rest of the world benefited in cheaper consumer goods and new markets for exporters, farmers and investment bankers eager to sell into an increasingly well-off consumer society.

This phenomenal economic growth transformed China. Structural change shifted many millions from labouring on farms in the countryside

Figure 3.1 GDP annual growth rates, 1978–2020

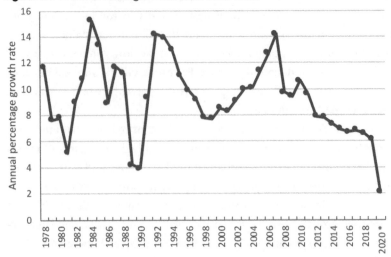

Note: *estimate for full-year growth in 2020 (*Financial Times*, 15 December 2020).
Source: CSY (2020: table 3.4); NSB 2020c.

Figure 3.2 Change in structure of GDP, 1980–2019

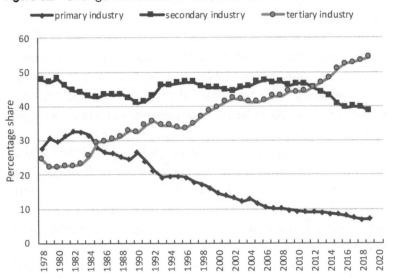

Source: CSY (2020: table 3.2); NSB 2020c.

to employment in industry and services in the cities. The shift in the structure of GDP is shown in Figure 3.2. China is now overall a service economy, with the tertiary sector eclipsing the share of secondary industry in 2012. Secondary industry has been around 40 per cent of GDP since the mid-2010s while the primary sector, which includes fishing and forestry, has steadily declined from a peak of 33 per cent in 1982 during the rapid change in the rural sector after the 1978 reforms, to just 7 per cent in the late 2010s.

Structural change and the internationalization of the once autarkic economy turned China into the dominant global exporter of manufactured goods, which became more sophisticated over time. These changes raised incomes, reduced poverty, and increased labour productivity. From among the ranks of the poorest economies in the late 1970s, China by 2010 had climbed the development stairway to overtake Japan as the world's second-largest economy and become an upper-middle-income economy set on becoming an advanced economy. Many other countries have stalled along this path to prosperity, stuck in the so-called middle-income trap (World Bank 2013). As Barry Naughton (2018: 3) noted, with the benefit of hindsight the enabling conditions for China were favourable at the start of the 1980s: China was a country of huge resources even if in per capita terms small at the time; the global division of labour welcomed China into the expanding production networks of the 1980s; there was a lot of catch-up potential from shifting underemployed surplus labour from agriculture to higher value-added manufacturing; and the government had a capacity to learn, despite favouring socialist planning and lingering Maoism that were slowly put to one side. Chapter 2 outlined these developments.

Measuring these developments is not straightforward. And, there is much scepticism about the veracity of official statistics. Rapid institutional change from a socialist planned economy to a market-oriented one was challenging for China's statisticians. Statistical reporting and methods have struggled to keep up with the change and the need for new statistical reporting (Chen & Ravallion 1999). Rawski (2001) was scathing of the

GDP data for the late 1990s, questioning increased output in the presence of a decline in energy consumption. Even the current premier, Li Keqiang, when party secretary of Liaoning province (2004–07) told a US diplomat the provincial GDP data were unreliable and instead used electricity consumption, rail freight and new bank loans to gauge the economic health of his province (*The Economist* 2010b). The problem with China's GDP data is that GDP growth forecasts are an input to policy, not an output measure of economic activity, and as a consequence, government officials will do whatever they need to deliver the policy goal, whether the activity is productive or not, as long as there are no hard budgets and bad debt is not booked (Pettis 2019). This will include activities that make no positive contribution, like bridges to nowhere, but still count as economic output. For that reason, China's growth data fails as a measure of economic performance.

Much maligned as the official statistics might be, and GDP growth data in particular, on balance most scholars agree the reported trends are reliable whatever the credibility of the specific numbers (Holz 2014). Officials have a vested interested in keeping roughly accurate data, despite the temptations to manipulate these for short-term political or personal gains. Overall, Kroeber (2016: 268) summed up the situation: "A government so dependent on sustained economic growth for its legitimacy, and so keenly aware (thanks to its own recent history) of the disastrous consequences of relying on bad data, has strong self-interest in maintaining statistics that are approximately right, at least with regards to trends, even if they do not meet the highest standards of modern statistical science".

A recurring issue in measuring the economy is prices, whether comparing China with other countries or one province with another. International comparisons are best made using purchasing power parity (PPP) estimates rather than exchange rate conversions of output and income.[2] This is because US$100 in China will buy a very different size basket of goods and services to $100 spent in the United States. In rich economies, capital is cheap (interest rates low) and labour dear (wages high), and the reverse in poor and developing economies. Similarly, in China ¥100 will go further in central and western China than in the richer eastern cities. Taxi fares begin, for example, in Shanghai from ¥14 in November 2019, whereas in Ningbo, which is two hours away by train, a taxi fare starts at ¥11, and in Chengdu, a three-hour flight further to the west, it is ¥8 (personal experience, 2019).

China has caught up and surpassed other developing and middle-income economies. How big is China's economy? Table 3.1 shows the relative size of GDP at current prices (US$ exchange rate) and PPP (2011 dollars) compared with selected other countries. At current prices, GDP was $13,605 billion in 2018 compared with the USA's GDP of $20,544 billion, while in PPP terms, China's GDP was $25,399 billion, which made it the world's largest economy. Between 1980 and 2018, in nominal terms the Chinese economy increased from just 1.7 per cent of the world economy to 15.8 per cent, and in purchasing power parity terms from 4.7 per cent to 18.6 per cent. Even at the start of the twenty-first century after two decades of reform, at exchange rate parity China was just 3.6 per cent of the world economy and one-eighth the size of the US economy.

That China has been hugely successful in growing its economy is obvious. Any regular visitor over the past four decades is aware of the changes in personal income, economic activity and the built environment. Not only has the level of urbanization tripled to 60 per cent, but the cities of the east coast have first-world skylines of office and residential towers along with metro-transit systems superior to most advanced economies. These urban centres are linked by freeways, high-speed trains and modern local airports, none of which existed four decades ago.

Too easily in viewing the modernity of the east coast an observer might think China has all but caught up with the advanced economies. That is far from the case. Plots of the PPP estimates for per capita GDP of selected high-income and middle-income economies in Figure 3.3 show China's ascendancy is a product of the rapid growth during the past two decades. China only overtook middle-income economies like the Philippines and Indonesia in the 2000s, still lagged behind Thailand and Malaysia in the early 2010s, and is well short of Hong Kong, Taiwan, South Korea or Japan.

Table 3.1 China and selected economies share of global output, 1970–2018 (% of world GDP)

Current US$	1980	1990	2000	2010	2018
China	1.7	1.6	3.6	9.2	15.8
India	1.6	1.4	1.4	2.5	5.8
Japan	9.9	13.9	14.5	8.6	3.2
United Kingdom	5.1	4.8	4.9	3.7	3.3
United States	25.6	26.5	30.6	22.7	23.9

PPP 2011 International $	1980	1990	2000	2010	2018
China	4.7	5.6	8.4	14.1	18.6
India	2.8	3.3	4.2	6.2	7.7
Japan	7.5	7.8	6.6	4.9	4.1
United Kingdom	3.5	3.1	2.9	2.4	2.2
United States	21.3	19.4	20.6	16.9	15.1

Notes: Current prices in US$ from the WDI; PPP in 2011 International $ from Penn World Tables except for 2018, which comes from WDI.

Sources: World Bank *World Development Indicators* (WDI), 2020 revision; Penn World Tables version 9.0.

Of the more than 100 countries that have become middle-income econo-mies since the 1960s, only a dozen escaped the middle-income group to join the ranks of high-income economies (World Bank 2013). Many have languished in the middle, such as Argentina. Some are at risk of falling back. Catching up is hard to do, even for a large country such as China with huge domestic resources and its openness to the international econ-omy, which has brought in a ready flow of capital and technology over the past 40 years.

China clearly has a way to go to catch up with the advanced economies

Figure 3.3 Comparative per capita GDP (PPP)

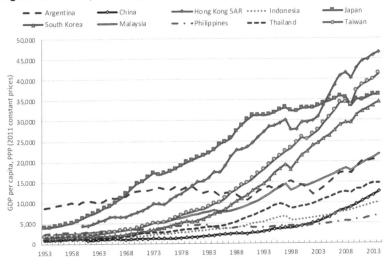

Source: Penn World Tables, version 9.0.

in per capita income, including its East Asia neighbours that were the "miracle" economies of the second half of the twentieth century. Figure 3.4 compares the change in the level of per capita GDP starting from the first year of high-speed economic growth. The vertical axis uses a logarithmic scale to show better the differences in the initial starting levels, which would otherwise be compressed with a linear scale.

China's high-speed growth phase began in 1978. The equivalent start year for Japan is 1954, the year following the Korean War; 1960 for Taiwan and 1962 for Korea. China began from a much lower level than Japan, South Korea and Taiwan. First, it was the poorest of the four, with a per capita GDP starting level of $1,305 (PPP 2011 dollars) in 1978 compared with Japan in 1954 ($4,163), Taiwan in 1960 ($2,070) and Korea ($1,577). Second, after four decades of high-speed economic growth these three East Asian economies had attained a far higher level of real per capita GDP than China, despite averaging nearly double-digit growth for the three decades to 2010. By these PPP measures, the catch-up growth has

Figure 3.4 China's growth compared to Japan, Taiwan and South Korea (per capita GDP in PPP 2011 constant $) from the start of their high-growth phase

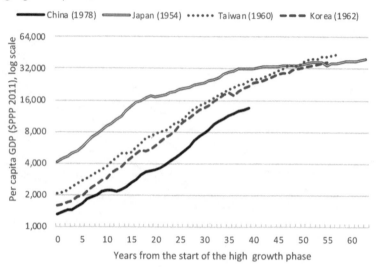

Note: The vertical axis uses a logarithmic scale, which makes clearer the initial level differences, but compresses the differences at higher values. The start year of the high growth phase for each economy is enclosed in brackets.

Source: Penn World Tables, version 9.0.

not been as spectacular as is often thought. Thirdly, the 1989–91 shock after the Tiananmen Square Incident of June 1989 slashed GDP growth rates (see Figure 3.1) and shifted the curve to the right, before resuming its climb. The impact of this shock on the growth in per capita GDP is far greater than the late 1990s downsizing of the state sector and the Asian Financial Crisis.

Per capita GDP in the United States, like it or not, is the common benchmark when we compare economic catch-up. China lags well behind. By the end of the fourth decade of high-speed growth, China in PPP terms had reached about 25 per cent of the US level compared with Japan reaching 84 per cent, Taiwan 55 per cent and South Korea 48 per cent (Figure 3.5). Part of that relative slowness in catch up can be attributed to the lower initial starting level – China was a lot poorer. But a part is due to institutional impediments in the early years of reform and opening. China simply muddled through, two steps forward and one step back, incrementally changing institutions and policies, often clinging to (and continuing to cling to) institutions and policies that supported vested state interests despite the upswell of innovation and market-led growth from farmers in the countryside and private entrepreneurs in towns and cities. Growth in per capita GDP was relatively slow in the 1980s and 1990s as shown in the gentle upward slope of the line in Figure 3.5 for China compared with the lines for Japan, South Korea and Taiwan at a comparable stage of development.

Figure 3.5 China's per capita GDP (2011 PPP$) as a percentage of the US level compared with Japan, Taiwan and South Korea from the start of their high-growth phase

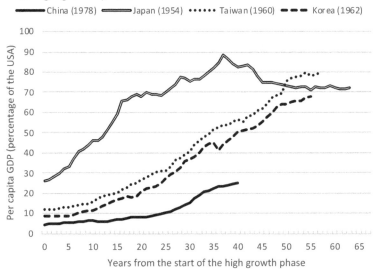

Source: Penn World Tables, version 9.0.

Accelerated growth relative to the United States picked up sharply after the radical reforms of the state sector in the late 1990s and the accession to the WTO, initiatives that were championed by the premier Zhu Rongji against party-state vested interests. By way of contrast, in Japan, Taiwan and South Korea the high-growth phase was marked by faster growth (the line is steeper), which was guided by visionary techno-bureaucrats who put in place economic institutions and government policies to grow rapidly their economies.[3] They also benefited from the military protection of the United States whose Cold War nuclear umbrella in East Asia reduced the need for defence spending.

China's continental size means there is wide variation in growth rates, the structure of the economy and living standards. National aggregates flatten the differences and conceal the challenges for future economic development inherent in the diversity among its provinces. Table 3.2 shows the size and structure of provincial GDP in 2018, with the third column indicating the provincial GDP rank order if the province was an independent country.

Table 3.2 Size and structure of provincial domestic product in China, 2018

	GDP (bil ¥)	GDP (bil US$)	world rank	Primary Industry	Secondary Industry	Tertiary Industry	GDP p.c. (US$)
National	90,031	13,605	2	7.2	40.7	52.2	9,769
Beijing	3,032	458	37	0.4	18.6	81.0	21,188
Tianjin	1,881	284	60	0.9	40.5	58.6	18,241
Hebei	3,601	544	31	9.3	44.5	46.2	7,219
Shanxi	1,682	254	65	4.4	42.2	53.4	6,850
Inner Mongolia	1,729	261	64	10.1	39.4	50.5	10,322
Liaoning	2,532	383	44	8.0	39.6	52.4	8,766
Jilin	1,507	228	72	7.7	42.5	49.8	8,404
Heilongjiang	1,636	247	67	18.3	24.6	57.1	6,539
Shanghai	3,268	494	36	0.3	29.8	69.9	20,398
Jiangsu	9,260	1,399	16	4.5	44.5	51.0	17,404

	GDP (bil ¥)	GDP (bil US$)	world rank	Primary Industry	Secondary Industry	Tertiary Industry	GDP p.c. (US$)
Zhejiang	5,620	849	21	3.5	41.8	54.7	14,907
Anhui	3,001	453	40	8.8	46.1	45.1	7,210
Fujian	3,580	541	33	6.7	48.1	45.2	13,781
Jiangxi	2,198	332	53	8.6	46.6	44.8	7,168
Shandong	7,647	1,156	18	6.5	44.0	49.5	11,525
Henan	4,806	726	24	8.9	45.9	45.2	7,579
Hubei	3,937	595	27	9.0	43.4	47.6	10,067
Hunan	3,643	550	30	8.5	39.7	51.8	8,001
Guangdong	9,728	1,470	13	4.0	41.8	54.2	13,058
Guangxi	2,035	308	58	14.8	39.7	45.5	6,270
Hainan	483	73	98	20.7	22.7	56.6	7,851
Chongqing	2,036	308	57	6.8	40.9	52.3	9,964
Sichuan	4,068	615	26	10.9	37.7	51.4	7,387
Guizhou	1,481	224	74	14.6	38.9	46.5	6,233
Yunnan	1,788	270	63	14.0	38.9	47.1	5,612
Tibet	148	22	144	8.8	42.5	48.7	6,558
Shaanxi	2,444	369	47	7.5	49.8	42.7	9,593
Gansu	825	125	85	11.2	33.9	54.9	4,735
Qinghai	287	43	119	9.4	43.5	47.1	7,207
Ningxia	371	56	110	7.6	44.5	47.9	8,175
Xinjiang	1,220	184	79	13.9	40.3	45.8	7,476

Notes: The provincial domestic (regional) product was converted to US$ using the average 2018 exchange rate. These provincial GDP estimates were merged with GDP estimates at current US$ for the world economies from WDI database to obtain equivalent world ranking as reported in the main text.

Sources: CSY (2019: tables 3.1, 3.2, 3.9, 18.8); World Bank, WDI, 2020 revision.

In 2018, the world's second largest economy had a GDP of US$13,605 billion at current prices and per capita GDP of US$9,769. The four largest provincial economies – all in East China – were Guangdong, Jiangsu, Shandong and Zhejiang. Were these independent countries they would rank as the world's thirteenth, sixteenth, eighteenth and twenty-first largest economies. They have been at the forefront of China's opening to the world. Guangdong benefited from its relationship with Hong Kong and became a hub for export-oriented manufacturing; Jiangsu and Zhejiang were historically hubs of manufacturing and innovation that regained their standing in the 1990s; and Shandong has benefited from close historical links to Japan and South Korea. Provincial per capita GDP of the four provinces is between 20 and 70 per cent above the national average.

The provincial-status metropolitan cities of Beijing, Tianjin and Shanghai are predominantly service economies, as shown in Table 3.2. They now have little residual agricultural activity; their rural countries having been converted to sprawling suburbs and dormitory towns. Beijing and Shanghai municipalities with more than 20 million inhabitants each would rank respectively as the thirty-seventh and thirty-sixth largest economy in the world. Their per capita GDP of $21,188 and $20,398 is more than twice the national average, which would rank them the fifty-third and fifty-fourth richest country in the world and on a level comparable with the Czech Republic and Greece (World Bank WDI).

The least developed and poorest provinces are in central and western China. The relative size of their primary sector is often twice the national average, the secondary sector is below the national average, and the per capita GDP about 60–80 per cent of the national average. For example, the primary sector is 14–15 per cent of the economies of Guangxi, Guizhou and Yunnan in southwest China. Their 2018 per capita GDP is $6,270, $6,233 and $5,612 respectively, which makes them equivalent to Fiji, Suriname and Iran (World Bank WDI). The poorest province is Gansu with a per capita GDP of $4,735, which is less than half the national average and one-quarter that of Beijing and Shanghai, and which puts Gansu on par with Azerbaijan in Central Asia (World Bank WDI).

Regional diversity of economic development in China is summarized in Table 3.3, which divides the country into eastern, northeastern, central and western regions. This table reports change in the per capita GDP by region in US dollars and the percentage level relative to the United States for 1980, 2000 and 2018. As already discussed, the change between 1980 and 2000 was slow and per capita GDP increased more slowly than GDP overall. In relative terms, the central and western regions even fell back a little. Rapid growth since 2000 has increased per capita GDP in current dollars to about 15.6 per cent of the US level by 2018; eastern China was 23.2 per cent of the US level and the northeastern, central and western regions had per capita income about half of eastern China, or around 12 per cent of the US level.

Table 3.3 Per capita GDP of regional China, selected years (1980, 2000, 2018)

	1980		2000		2018	
	US$	% US level	US$	% US level	US$	% US level
United States	12,575	100	36,335	100	62,641	100
China	195	1.5	959	2.6	9,771	15.6
East	577	4.6	1,739	4.8	14,552	23.2
Northeast	433	3.4	1,080	3.0	7,900	12.6
Central	243	1.9	655	1.8	7,809	12.5
West	238	1.9	612	1.7	7,458	11.9

Note: Per capita income in current US$ (exchange rate) and comparisons of the per capita GDP of each region with the US is converted at exchange rate parity. China regional classification follows official definitions of broad regions: East (Beijing, Tianjin, Hebei, Shandong, Shanghai, Jiangsu, Zhejiang, Fujian, Guangdong, Hainan), Northeast (Liaoning, Jilin, Heilongjiang), Central (Shanxi, Henan, Hubei, Hunan, Anhui, Jiangxi) and West (Inner Mongolia, Sichuan, Chongqing, Guizhou, Guangxi, Yunnan, Tibet, Shaanxi, Gansu, Qinghai, Ningxia, Xinjiang).

Source: World Bank, WDI, 2020 revision.

The regional gap in per capita income between East China and the rest widened from 1980 to 2000 (see Table 3.3). Since 2000, the relative level of Central and West China has improved with income rising to 54 per cent and 51 per cent respectively of East China, but the Northeast – home to the rustbelt industries that bore the brunt of the reform of state sector firms in the late 1990s – has continued to decline and was only 54 per cent of the East China level in 2018. Regional inequality is discussed in detail in Chapter 5.

POPULATION AND LABOUR

Population momentum has driven economic and social change in China for the past few centuries. Between the late-seventeenth and mid-nineteenth centuries the population tripled, reaching about 430 million in 1850 (see Chapter 1). Without a commensurate increase in arable land or compensating increase in agricultural productivity or new off-farm industry, living standards fell and the once highly integrated markets fragmented (Bernhofen *et al.* 2015; Broadberry *et al* 2018). These changes were the domestic catalysts that drove the upheavals over the century to the founding of the PRC in 1949. In the second half of the twentieth century population again accelerated, more or less doubling between 1950 and 1980. Concerns about population growth developed in the 1970s. Birth control shifted to aggressive intervention with the one-child policy (OCP) in 1980, despite the steep decline in total fertility during the 1970s (Banister 1987; Zhang 2017). The policy reduced fertility far faster than economic development would inevitably have done and bequeathed China a prematurely aged population.

China's population will peak at 1.46 billion between 2025 and 2030, according to UN (2019) population projections, and then begin to decline.[4] The workforce is already shrinking, having peaked around 2010–11, while the population is ageing rapidly. Figure 3.6 show these trends ordered by the following broad age groups, 0–14, 15–24, 25–49, 50–64 and 65 years and above. The rapid acceleration in ageing from around 2010 is clear. Recent projections show the population of those older than 60 years will increase 5–7 percentage points each decade from 2010 to 2050. The early age of retirement in China for those in formal urban employment – 55 years for women and 60 years for men – will increase the burden on the state to provide pensions and healthcare. The universal pensions and widened welfare safety net introduced in the second half of the 2000s (see Chapter 5), which have made a big difference to elderly Chinese, will not be sustainable without changing the age of retirement and the fiscal system to fund increased elderly-care expenditure.

Figure 3.6 Age structure of China's population, 1950–2100

a) Change in population by broad age groups (thousands)

b) Change in age composition of population (percentage)

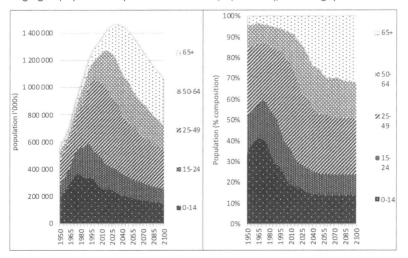

Source: UN *World Population Prospects* (2019).

Over the next three decades population ageing will resize the workforce, increasing the gross dependency level (the ratio of non-working to working population). Table 3.4 shows that between 2020 and 2050 the population under 25 years of age is projected to shrink by about 88 million. Those aged 25–49, the most productive adult years, will shrink by 140 million, while those 65 years and older will increase by 193 million, or about three times the population of the UK. By 2050, for every 100 people aged 20–64 working there will be 82 dependents. In 1970 when the total fertility rate began to turn downward the median age was just 19 years and the 20–64 gross dependency level was 124 for every 100 working, which reached a low of about 51 in 2015. Median age had increased to 35 years by 2010 and will reach 48 years in 2050. Japan in the same year will have a median age of 55 years. The UN projections show China's population structure will not be as aged as Japan, Korea and Taiwan in the mid-twenty-first century, where the dependency level is expected to be around 100 or higher, with more people not working than working, but it will be far older than the population in India, Indonesia and most countries in Asia (UN 2019).

Table 3.4 Change in population age structure to 2050 (millions)

Age group	2020	2030	2040	2050	net diff 2020–50
0–14	254.9	230.9	206.8	198.4	
– change		−24.1	−24.0	−8.5	−56.5
15–24	169.5	169.8	158.8	138.5	
– change		0.3	−11.0	−20.4	−31.0
25–49	542.9	490.0	429.1	403.0	
– change		−52.9	-60.9	−26.1	−139.9
50–64	299.7	326.7	310.4	296.9	
– change		27.0	−16.3	−13.6	−2.8
65+	172.3	247.0	343.8	365.6	
– change		74.7	96.8	21.8	193.4

Source: UN *World Population Prospects* (2019).

China – and indeed East Asia for most of the second half of the twentieth century – benefited from the one-off gain from the population transition and "population dividend" (Bloom & Williamson 1998; Cai

2016; Naughton 2018: 188–9). An expanding workforce of young workers drove down the dependency ratio and raised labour productivity, aggregate GDP and per capita income. From 1970 until the later 2000s, China's workforce entrants were not only young, but possessed higher human capital; they were increasingly better educated, healthier and productive (Heckman 2005; Liu *et al.* 2008). The above effects of the surge in young workers and the population dividend are well and truly over. Like a pig swallowed by a python the larger sized cohorts will pass through the age distribution, increasing the elderly population. Figure 3.7a shows graphically the projected demographic changes, the shrinking of the workforce aged 20–60 years and increase in the elderly population.

China's OCP accelerated the fall in the total fertility rate (TFR), the number of children on average a woman can be expected to give birth to during her life, and in turn accelerated the ageing process.[5] The TFR had fallen dramatically from an estimated 6.5 children per woman in 1970 to about 2.9 children in 1980 when the OCP was introduced, but was already below the replacement level of 2.1 children for women in cities (Cai 2016: 59; Zhang 2017; Naughton 2018: 190–92). Fertility in both rural and urban areas would have fallen after 1980 with economic growth, prosperity and urbanization as has occurred in the rest of East Asia, so whether the OCP had any long-term impact on fertility outcome is moot.

The main effect of the OCP birth control measures, however, was to quicken very rapidly the decline in fertility, especially in the countryside. By the mid-1990s, the TFR in both rural and urban China was below replacement level and the annual population growth rate reached an all-time low. But it came at a huge cost, as explained by Wang (2005: 1): "a growing proportion of elderly with inadequate government or family support, a disproportionately high number of male births attributable to sex selective abortion, increased female infant and child mortality rates, and the collapse of a credible government birth reporting system [because illegal births were often hidden from officials and census takers]".

China belatedly (and reluctantly) came to realize the consequences of the OCP for its future, despite the warning of demographers and labour

Figure 3.7 The end of China's demographic dividend

a) Simplified population age trends
for China, 1950 to 2100

b) Fertility and relative per capita GDP
from the start of high-speed growth

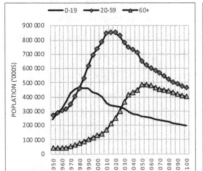

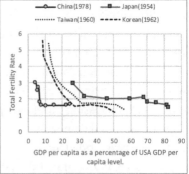

Note: Figure 3.7a reflects the current employment regime that most people in formal urban employment retire by 60 years of age. In Figure 3.7b, each line shows the total fertility rate at five-year intervals (y axis) relative to percentage level of the per capita GDP in the United States for the first four decades of high-speed economic growth. For China, from 1978; Japan from 1954; Taiwan from 1960; and South Korea from 1962.

Sources: Figure 3.7a UN *World Population Prospects* (2019); Figure 3.7b total fertility rate from the UN *World Population Prospects* (2019) and GDP per capita from the Penn World Tables, version 9.0 (PPP$ 2011).

economists (Cai & Yang 2013; Wang 2005, 2010). It was finally abandoned in 2016. Compared with other high-growth East Asian economies, fertility in China fell far faster to reach a lower TFR at a much lower relative per capita GDP than the other selected economies shown in Figure 3.7b. China's fertility rate reached a low of 1.61 births per woman in the early 2000s when its per capita GDP was just 11 per cent of the United States. Japan did not reach the equivalent level of fertility until its GDP was more than 80 per cent of the USA. China in effect depleted its youth advantage many decades before other countries in East Asia and at a lower relative per capita GDP. The inescapable conclusion is the population dividend was banked far too early.

These demographic changes have enormous implications for future growth, per capita incomes and the wherewithal of the government to support the elderly. Living standards in real terms might decline.[6] A major source of growth in any economy over the past two centuries has come from an expanding population, their demand for goods and services, and their employment in producing these. This growth factor in China is in reverse now. The challenge for China is how to sustain future economic growth and in turn the standard of living in the face of these demographic challenges.

Employment has changed markedly over the past four decades. In 1980, most people lived in the countryside and worked in collective agriculture (Table 3.5). Primary sector employment accounted for 69 per cent of the 423.6 million people in employment. The rural workforce, which numbered 318 million, made up three-quarters of the total employment. Only 18 per cent of the workforce was employed in secondary industry and just 13 per cent in services. In the cities, most people were employed in the state sector, which accounted for 76 per cent of the then 105 million urban employees. The rest of the urban workforce worked in collective enterprises, which were in practice state owned but outside the planning mechanism. There was no labour market – jobs were assigned by the local state labour bureau.

By 2019, China's workforce was 775 million, the world's largest, and the employment mix was very different. The state-owned sector accounted for only 12.4 per cent of urban employment. Half of the workforce, some 405 million in urban and rural areas worked for private firms or were self-employed. This was a five-fold increase since 2000. Primary sector employment was 195 million (25.1 per cent of the workforce), secondary industry numbered 213 million employees (27.5 per cent) and tertiary employment had risen to 367 million (47.4 per cent). As shown in Table 3.5, the change in the structure of employment has been especially quick over the past two decades. In 2000, the primary sector still accounted for half of all employed persons, while the private sector and self-employed narrowly defined employed 74.8 million, about 10.4 per cent of the workforce. Nevertheless, 44 per cent of the workforce was still employed in areas designated rural, which is an anomalous classification these days in the context of huge mega-city urban regions (see Chapter 6).

Table 3.5 Employment by sectors, rural–urban and ownership classification, selected years

	1980	1990	2000	2010	2019
Total employed persons (millions)	423.6	647.5	720.9	761.1	774.7
Primary Industry	291.2	389.1	360.4	279.3	194.5
% share	68.7	60.1	50.0	36.7	25.1
Secondary Industry	77.1	138.6	162.2	218.4	213.1
% share	18.2	21.4	22.5	28.7	27.5
Tertiary Industry	55.3	119.8	198.2	263.3	367.2
% share	13.1	18.5	27.5	34.6	47.4
Employed persons by urban and rural area (millions)					
Urban employed persons	105.3	170.4	231.5	346.9	442.5
Rural employed persons	318.4	477.1	489.3	414.2	332.2
% share	75.2	73.7	67.9	54.4	42.9
Employed persons in urban non-private units (millions)					
State-owned units	80.2	103.5	81.0	65.2	54.7
% share urban employment	76.2	60.7	35.0	18.8	12.4
Urban collective-owned units	24.3	35.5	15.0	6.0	3.0
Cooperative units			1.6	1.6	0.6
Joint ownership units		1.0	0.4	0.4	0.1
Limited liability corporations			6.9	26.1	66.1
Share-holding corporations Ltd			4.6	10.2	18.8
Hong Kong, Macao & Taiwan		0.0	3.1	7.7	11.6
Foreign funded units		0.6	3.3	10.5	12.0
TOTAL	104.4	140.6	115.9	127.7	166.9*
Employed persons in private enterprises and self-employed industrial and commercial units (millions)					
Private enterprises in urban areas		0.6	12.7	60.7	145.7
Self-employed in urban areas	0.8	6.1	21.4	44.7	116.9
Private enterprises in rural areas		1.1	11.4	33.5	82.7
Self-employed in rural areas		14.9	29.3	25.4	60.0
Township & village enterprises (**)	30.0	92.7	128.2	158.9	
TOTAL	30.8	115.4	203.0	323.2	405.26

Notes: *The discrepancy between this total and Table 4.5 provincial total of employed persons in urban non-private units is not explained by the NSB.

**TVEs were commune and brigade industries in 1980; by 2013, these had been transformed into private-owned entities and reclassified.

Sources: CSY (2020: tables 4.1, 4.2); CSY (2011: table 4.2).

In general, the numbers employed in the primary sector are probably overstated and may be only around 10 per cent. Another 128.2 million in 2000 were employed in township and village enterprises, which were ostensibly collective owned enterprises but often in practice private-run firms (see Chapter 4).

Differences between the provinces in the size and structure of their human resources are large, much as we have seen with the level and structure of GDP. Some of these differences are summarized in Table 3.6. The three province-level megacities of Beijing, Tianjin and Shanghai are overwhelmingly urban, their once rural areas accounting for less than 20 per cent of the population and transformed into dormitory suburbs. Other highly developed East China provinces such as Guangdong, Jiangsu and Zhejiang have an urbanization level about 10 percentage points above the national average of 60.6 per cent. Urbanization in West China has increased rapidly over the past decade or two and spurred on the past decade by the poverty alleviation programme that has relocated millions from remote villages to towns, but is well below the national average: Guizhou is 49 per cent, Yunnan 48.9 per cent, Gansu 48.5 per cent and Xinjiang 51.9 per cent. Urbanization is considered in more detail in Chapter 6.

Chinese working lives for the past two decades have been governed by increasingly efficient labour markets. Gone are the once all-encompassing *danwei* (work unit), which provided cradle to grave welfare for urban workers, the "iron rice bowl" (*tie fanwan*), and the allocation of jobs by labour bureaux. Gone also are the compressed wage bands, the almost zero return to education and the restrictions on internal migration.

Wages grew slowly from the 1980s through the 1990s, although in international comparative terms annual manufacturing real wages barely changed because of the adjustment in China's exchange rate over the period (Li *et al.* 2012).[7] Beginning in the late 1990s real wage growth accelerated in part due to labour market reforms that allowed stronger growth of the private sector and in part due to increased openness of the economy that led to an inflow of foreign firms. From around 2004, demand for unskilled labour began to exceed the supply from the countryside and the

Table 3.6 Population and employment by province, 2019

	Population			Selected employment types	
	Total (million)	Urban (million)	Urban (%)	Urban non-private employment (millions)	Private enterprise & self-employed employment (millions) *
NATIONAL TOTAL	1,400.1	848.4	60.6	171.6	405.2
Beijing	21.5	18.7	86.6	7.9	11.9
Tianjin	15.6	13.0	83.5	2.7	2.3
Hebei	75.9	43.7	57.6	5.8	14.1
Shanxi	37.3	22.2	59.6	4.4	6.9
Inner Mongolia	25.4	16.1	63.4	2.8	6.2
Liaoning	43.5	29.6	68.1	5.0	10.4
Jilin	26.9	15.7	58.3	2.8	8.2
Heilongjiang	37.5	22.8	60.9	3.5	5.4
Shanghai	24.3	21.4	88.3	7.2	15.6
Jiangsu	80.7	57.0	70.6	13.3	35.3
Zhejiang	58.5	41.0	70.0	9.9	27.8
Anhui	63.7	35.5	55.8	5.8	15.7
Fujian	39.7	26.4	66.5	6.4	16.8
Jiangxi	46.7	26.8	57.4	4.5	11.0
Shandong	100.7	61.9	61.5	10.7	37.6
Henan	96.4	51.3	53.2	9.7	18.8
Hubei	59.3	36.2	61.0	6.5	19.1
Hunan	69.2	39.6	57.2	6.0	10.5
Guangdong	115.2	82.3	71.4	20.6	50.7
Guangxi	49.6	25.3	51.1	4.0	10.3
Hainan	9.5	5.6	59.2	1.0	2.4
Chongqing	31.2	20.9	66.8	3.7	13.8
Sichuan	83.8	45.1	53.8	7.9	13.3
Guizhou	36.2	17.8	49.0	3.2	8.3
Yunnan	48.6	23.8	48.9	3.7	9.2
Tibet	3.5	1.1	31.5	0.4	0.9
Shaanxi	38.8	23.0	59.4	5.0	10.3
Gansu	26.5	12.8	48.5	2.5	5.2
Qinghai	6.1	3.4	55.5	0.7	1.2
Ningxia	7.0	4.2	59.9	0.7	1.5
Xinjiang	25.2	13.1	51.9	3.2	4.8

Note: *Industrial and commercial activity only, including both urban and rural.

Sources: CSY (2020: tables 2.8, 4.5, 4.6).

wages rose. Real wages for migrant workers grew about 7.8 per cent a year from 2003 to 2007 and increased to 12.4 per cent a year from 2008 to 2015. The four-fold increase in unskilled wages over this period eroded the profitability of labour-intensive export-oriented manufacturers (Naughton 2018: 230–31).

In 2018, the average annual wage of employees in the urban "non-private units" (*fei siying danwei*) was ¥82,413 ($12,455), while for those in the private sector (private firms and self-employed, *siying he geti*) the annual wage was ¥49,575 ($7,492).[8] Both had increased more than 2.5 times over the ten years to 2018 (CSY 2019: tables 4.15 and 4.16). Regional differences were large. Wages on average were highest in Beijing – ¥145,766 for the non-private sector and ¥76,908 for the private sector – as indeed were living costs too, and the lowest in Heilongjiang (¥60,780) and Shanxi (¥34,535) respectively. Sectoral differences compounded regional ones. Financial sector non-private employees in Beijing were most highly rewarded in 2018 and took home on average ¥266,921, while the lowest paid were Hebei employees for primary producers earning just ¥23,402 a year, about $3,536. Manufacturing private sector wages in the coastal provinces in 2018 were 34 per cent higher on average than for workers in the inland provinces (computed from CSY 2019: table 4.16).

China's labour markets remain dualistic, split between rural and urban, and within the urban sector between those who have an urban household registration (*hukou*) and migrant workers. Rural–urban migration has played a pivotal role in the post-1980 economic growth of China, increasing the level of urbanization from less than 20 per cent to 60 per cent by 2020. Migrants filled the jobs on construction sites building the offices, apartments, shopping malls and infrastructure of the cities, and in the export-oriented factories that made China the workshop of the world by the early 2000s. But the household registration (*hukou*) system, introduced in the late 1950s to control rural–urban migration, continues to impede rural migrants settling in cities and contributes to the persistent large gaps between rural and urban incomes, education and health, which are discussed in Chapter 5.

Measuring rural–urban migration flows is imprecise. The main metric is the "floating population" (*liudong renkou*), which refers to those living away from their household registration for more than six months. It does not capture short-term and short-distance migrants. In 1982, less than 1 per cent of China's population was floating; this level increased rapidly during the 1990s and 2000s, reaching 121 million in 2000 (9.6 per cent) and peaked at 253 million (18.9 per cent) in 2014 (CSY 2019: table 2.3). The largest population flows were from central provinces – about half from Sichuan, Anhui, Henan and Hunan – to Guangdong in South China and Shanghai, Jiangsu and Zhejiang in East China. In recent years the floating population has declined slightly. The reasons are unclear. Partly this is due to better paid jobs at inland factories, which have been relocated from the coastal provinces as wages rose from the mid-2000s. Partly the trend also reflects migrants settling down and the formation of migrant households in cities, despite the *hukou* difficulties. One-third of the census-counted 2000 floating population was still in the cities in 2010 and only 27 per cent of them were single, the remainder with a sibling or a spouse (30 per cent), children (38 per cent) or a parent (5 per cent) in their household (Naughton 2018: 140–1).

Official unemployment levels are low, even below the level that would be considered full employment in market economies.[9] These data only report registered unemployed in urban areas. In 2018, the reported level was 3.1 per cent (CSY 2019: table 4.17). Others who might be looking for work are unrecorded. In the early 2000s, several studies reported urban unemployment two to three times higher than official data. Between 1993 and 2003, the downsizing of SOEs – "grasp the big, let go the small" (*zhuada fangxiao*) – laid off almost 50 million workers or about 40 per cent of the public enterprise workforce. Unemployment peaked in 1997 at 10 per cent, comprising about 5 million registered unemployed and 11 million laid off workers (Naughton 2018: 209, 214–16). Regional variations in urban unemployment are relatively large, from just 1.4 per cent in Beijing in 2018 to 4 per cent in Heilongjiang, which with the other two provinces of the Northeast have the highest average unemployment in urban China of 3.8 per cent (CSY 2019: table 4.17). Rural under- and unemployed are matters of guesswork and not enumerated.

INTERNATIONAL TRADE AND FOREIGN INVESTMENT

China and the world economy were joined over the past 40 years in ways that profoundly changed both. In 1978, China was an isolated economy. Its international trade was less than 1 per cent of world trade. Foreign investment was negligible. China became the world's largest exporter in 2006 and the world's largest trader in 2012. Since the 1990s China has been one of the largest destinations for foreign direct investment (FDI). The openness of China has been exceptional for a continental-sized economy. Its experience is a classic example of how economies with different factor endowments can benefit from trading with each other. China is a labour-rich and land-poor (resources) economy. Opening up to trade enabled China to produce labour-intensive exports in firms that were often foreign-invested and import essential food, raw materials and intermediate products. As China became more integrated into the global economy it imported capital- and technology-intensive goods, which in turn enabled China to increasingly move up the value chain. China's rapid economic growth after 1978 would be unimaginable without this trade (Lardy 1992, 1994, 2002).

China's emergence as a global trading power is shown in Figures 3.8 and 3.9. Exports and imports grew strongly from the late 1970s, increasing from 5 per cent of GDP in 1978 to 20 per cent in the mid-1990s and 2000s, with a dip in between. Trade surged after China's 2001 entry to the WTO (Figure 3.8). Exports reached 35 per cent of GDP in 2006–07 and imports 29 per cent. This opened up a huge merchandize trade surplus, which peaked at 7.4 per cent of GDP in 2007 (Naughton 2018: 401). Around 2001–02 China had caught up with average world levels of openness (Figure 3.9) and thereafter was more open until 2007. Although China's export/GDP ratio fell back in the 2010s, China's share of world exports continued to rise, peaking at 11.1 per cent in 2015, and has remained above

Figure 3.8   Exports and imports as a share of GDP (%)

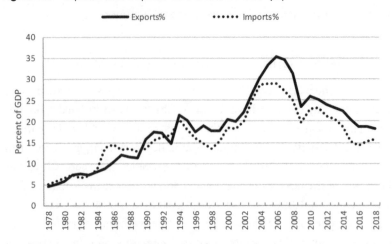

Sources: CSY (2001: table 17.2); CSY (2019: tables 3.1, 11.2).

Figure 3.9   China's exports in global perspective

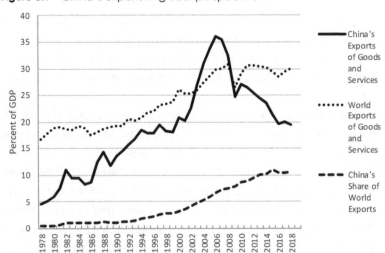

Source: World Bank WDI, 2020 revision.

10 per cent. Since 1978 China has experienced only three periods of short downturns in exports: 1983, 2009 and 2015–16. China ran a trade deficit 11 times between 1979 and 1994, but none since. The export surge after joining the WTO – coupled with currency controls – quickly saw China run up a foreign exchange reserve that topped out at $3.8 trillion in 2013–14 from just $166 million in 2000. This rise contributed to the global imbalances of the period and the on-going friction with trading partners that boiled over into the US President Trump "trade war" with China.

Among the top-20 trade partners for 2018, shown in Table 3.7, China runs a huge trade surplus with the United States ($323 billion), Hong Kong ($294 billion) and lesser surpluses with the Netherlands, India and the UK. It has a large trade deficit with 11 of them, the largest of which is Taiwan ($129 billion), South Korea ($96 billion) and Australia ($58 billion). The data reflects a pattern on one hand similar to other East Asian countries – a reliance on imports of raw materials and energy – and on the other China's place in the global supply chains as an assembler of manufactured goods. Australia, Brazil, Saudi Arabia and other resource-rich countries supply iron ore, alumina, oil, among other materials, while Taiwan, Korea, Japan, Germany and the like supply the intermediate components for assembly or superior technological goods. Many of these intermediate components and superior goods come from the United States, but it consumes about $3 of Chinese manufactures for every $1 it exports to China.[10]

Countries that are heavily dependent on China as an export market might be perceived as hostage to China and retaliation by the government unhappy with their policies, but that neglects China's own vulnerabilities. For example, China has been Australia's number one export market for more than a decade, and accounts for about 40 per cent of its exports, but quick diversification for China would be difficult and quite a few of the Australian exporters are actually owned by Chinese interests. Shifting assembly out of China has been mooted as trade friction between China and the United States escalated in the late 2010s (*Nikkei Asian Review* 2020). That was already underway for low-tech products – even PRC companies have moved offshore to tap cheaper labour markets rather

Table 3.7 China's top-20 trading partners in 2018

REGION	Merchandise trade in US$ billion				Rank order	
	Total	Exports	Imports	BoT*	Exports	Imports
United States	633.5	478.4	155.1	323	1	4
Japan	327.7	147.0	180.7	−34	3	2
South Korea	313.4	108.8	204.6	−96	4	1
Hong Kong	310.5	302.0	8.5	294	2	39
Taiwan	226.2	48.6	177.6	−129	11	3
Germany	183.8	77.5	106.3	−29	6	5
Australia	153.1	47.3	105.8	−58	13	6
Vietnam	147.8	83.9	64.0	20	5	8
Brazil	111.2	33.7	77.6	−44	20	7
Malaysia	108.6	45.4	63.2	−18	14	9
Russia	107.1	48.0	59.1	−11	12	10
India	95.5	76.7	18.8	58	7	27
Thailand	87.5	42.9	44.6	−2	17	12
Netherlands	85.2	72.8	12.3	61	8	32
Singapore	82.8	49.0	33.7	15	10	15
United Kingdom	80.4	56.5	23.9	33	9	21
Indonesia	77.3	43.2	34.1	9	16	14
Canada	63.5	35.2	28.4	7	18	17
Saudi Arabia	63.3	17.4	45.9	−28	28	11
France	62.9	30.7	32.2	−2	22	16

Note: Countries are ranked by the size of total trade (exports and imports); BoT = the balance of trade between China and the respective trade partner.

Source: CSY (2019: table 11.5).

than move inland – but it might prove more difficult for hi-tech products, which rely on a sophisticated industrial ecology in China, where intermediate components come from both local and foreign suppliers as well as the availability of a suitable workforce and excellent logistics infrastructure (CSY 2019: tables 28.15, 28.16, appendix table 11.5; CIA 2020; IMF 2020).

Table 3.8 Regional origin of exports, percentage share and per capita value (US$)

	2000		2009		2018	
	% share	p.c.$	% share	p.c.$	% share	p.c.$
East	85.8	481	88.9	2,155	82.1	3,798
Northeast	5.8	136	3.5	389	2.8	632
Central	4.2	30	3.7	125	7.7	513
West	4.1	29	3.9	129	7.5	493

Note: See Table 3.3 for the provincial composition of the regional classification scheme.
Source: CSY, various years.

In domestic terms, international trade helped fuel economic growth, but the impact was uneven across China's provinces. Most exporters, many of which are foreign invested, are located in East China. The East China share of total exports by value has barely changed since 2000 and remains above 80 per cent (Table 3.8). Relocation inland of labour-intensive manufacturing over the past decade has pushed up the share of central China to 7.7 per cent in 2018 and West China to 7.5 per cent, but the share of the Northeast has declined since 2000. The per capita value of exports from East China was $3,798 in 2018, six times that of the Northeast, seven times that of central China and almost nine times that of West China.

Foreign investment

Opening up China to foreign trade in 1978 was twinned with opening China to FDI. China sought to woo foreign firms to come to China, to partner with local firms, to transfer technology to them and to engage in export-oriented manufacturing. This policy was a radical departure from the autarky of the past. China's model of export-led modernization followed the experience of Southeast Asian countries such as Singapore, Thailand and Malaysia, which had developed policies to attract multinational enterprises (MNEs). This contrasted with the Northeast Asia approach: Japan, South Korea and Taiwan had shunned FDI and MNEs had played little role in their periods of fast-growth economic development.

FDI inflows were modest throughout the 1980s and development loans were nearly double the value of investment flows in most years (see Figure 3.10). Foreign investors were wary of the regulatory regime, including official emphasis on joint ventures, the lack of safeguards for intellectual property and controls on the remittance of profits. Most investment was limited to the Special Economic Zones (SEZs) or the then rural prefectures in the Pearl River Delta between Guangzhou and Hong Kong. FDI inflows picked up from the mid-1980s in response to policy inducements. In 1984, 14 coastal cities and Hainan Island were opened to FDI; in 1988 economic and development zones opened up most of the eastern China coastal provinces; and a raft of more liberal policies were also adopted.[11]

FDI surged in the 1990s, as shown in Figure 3.10, following Deng Xiaoping's 1992 "Southern tour".[12] Between 1990 and 1992, FDI tripled to $11 billion a year in spite of the negative sentiment after the 1989 Tiananmen Square Incident and reached $45.5 billion in 1998 before the Asian Financial Crisis pegged it back to $40 billion for 1999–2000. After China joined the WTO, FDI surged again from $46.9 billion in 2001 to $92.4 billion in 2008 and has grown most years to reach $138 billion in 2019, apart from minor contractions in 2009 and 2012.

Asia has been the major source for FDI since the start of China's opening and over the past decade has even increased, as shown in Table 3.9. Hong Kong has been the number one "foreign" investor. The Newly Industrial Economies (NIEs) of Hong Kong, Singapore, South Korea and Taiwan have accounted for more than 60 per cent of all FDI in China since

Figure 3.10 Foreign direct investment and loans to China, 1979/82–2019

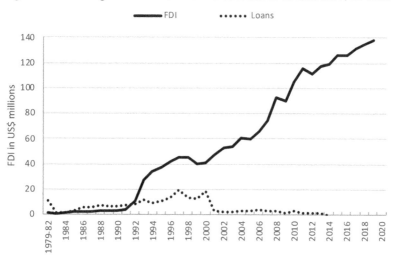

Note: Loans also include other minor non-equity foreign investment in some years.

Source: CSY (2020: table 11.13).

the 1990s except for the two years of the Asian Financial Crisis.[13] Europe and North American FDI in China peaked during the late 1990s and early 2000s. The US was the second-largest source of FDI after Hong Kong in 2000 but slipped to the fifth largest in 2010 and the eighth largest in 2018. In the late 1990s, FDI from Hong Kong declined to 40 per cent in 1998 and 38 per cent in 2000, but since has grown to account for 67 per cent of all FDI in 2018. The Asian share of FDI rose rapidly after China joined the WTO. Taiwan and Korean firms in particular relocated their manufacturing lines for high-technology products, such as laptops and mobile phones, many of which were produced for global brands. In 2005, China surpassed the United States to become the world foremost high-tech exporter (Naughton 2018: 376).

Two intriguing facets of China's FDI became clearer in the 2000s: the role of tax havens and Hong Kong, which since 1997 has been a special administrative region of the PRC, but treated as a separate country for purposes of international trade and investment.[14] By the mid-1990s, the

Table 3.9 Foreign direct investment in China by investor origins, 1990–2018

	1990 $ million	1990 %	2000 $ million	2000 %	2010 $ million	2010 %	2018 $ million	2018 %
World	3,487	100	40,715	100	105,732	100	134,966	100
Asia	2,724	78.1	25,482	62.6	77,592	73.4	107,013	79.3
Europe	151	4.3	4,765	11.7	5,922	5.6	11,194	8.3
Latin America	7	0.2	4,617	11.3	13,526	12.8	9,026	6.7
North America	464	13.3	4,786	11.8	4,014	3.8	5,148	3.8
Oceania	50	1.4	694	1.7	2,328	2.2	1,909	1.4
Africa	<1	0.0	288	0.7	1,280	1.2	610	0.5

Top-15 Sources of foreign investment in China (based on the 2018 rank order)

	1990 $ million	1990 rank	2000 $ million	2000 rank	2010 $ million	2010 rank	2018 $ million	2018 rank
Hong Kong	1,913	1	15,500	1	60,567	1	89,917	1
Singapore	50	6	2,172	6	5,428	3	5,210	2
Virgin Islands	N.R.*		3,833	3	10,447	2	4,712	3
South Korea	N.R.		1,490	7	2,692	6	4,667	4
Cayman Islands	N.R.		624	12	2,499	7	4,068	5
Japan	503	2	2,916	4	4,084	4	3,798	6
Germany	64	5	1,041	9	888	13	3,674	7
United States	456	3	4,384	2	3,017	5	2,689	8
United Kingdom	13	11	1,164	8	710	14	2,482	9
Bermuda	N.R.		122	24	360	20	2,167	10
Samoa	N.R.		283	15	1,773	8	1,554	11
Taiwan	222	4	2,297	5	2,476	9	1,391	12
Macao	N.R.		347	13	655	15	1,280	13
Netherlands	16	10	789	11	914	12	1,273	14
France	2106	9	853	10	1,238	10	1,011	15
NIE-4	2,186	62.7%	21,458	52.7%	71,163	67.3%	101,186	75.0%

Notes: In 1990, the Taiwan investment was reported in the "Other" category in the CSY. My estimate comes from Deng (2000). The Other category probably also included small FDI flows from Africa and Latin America. Panama was the only tax haven reported. Australia was the seventh largest investor in 1990 and was a prominent investor throughout the 1990s. NIE-4 comprises the four newly industrialized economies of Hong Kong, Singapore, South Korea and Taiwan. South Korean FDI before its recognition of the PRC in 1992 was unofficial. NR = not reported. *Sources*: CSY (1991, 2001, 2011, 2019); Deng (2000).

tax havens of the Virgin Islands, Cayman Islands and Samoa were increasingly important sources of foreign investment.[15] For the past two decades these three tax havens have been among the top 15 sources of FDI in China – the Virgin Islands has been the second or third most important source (see Table 3.9). Other tax havens have also figured at different times over the past two decades, including Bermuda, Barbados, Belize, and Panama in the Americas; Mauritius and the Seychelles in the Indian Ocean; and Vanuatu in the Pacific.

Many of the China-investing firms from the tax havens no doubt have principals in Western countries, but many are also Chinese owned. That means a lot of China's FDI is "round-tripping" Chinese money, which leaves China by one way or another and returns dressed up as "foreign" investment. Hong Kong serves a similar purpose for subsidiaries of PRC firms and those of large Southeast Asian conglomerates such as Indonesia's Lippo Group, among many others. These firms use their Hong Kong subsidiaries to manage investments in China. That has allowed Hong Kong to rank consistently as the number one foreign investor in China. Macau has also been among the top-15 investors since 2000.

In the early 1980s, FDI was in almost equal proportion in three ownership forms: equity joint ventures (EJV), contractual joint ventures (CJV) and joint exploration (see Table 3.10). Joint exploration investments, which accounted for 29 per cent of the $1.6 billion in FDI in 1985, were wholly in minerals extraction, mostly offshore oil exploration projects in collaboration with major oil firms, but rapidly dwindled over the decade. EJVs and CJVs accounted each for 35 per cent of FDI in 1985, then valued at slightly under $0.6 billion.

China's preferred FDI vehicle was the EJV, a joint venture between one or more foreign firms and one or more Chinese firms. The Chinese partner firms were at this time all state-owned. Foreign MNEs were in effect partnering with the Chinese state via SOEs. Another type of foreign-invested venture, the CJVs – reported in official statistics as cooperative operation enterprises – were non-equity relational contracts mostly used by Hong Kong firms in partnership with township organizations in the Pearl River

Delta of Guangdong. The Chinese partner provided the buildings and the workers and the Hong Kong partner the materials, technology and management. During the 1980s nearly all of Hong Kong's manufacturing industry moved to Guangdong. This created a sophisticated export hub where the labour-intensive assembly and processing was done in South China and the high value design, marketing, finance and trade aspects of the product were handled in Hong Kong, as well as some of the capital-intensive finishing processes. Taiwan traders and investors also entered China via Hong Kong, which joined South China, Hong Kong and Taiwan in a "China Circle" of integrated manufacturers (Deng 2000; Naughton 2018: 437–8, 448).

Although wholly foreign-owned enterprises (WFOEs) were reluctantly allowed from the start, and insisted on by some big MNEs, in 1985 the sum of all FDI in this form was less than 1 per cent (see Table 3.10). As China opened and the economy grew Chinese officials came to realize that the transfer of technology and managerial know-how could occur without insisting on equity participation. WFOEs increased rapidly from the late 1980s to become the main ownership form by 2000 (47.3 per cent). By 2010, WFOEs accounted for 76.6 per cent of all FDI. Meanwhile, the share of the CJVs had shrunk to 16.2 per cent by 2000 and to 0.6 per cent in 2018. In recent years new forms of FDI ownership have emerged, including FDI Shareholding Enterprises and Partnerships, which account for 6.1 per cent and 0.6 per cent respectively in 2018. Foreign-invested firms including those from Taiwan, Hong Kong and Macau are significant employers providing 23.6 million jobs in 2018 (see Table 3.5).

FDI was concentrated in the provinces along the eastern seaboard, in the developed Yangzi River Delta regional economy centred on Shanghai and neighbouring Jiangsu and Zhejiang, and in the SEZs in Fujian and the Guangdong Pearl River Delta. In 2000, East China accounted for 80.2 per cent of all FDI and the per capita value ($82.40) was more than twice any other region (see Table 3.11). Over the past two decades FDI has increasingly shifted to inland provinces, mostly in response to changes in the labour market, which was discussed above. Between 2000 and 2018,

Table 3.10 Foreign direct investment by ownership form, selected years 1985–2018

	1985		1990		2000		2010		2018	
	(USD bill)	%	(USD bill)	%	(USD bill)	%	(USD bill)	%	(USD bill)	%
Foreign Direct Investments	1.66		3.49		40.7		105.7		135.0	
Equity Joint Venture	0.58	35.0	1.89	54.1	14.3	35.2	22.5	21.3	34.5	25.6
Contractual Joint Venture	0.59	35.2	0.67	19.3	6.6	16.2	1.6	1.5	0.8	0.6
Wholly Foreign-owned Enterprise	0.01	0.8	0.68	19.6	19.3	47.3	81.0	76.6	89.4	66.2
FDI Shareholding Enterprise	—	—	—	—	0.1	0.3	0.6	0.6	8.3	6.1
Joint Exploration (Coop Dev)	0.48	29.0	0.24	7.0	0.4	0.9	—	—	1.2	0.9
Partnership	—	—	—	—	—	—	—	—	0.8	0.6

Notes: Data for 1985 and 1990 are from Ministry of Foreign Trade and Economic Cooperation reported in the CSY. The FDI value is the FDI used (committed) in that year and is less than the reported contracted value, which may be realized in subsequent years. It is a flow measure. Contractual Joint Ventures were also known as Cooperative Operation Enterprises while Joint Exploration Enterprises were also called Cooperative Development Enterprises.

Sources: CSY (1986, 1991, 2001, 2011, 2019).

central China's share of FDI increased 5.5 times from 6.4 per cent to 35.6 per cent and the per capita value reached $210.10, slightly above that of East China. Even the remote West China almost doubled its share by 2018, but the Northeast, which had increased its share in the 2000s, received less FDI than in 2000.

Table 3.11 Regional distribution of FDI, percentage share and per capita value (US$)

	2000		2009		2018	
	% share	p.c.$	% share	p.c.$	% share	p.c.$
East	80.2	82.4	64.4	199.3	50.4	205.3
Northeast	8.7	37.4	12.3	173.7	5.0	100.1
Central	6.4	8.3	14.0	60.3	35.6	210.1
West	4.7	6.0	9.3	39.3	9.0	52.1

Note: See Table 3.3 for the provincial composition of the regional classification scheme.
Source: CSY, various years.

China has not only been a major importer of capital through FDI but had begun to export capital from the first decade of its opening. An early investment was the US$100 million purchase of an interest in the Channar iron ore mine in Western Australia in 1987, which would remain China's largest overseas investment for many years.[16] China's early outward foreign direct investments (OFDI) sought to acquire raw materials, such as minerals, but also to gain managerial expertise through joint operation of these ventures. Seconded staff rotated through these overseas ventures would return to the parent company in China having gained experience abroad in modern management and international operations, an exceptionally valuable although difficult to quantify knowledge transfer that has contributed hugely to the growth of the Chinese economy.

In 2002, China began to encourage domestic firms to "go out" (*zou chuqu*). OFDI picked up quickly in the 2000s and surged after the GFC. It increased nearly four-fold from $55.9 billion in 2008, which was twice the level of 2007, to $196.2 billion in 2016 (see Figure 3.11). The rise took China from the seventeenth-largest overseas investor in 2007 to the second largest. Outward FDI in 2015 surpassed inward FDI, making China a net capital exporter. In recent years state and private firms have aggressively acquired firms abroad. Their motivation was to seek advance technology, brands and product markets through their acquisitions, which will be explored in more detail in Chapter 4. The total stock of OFDI (Figure 3.11) has increased from $29.9 billion in 2002 to $2,198.9 billion in 2019.

Figure 3.11 China's outward foreign investment flow and stock, 2002–19

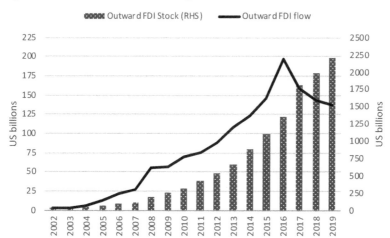

Note: Data for 2002–05 includes only non-financial outward FDI.

Sources: CSY (2020: table 11.19); Statistical Bulletin of China's Outward Foreign Direct Investment (http://fec.mofcom.gov.cn/article/tjsj/tjgb/).

In 2017, China's central government cracked down on the rampant expansion offshore, which resulted in OFDI declining from a peak of $196.2 billion in 2016 in each successive year to $136.9 billion in 2019. Many conglomerates were made to divest overseas holdings; entrepreneurs were arrested and imprisoned.[17] Nevertheless, China still accounts for 10 per cent of global FDI flows the past four years and in 2019 ranked third after the United States and the Netherlands (MofCom 2020). About

70 per cent of OFDI in both years was in leasing and business services, manufacturing, wholesale and retail, and finance (MofCom 2018, 2019, 2020). Chinese OFDI can be found in more than 180 countries, but 92 per cent is concentrated in just 20 countries (MofCom 2019, 2020). OFDI flows have gone primarily to Asia – 73.8 per cent in 2018, of which 82 per cent was to Hong Kong – and next Latin America, the major tax havens of the Cayman Islands and Virgin Islands with 3.8 per cent and 5 per cent of the total respectively. The United States received 5.3 per cent (CSY 2019: table 11.19).

The distribution of China's OFDI has remained fairly consistent since the mid-2000s. The Cayman Islands and Virgin Islands have been among the top-5 destinations for foreign investment most years, except 2018 when there was a negative flow for the Cayman Islands – $6.61 billion was repatriated to China. But these tax havens are way stations for Chinese capital flow to another destination – and often back to China. Hong Kong has been the leading destination almost every year, sometimes pipped by a tax haven. Most of the top-15 destinations are advanced economies such as Australia, the United States, Canada, Germany, the UK, Singapore and Japan. Several are major sources of energy and raw materials, including Australia, Indonesia and Russia.

African destinations for OFDI were relatively prominent in the 2000s. Algeria, Guinea, Nigeria, Sudan and South Africa were often in the top-15 destinations. Since 2010, OFDI flows to Africa have been lower than media reporting of China's investments in the continent would suggest (CSY 2006, 2011, 2018, 2019). Africa nevertheless is a focus of geopolitical gamesmanship with strategic investments in selected ports and infrastructure. More than a million Chinese work or run businesses in Africa (French 2014; Mohan *et al.* 2014). China has also sought to win the hearts and minds of the continent through "soft power" diplomacy and media engagement (Zhang *et al.* 2016), as well as through aid and investment. China's aid to Africa is a mix of conventional aid, debts and trade credits, and project partnerships (Brautigam 2009). A high-profile initiative is the Forum on China–Africa Cooperation (FOCAC) at which major projects are often announced. While China has made positive contributions to the development of countries in Africa, building infrastructure and providing employment and training (Calabrese & Tang 2020), it is not a major aid donor in a conventional sense because the support is largely in the form of export credits, supplier credits, or commercial (non-concessional) loans (CARI 2020). Since the 2000s, China has become the biggest bilateral lender to Africa, increasing sovereign debt. This became painfully clear in 2020 as the coronavirus pandemic reduced the ability of many countries to service their debt, pushing Zambia into default in November. The IMF, World Bank and major Western creditors have criticised China's lack of willingness to engage in debt relief measures (*Financial Times* 2020o; WSJ 2020; World Bank 2020a).[18]

None of the focal BRI countries of Central, South or West Asia figure prominently as destinations for China's OFDI, despite the official claim that 10,000 China-invested enterprises had been established in BRI countries (MofCom 2019).[19] This is not surprising. In 2013 when the BRI was first announced, the initiative was conceived as an infrastructure development programme, although one of the primary goals was to create an outlet for China's surplus capacity in aluminium, cement and steel, as well as power plant design and constructions services, among others.[20] The projects would connect China westward overland via Central Asia to Europe and southwards via both maritime and land routes through Southeast and South Asia to West Asia, Africa and beyond to Europe. China's goal, however, was primarily domestic: to find outlets for its huge over capacity in the aluminium, cement and steel industries and to strengthen security around its western borders with Central Asia. The main agents of China's BRI investments are the state policy banks, such as the China Development Bank and the China Exim Bank, and large state firms acting on official direction. Few non-state firms appear willing to invest in countries which are high risk and fragile in economic, environmental, political and social terms. Lending and investment to these countries are therefore mostly outside of the OFDI framework. Collier (2018: 71) observes that the discrepancy between China's rhetoric and actual OFDI in BRI "is quite striking".

In recent years the scope of BRI has expanded to embrace nearly all of China's aid and investment around the world without the geographical boundaries implied in the original concept. Many projects that began well before the BRI was announced, such as the Gwadar Port in Pakistan, are now an integral part. In 2019, MofCom reported non-financial China FDI to 56 BRI countries was $15.04 billion, down 3.8 per cent on the $15.64 billion of the previous year and accounting for 13.6 per cent of total OFDI. The BRI-area funds during these two years were mainly invested in Singapore, Vietnam, Laos, Indonesia, Pakistan, Thailand, Malaysia, UAE, Cambodia, Russia and Kazakhstan. Newly signed overseas engineering project contracts (*duiwai chengbao gongcheng xiangmu hetong*) were ten times the value of the OFDI flow for 2019, totalling $154.89 billion in 62 countries, which accounted for about 60 per cent of all such projects (MofCom 2019, 2020). These are mostly state-to-state agreed projects, delivered by large SOEs and financed through China's policy banks.

BANKING, FINANCE AND MONEY

The remaking of the modern banking and finance system in China has played a positive role in the remarkable growth of the real economy. There has been a huge financial deepening, the creation of new assets (saving deposits, stocks and bonds) that grow savings more rapidly than GDP. A common measure of the depth of the financial system is the ratio of broad money (M2) to GDP. M2 grew from just 32 per cent of GDP in 1978 to 162 per cent in 2003, paused for a few years, and resumed growing after 2011 to surpass 200 per cent (Naughton 2018: 480–1). Household savings deposits as a ratio of GDP have tracked a similar trajectory, rising from about 5 per cent in the late 1970s to about 80 per cent in the late 2010s. The diversification – broadening – of the financial system has been slower; banks dominate, and savers have still too few alternatives for higher returns on their savings, a typical characteristic of the "financial repression" facing Chinese households.[21]

Between 1952 and 1978, China had a mono-bank system. The People's Bank of China (PBOC) – for many years little more than a bureau of the Ministry of Finance – was the accountant and cashier for the planned economy, taking in payments and allocating funds to state enterprises according to the plan. Mao's economy did not need financial intermediation between savers and borrowers to allocate capital efficiently. The savings of ordinary Chinese were meagre. In 1979, Deng Xiaoping realized that China would need "real banks" that could "be levers of economic development and technological upgrading" (cited in Stent 2017: 64). The ensuing transformation of banking has created what Stent (2017) called a set of "hybrid" banks that are neither market nor state in their characteristics, which since the 2000s have combined the best practices of modern banking with the collectivist cultural values of China and the development goals of the party-state to grow the real economy.

The first step in building a new banking system was the separation of the central and commercial banking functions of the PBOC and the Ministry of Finance. Four state commercial banks were formed, each focused on a specialized area: the Agricultural Bank of China (ABC 1979); the Bank of China (BOC 1979), which had previously existed to handle foreign exchange and provide a window to the world via its Hong Kong subsidiary; the China Construction Bank (CCB 1979), and the Industrial and Commercial Bank of China (ICBC 1984).[22] The "Big Four" commercial banks were later joined by the Bank of Communications (BoCom).

Between 1984 and the mid-1990s, the Big Four became diversified commercial lenders to the whole economy. Meanwhile, a dozen large joint-stock banks were created, including several with substantial private capital (Shenzhen Development Bank, China Everbright Bank and China Minsheng Bank) and more than 100 provincial and city banks. Non-bank financial institutions, the first of which was the China International Trust and Investment Company (CITIC), proliferated. New laws were passed in 1994–95 to set up a legal framework for the commercial banks and the PBOC along with three policy banks – the China Development Bank (CDB), the Agricultural Development Bank and the China

Export-Import (China Exim) Bank. These were established to free the Big Four of politically guided "policy lending", such as loans for infrastructure projects at home or abroad. In 2003, the China Bank Regulatory Commission was established and took over the regulatory role of the PBOC.

By the middle 1990s, the inadequacies of the new banking system to meet the needs of the new mixed economy were apparent. About 80–85 per cent of all credit extended by state banks went to SOEs, yet by 1994 the non-state sector contribution to the gross value of industrial output had risen to 63 per cent and the annual contribution of state firms had fallen from about 90 per cent to less than 20 per cent (Stent 2017: 73, 76). Productivity in the private sector was two–three times higher than the state sector (Lardy 2014: 95). In addition, the banking system was weighed down with non-performing loans (NPLs) owed by SOEs. These bad loans were estimated to account for as much as 40 per cent of the balance sheet, which meant the banks were technically insolvent (Kroeber 2016: 130; Stent 2017: 76).

In 1997–98, the twin shocks of the Asian Financial Crisis and the collapse of the Guangdong International Trust and Investment Company, along with other trusts and small rural savings institutions, precipitated action. Premier Zhu Rongji struck out with two radical initiatives: he quickened the restructuring of SOEs (see Chapter 4) and took on the banking sector. The NPLs were stripped from the balance sheets of the Big Four and warehoused in four asset management companies (AMCs), one for each of the banks, which bought the bad loans at face value for an estimated cost of 15 per cent of the 2001 GDP (Naughton 2018: 493). The banks were restructured (corporatized and housed in an AMC-like bank holding company called Central Huijin), then recapitalized and finally listed on overseas stock exchanges. The latter was a brilliant move: it forced the banks to reform management processes to secure international investor confidence. The CCB was listed on the Hong Kong exchange in 2005, valuing it at a $67 billion, the BOC and ICBC in 2006, and the ABC in 2010. The ICBC is the largest bank in the world – with $4 trillion in assets, $42.3 billion in profits and 453,000 employees (Fortune Global 500 2018). The Big Four banks were ranked among the world's top-10 profitable companies in size in 2018.

By the mid-2010s, the Chinese banking system was the largest in the world, bigger than all of Europe's combined (Naughton 2018: 481). Although the financial system is still dominated by banks, change has gathered pace with the entry of new lenders. Table 3.12 shows the steady decline in the share of assets held by large state commercial banks until the mid-2010s, but thereafter they have increased their share again (Bisio 2020). Foreign banks account for very little of total assets despite promises in the WTO entry agreement that the financial sector would open to foreign participants. In 2019–20, there was some movement as Beijing approved several major investment houses taking 100 per cent control of their securities JVs.

Broadening of the financial system picked up from 2000. Bank loans were more than 90 per cent of "social financing" in the early 2000s (see Figure 3.12), which declined to 55 per cent in 2013, apart from the huge state-mandated disbursement of loans as part of the stimulus package during the GFC. Since 2013, however, banks loans have steadily regained share. Bank deposits and lending are still the main form of intermediation for funds provided to the corporate sector. Stocks and corporate bonds were an insignificant source of new lending until the 2010s. Consumer lending was negligible in 2000 but in the form of mortgages now accounts for about one-fifth of all lending. In the later 2000s, shadow banking grew strongly, but most of this was initially controlled by the banks at all tiers offering higher interest-bearing wealth management products routed through lightly regulated trusts. E-commerce giant Alibaba also entered the fray through its Yuebao saving product that sought to leverage its successful online payment system, Alipay, becoming one of the world's largest money-market funds. Peer-to-peer lending also emerged. Lending from these trusts and money-market funds ramped up non-bank credit to borrowers outside the regulated (and repressed) financial system (Kroeber 2016: 129, 139–40; Naughton 2018: 480, 504–05).

Table 3.12 Banking sector assets by bank type (%)

	number	2003	2007	2010	2013	2015	2020*
Policy Banks	3	7.7	8.1	8.0	8.3	9.7	10.6
Large state commercial banks	5	58.0	53.7	49.2	43.3	39.2	42.1
Joint stock commercial banks	12	10.7	13.7	15.6	17.8	18.6	18.8
City commercial banks	133	5.8	6.5	8.2	10	11.4	14.3
Rural banks and RCCs	2,303	9.7	10.5	11.2	12.1	12.4	14.3
Non-bank financial institutions		3.3	1.8	2.2	2.6	3.3	
Foreign banks	40	1.5	2.4	1.8	1.7	1.3	
Postal Savings Bank		3.2	3.3	3.7	4.1	4.2	

Note: *Data are for January 2020, while the policy bank data are from the 2018 annual reports for these banks. The large commercial banks numbered six, which now include the Postal Savings Bank. *Sources*: Naughton (2018: 489); CBRC 2019; Bisio 2020.

Stock markets were established in Shenzhen in 1990 and Shanghai in 1991. They are now among the largest in the world by market capitalization and turnover. In March 2020, the Shanghai Stock Exchange was ranked fourth largest with a capitalization value of $4.7 trillion and the Shenzhen Stock Exchange was ranked seventh with a value of $3.3 trillion.[23] Twenty years ago their combined market capitalization was under $200 billion, less than one-fortieth of current value. China is today the second-largest equities market after the United States. Trading is technically efficient for the tens of millions of Chinese stockholders and disclosure of information about firms far better than for non-listed firms. Nevertheless, state intervention to ensure financial stability warps incentives and investor behaviour, encouraging belief that poorly performing firms will be bailed out.

Figure 3.12 Structure of financial flows: annual new financing by type (%)

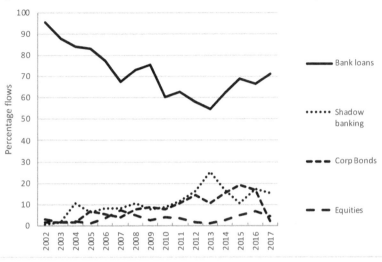

Notes: The percentages report the annual flow by type of "social financing", most recently described as the "aggregate financing to the real economy (flow)". Definition changes make the 2018 data not comparable to the earlier data, therefore excluded. Loans includes RMB and foreign loans in RMB equivalent; "shadow banking" is the recorded flows from trusts; bonds are corporate bonds (local government bonds are not included); and equities are stock market financing of non-financial securities.

Source: CSY (2019: table 18.3).

There were 3,777 companies listed on the main boards of the two exchanges at year-end 2019 (Figure 3.13). New listings increased from 2009 after several dull years: the number of firms on the Shenzhen main board increased 2.5 times and Shanghai's 1.7 times. Market capitalization has increased markedly, as has trading volume. The market capitalization of tradable (negotiable) stock was quite tiny until the mid-2000s. Total market capitalization increased from just $15 billion (¥86 billion) in 1993 to $99 billion in 1999. By 2007 capitalization had risen to $1,224 billion (¥9,306 billion) on the back of rampant speculation. After a fallback in 2008 because of the GFC, new listings pushed the combined market capitalization higher and propelled the China stock exchanges into the global top 10.

Figure 3.13 Companies listed on the Shanghai and Shenzhen Stock Exchanges and combined market capitalization, 1990–2019

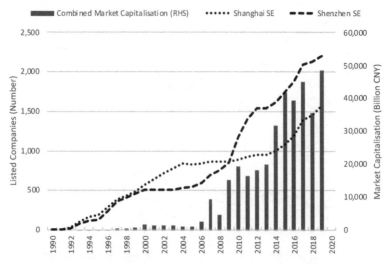

Sources: For market capitalization, CSY (1999: table 19.13), CSY (2001: table 19.14), CSY 2006: table 20.19), CSY (2012: table 19.15), CSY (2020: table 18.17); for listing numbers CSY (2020: table 18.15).

There are secondary boards that list thousands of small- and medium-sized enterprises. An over-the-counter board, the National Equities Exchange and Quotation, was introduced in 2012 that allowed trades in some 10,000 public limited firms that are not listed on either of the main exchanges. Shenzhen is the more innovative exchange, which reflects the private sector and technology activities in the SEZ, but smaller in total market capitalization. In 2009, Shenzhen introduced a special board to list firms from the high-growth electronic and pharmaceutical sectors. The Shanghai exchange in July 2019 launched a new science and technology-focused equities market billed as China's answer to the Nasdaq in New York. When the new board plan was unveiled in late 2018 Xi Jinping said it would "support Shanghai in cementing its position as an international financial centre and a hub of science and innovation" (*Financial Times* 2019).

Most of the large firms on the Shanghai exchange are state owned. And herein lies one of the big problems with the China equities market: unlike those in developed economies, the China market is not a market for corporate control because many shares are closely held by state-linked parties that block private investors gaining control. Although the number of shares technically tradable has increased from around 25–30 per cent of shares issued in the early 1990s to more than 70 per cent since 2010, in effect far fewer trade freely. Moreover, the movement in prices is driven more by government policy and the speculation of private investors second-guessing policy directions than market signals. The underlying fundamentals of the listed firms are almost irrelevant for their pricing. In the event of market weaknesses when private investors might dump shares, such as in mid-2015 when the market dropped 40 per cent in a few days, the government will intervene to tell the big state firms and domestic securities companies to buy stock.

As Naughton (2018: 498) observed, the volatility, high turnover and policy driven characteristics of the China stock markets reflects the lack of institutional investors – pension funds, mutual funds and insurance companies – that hold only about one-seventh of total shares. These types of investors, who hold shares for the long term are the foundation of stable capital markets in developed market economies. Private investors, contrary to popular belief, only hold about a quarter of all shares in China. About 60 per cent of shares are held by "general institutions", which comprise the parent companies of listed firms, such as the holding companies under the central government SASAC (see Chapter 4), and funds managed by securities firms. Planned liberalization of China's stock markets were put on hold after the 2015 meltdown. Internationalization – non-Chinese ownership of shares – is just 2 per cent when full internationalization would push it probably to the order of 20–40 per cent.

Often bond markets are bigger than stock markets in developed economies and their market capitalization is larger than GDP. China's bond market has grown rapidly since the mid-2000s to account for more than 60 per cent of GDP by the mid-2010s (Naughton 2018: 500). An unusual feature of the Chinese bond market is that most sellers of bonds are government actors. Government entities comprised more than half the bonds issued. About 28 per cent of issues were tied to the state-owned policy banks (the CDB had an outstanding issue of ¥71 trillion in 2016). Corporate bonds amounted to around 5 per cent of GDP compared with more than 50 per cent in the United States. Corporate bond issues also need regulatory approval, which is easier for SOEs (Naughton 2018: 501).

Aggregate debt has increased quickly since the GFC. Before 2008, the non-financial debt-to-GDP ratio, the debt owed by households, firms and governments, was around 140 per cent, which made China a relatively low-debt country. Debt increased to 179 per cent of GDP in 2012, reached 236 per cent by the end of 2016 and recent studies have put it at greater than 300 per cent (Naughton 2018: 508; Magnus 2018: 77). Most of the debt is owed by corporations and local governments, which in 2017 exceeded 200 per cent of GDP compared with the central government's 15 per cent and households' around 100 per cent (Magnus 2018: 78–9). The catalysts for this rapid build-up in debt was the ¥4 trillion ($586 billion) GFC stimulus package issued in November 2008. Short-term this stimulus was successful. It substituted for the fall in global demand and private domestic demand, which allowed the Chinese economy to rebound in 2009 and contributed notably to global economic recovery. Long term it has undone much of the success of the late 1990s in enforcing hard budget constraints on SOEs, state banks and local governments.

Local government debt is particularly conspicuous yet lack transparency. A lot of this debt is concealed in off the balance sheet obligations held in local government financing vehicles (LGFV) that were created to manage the projects funded by the GFC stimulus. LGFVs are development companies run by local governments, which have played a big role in local economic development and which the central government had previously kept under tight rein. Their projects were mostly funded through local government sale of land. After the GFC these proliferated as instruments for the dispersal of stimulus funds, which were poured into the queue of projects most local governments had planned but lacked the funds to proceed. These projects were ready-made to take the stimulus and explain the rapid uptake of the stimulus. The main problem was the LGFVs were in a legal limbo. Before 2014, local governments could not legally borrow or guarantee in their own name, yet the central government's acknowledgement carried an implicit guarantee. Responsibility for the debt was diffused and there were no obvious mechanisms to manage debt or default of LGFV debt. The 2014 budget reforms gave local government the right to borrow and to issue bonds, which became a means to offload debt as local government bonds. However, potential buyers often considered the bond interest rates non-competitive and state banks were forced to buy the debt. In 2015–16, some ¥8 trillion (about 10 per cent of GDP) was converted to local bonds, put on the state bank balance sheets and made the responsibility of the provincial governments (Naughton 2018: 533–4).

After four decades of reform the financial system remains the weakest link because there is insufficient breadth and diversity to intermediate the savings in the economy. Banks still dominate financial intermediation, the reallocation of capital from savers to borrowers, despite fintech innovations like the mobile payment systems of Alibaba and Tencent and other market driven disintermediation. Chinese citizen savers do not have sufficient viable outlets for their money other than squirreling away in banks or buying real estate. The rise in bank lending as a proportion of all lending to the corporate sector since the mid-2010s (Figure 3.12) points to the slowing of financial liberalization and growing conservativism that has become associated with Xi Jinping's general preference for favouring the state-owned sectors over the private.

CONCLUSION

Forty years on from the start of economic reforms in 1978–79 China's economy and society is almost unrecognisable. China was transformed from a very poor country that barely participated in international trade and investment to become the second-largest economy that demands a greater say in how the world is governed, not just the global economy.

Predictions about the future are inevitably prone to error. But there are several factors that have locked in China's future, not least its population structure. A shrinking workforce and ageing population mean that important drivers of past economic growth are actually going in the wrong direction and pose huge questions about how to grow in the future (see Chapter 6).

Sustaining China's economic growth is vital to the future of the party-state leaders in Beijing and to every household in the country; it is vital also for the global economy. The integration of China into global supply chains since the 1980s has lowered worldwide the price of goods, spurred innovation and delivered an unimaginable lift in prosperity for China. As China enters the third decade of the twenty-first century, it is intent on staking its claim to shaping the future of the global economy across many dimensions. This can be seen in the pronouncements such as those of Xi Jinping at Davos in 2017 where he asserted China would defend globalization in the face of the US President Donald Trump turn inward and his trashing of the international norms that had governed global trade since the middle of the twentieth century (Xi 2017). China wants to be recognized as a global superpower and stamp its vision on the global economy, reshaping the rules of the global economy and technical standards. This will be a "New Era", as Xi has proclaimed his strategy. A strong economy will be essential to fulfil his strategic ambitions. Innovation is at the heart of making China a more productive and richer country, but so too is the need for better governance and more competitive firms, a more equitable and fairer society, and a more sustainable energy footprint for an increasingly urbanized China. These challenges are the topics of the next chapters.

4

Form of the economy: business and government

China's economy today is a hybrid capitalism. The private or non-state sector is the primary driver of economic growth: the most profitable, the most innovative and the major employer that has delivered the stellar growth of recent decades.[1] Yet state sector firms remain important, especially in sectors vital to the interests of the party-state. They are the largest firms in many sectors of the economy and the biggest are included on the Fortune Global 500. But their contribution to employment has vastly diminished, their inefficiency holds back potential growth, and their lacklustre innovative capacity puts at risks China's aspirations has to become an advanced economy. Despite these deficiencies the state sector is privileged; their leaders are at the centre of the party-state, both corporate titans and powerful party officials, who profoundly influence the country's industrial policy.

Explanation for these contradictions rest in the dominance of the Communist Party of China (CPC) over business and economic life. Although the state abandoned economic planning in the 1980s and stepped back from day-to-day involvement in the economy, in what Barry Naughton (1995) called "growing out of the plan", still everywhere the party-state's hand is at work in shaping the economy and the business opportunities of firms and individuals. And that hand has strengthened. Under Xi Jinping, the General Secretary of the CPC, the appetite for reform has waned during the 2010s and support for the state sector increased, or as the Chinese would put it: "the state advances, the private sector retreats (*guo jin min tui*)". Few countries highlight as clearly as China the tension between the role of the state and that of the market in economic development. For this reason, the chapter begins with an overview of the organization of the government administration and the CPC.

This contemporary business configuration described above is not a simple story of a dual economy. Both state sector and private firms are tied together in complex webs of social networks based on personal and particularistic relationships that are a central trait of Chinese societies and indeed of most of Asia. Chinese business – whether state enterprise, private conglomerate or family firm – will thrive or perish on the strength of their personal networks. Capitalism in China today is a blend of deep-seated culturally influenced business behaviour mapped onto a unique political economy shaped by an ever-present party-state. We need to understand these networks and their roots in the social relations of everyday life to grasp the complexity of the business–state dynamics in China. The chapter will therefore analyse the nature of interpersonal relations, known as "*guanxi*" (connections), not as something culturally peculiar to Chinese society, but as a rational economic response to high levels of uncertainty in business and society, which reflect the weakness of institutions and the low levels of trust.

The remaining sections of the chapter will first discuss the reorganization of the state sector since the late 1990s, focused on the emergence of gigantic firms in key sectors over which they exercise monopolistic or oligopolistic control. Next, the focus turns to the private sector, whose re-emergence from the 1980s is one of the most remarkable and contradictory aspects of contemporary China. We will conclude with a brief look at the development of a modern corporate governance that has proved difficult for both private and state firms because of the personal particularistic practices rooted in a collectivist-oriented network society like China, on the one hand, and the pervasive reach of the party-state into business, on the other.

STATE, PARTY AND GOVERNANCE

China is a unity state comprising 31 provincial entities in 2018, including 22 provinces (official PRC sources count Taiwan to make the tally 23), five autonomous regions, four municipalities directly under the central government, and two Special Administrative Regions (Hong Kong and Macau). Beneath this upper administrative provincial structure there are 333 prefectures including 293-prefecture level cities, 2,851 counties with 375-county-level cities and 39,945 towns and townships (CSY 2019: table 1.1). State and party are separate but intertwined, which is the reason party-state is used interchangeably for government in this book. A party official at a particular level will have more sway than a state official: the party secretary of a province trumps the provincial governor, the party secretary of a municipality the mayor, and so on down to the township and village level. The authority of the current leader of China, Xi Jinping, derives from his position as the General Secretary of the CPC rather than President of China, the head of state. He is also chair of both the state and the party Central Military Affairs Commission, making him the commander in chief of the People's Liberation Army, which is in effect the armed wing of the party.

Economic policy might be executed by the government at central and lower levels, but the making of it invariably involves the party, which sets the national development goals, although the party's internal secrecy rarely renders this process visible to outsiders. The CPC is the world's largest communist party with about 91 million members (*China Daily* 2020). The party is committed to a Leninist model of political control and will ruthlessly suppress any perceived threat to its control, yet in so many ways economic reform has changed and challenged the party.[2] Paradoxically the party is highly adaptive, such as opening up membership to entrepreneurs in the early 2000s and embracing social media as a means for control, although always stridently defensive of its mandate to lead China, shutting down debates and imprisoning contrarian voices perceived to be a threat. Since 1949, the CPC has been dominated by successive "paramount leaders": Mao Zedong, Deng Xiaoping, Jiang Zemin in his later years, and Xi Jinping, who has become the most powerful leader in China since Deng if not Mao. The self-effacing Hu Jintao lacked presence as the General Secretary during his tenure from 2002 to 2012. Personal power and relationships dominate the party and its governance of China – "the leadership is riddled with networks of personal relations and is dominated by patron-client ties" (Saich 2015: 89). This ironically makes the political leadership more unstable and the party more vulnerable to sudden collapse than the public image of its authoritarian control would suggest.

The CPC's top-level decision-making body is formally the National Party Congress, or its Central Committee (CC) when the congress is not meeting. Its meetings every five years brings together about 2,300 delegates. The Nineteenth Party Congress CC (2017–22) has 204 members. In practice, power lies with the Political Bureau (Politburo: 24 members) and its Standing Committee (SC) of seven members led by General Secretary Xi Jinping (CPC website).[3] These senior leaders control decision making in the party. They are supported in their work by a Secretariat and a dozen Leading Small Groups, each focused on areas vital to party power such as the economy, law, media and the internet, and so on, many of which are also chaired by Xi. An important and much feared agency at the same level as the CC is the Central Discipline Inspection Commission (CDIC), which has spearheaded Xi's crackdown on party corruption, whose secretary, Zhao Leji, is a member of the Politburo SC.

Two other agencies instrumental in sustaining party power and control over members, their thoughts and their activities are the Central Organization Department and the party schools. The Central Organization Department is the human resources department for the CPC. It plays a vital role in selecting leaders and overseeing their training, including all senior government ministry officials, senior judiciary positions, the executives of large state firms, the presidents of universities such as Beijing and Tsinghua, editors of party papers, and so on. As Saich (2015: 99) observed, the Organization Department's influence "is pervasive and party members bend over backwards to please and flatter its staff". The CPC Central Party School (*zhonggong zhongyang dangxiao*) in Beijing – now styled as the National Academy of Governance (*guojia xingzheng xuexiao*) – and its 2,500 lower level affiliates educate party members in the way they should behave, creates an esprit de corps and prepares them for promotion. These deliver courses ranging from executive style short courses through undergraduate to doctorate programmes. It is a venue where officials are exposed to diverse ideas that would otherwise not be allowed in party venues or elsewhere and accordingly may produce new policies. Parallel to the party schools is an administration school system focused on the practical issues of governance.

A cursory glance at the official biographies of the Politburo or the CC members reveal how the upper ranks of party and government are fused and primacy accorded the party over the state in pursuing reforms and promoting China's future. The breadth of Xi's authority is obvious, spanning party, military and government, but so too is that of the others (see Table 4.1). Li Keqiang is Premier, the head of the State Council, which is the equivalent to the cabinet or government executive, and secretary of the party committee in the State Council; Li Zhanshu is the nominal head of the Chinese parliament, the National People's Congress; Wang Yang is chair of the next most important political body, the Chinese People's Political Consultative Conference; Wang Huning runs the party's core ideological agencies; Zhao Leji is the party's super cop in charge of the corruption-busting CDIC, and Han Zheng is a vice premier and deputy party secretary to the State Council.

The current 1982 Constitution of the PRC – the fourth since 1949 – upholds in name many values ignored in the practice of governance, yet it indicates the direction of thinking within the political leadership, such as the amendments from 1988 that increasingly accepted the role of the non-state sector and the 1993 definition of the PRC economic system as a "socialist market economy".[4] Although the state was formally separated from the grip of the party before 2018, "the state's freedom for political manoeuvre remains circumscribed and limited" (Saich 2015:

Table 4.1 Membership of the Standing Committee of the Politburo, CPC, 2017–22

Title	Name	Key roles
General Secretary	Xi Jinping	General Secretary, CPC. Chair CPC Central Military Commission, President PRC, Chair PRC Central Military Commission
Premier	Li Keqiang	Premier (Prime Minister). Party Secretary of the State Council
Member	Li Zhanshu	Chairman, Standing Committee, 13th National People's Congress
Member	Wang Yang	Chairman, 13th National Committee of the Chinese People's Political Consultative Conference
Member	Wang Huning	Secretary of the Central Secretariat; director, Central Policy Research Office; director, the Office of the Central Leading Group for Comprehensive Deepening Reform.
Member	Zhao Leji	Secretary of the 19th Central Commission for Discipline Inspection
Vice Premier	Han Zheng	Deputy Premier of the State Council and deputy secretary of the party group of the State Council.

Note: Members were elected at the Nineteenth Party Congress in October 2017 for a five-year term. The full name is the Standing Committee of the Politburo (Political Bureau) of the Central Committee of the CPC.

Source: CPC website; http://cpc.people.com.cn/GB/64162/.

125). During the 1980s there was discussion of the separation of the party and state, but after the upheavals of 1989 this was quietly shelved. Former Premier Jiang Zemin in the 1990s sought to fuse the party and government to ensure reciprocal accountability, locking government and party, which would force state actors to implement the party visions for national development.[5] The 2018 amendment to Article 1 did away with any pretence of independence and inserted the sentence: "The defining feature of socialism with Chinese characteristics is the leadership of the Communist Party of China". Mention of the CPC had only previously appeared in the Preamble, the substance of which may have had little legal force, unlike the articles.[6] The change reflects Xi Jinping's push for "party-state integration" (*dangzheng ronghe*), a shuffling of party and state roles. It includes the merging of the State Civil Servants Bureau and the CPC Central Organization Department, which will subject civil servants to the party's authority whether they are members or not. This is "a sharp volte-face on the trend begun by Deng Xiaoping toward state management of civil servants" (Snape & Wang 2020).

The State Council is the executive of the PRC government led by the Premier, Li Keqiang since 2013, with four vice premiers and five state counsellors (State Council website).[7] Two are members of the CPC Politburo Standing Committee, five are members of the Politburo and all seven are members of the Central Committee. Four of the five state councillors hold ministerial responsibilities for defence, foreign affairs, finance, and public security (see Table 4.2). The premier is conventionally the lead minister for economic affairs, but the team is strong in economics and finance. Vice premier Liu He, for instance, directs the party's Central Finance Leading Group. He was formerly deputy director of the National Development and Reform Commission, the leading government economic think tank, and was the chief negotiator with the United States in the 2018–20 "trade war".

Below the State Council in 2020 there were 25 ministries and commissions and another 52 organizations, offices, institutions, bureaux and agencies that made up the central government. These include the State-Owned Asset Supervision and Administration Commission (SASAC), which is the giant holding company that controls the largest central state enterprises (*zhongyang qiye* or *yangqi*). They in turn direct the lower-level counterparts in the provincial governments (see Saich 2015: Chapter 6, for an analysis of lower-level government and central–local relations).

Table 4.2 Membership of the State Council, 2018–23

Title	Name	Politburo SC of CC	Politburo	CC SC	CC	Ministry
Premier	Li Keqiang	Y	Y	Y	Y	Premier
Vice Premiers	Han Zheng	Y	Y	Y	Y	Vice Premier
Vice Premiers	Sun Chunlan (F)		Y	Y	Y	Vice Premier
Vice Premiers	Hu Chunhua		Y	Y	Y	Vice Premier
Vice Premiers	Liu He		Y	Y	Y	Vice Premier
State Counsellors	Wei Fenghe				Y	Defence
State Counsellors	Wang Yong				Y	No portfolio
State Counsellors	Wang Yi				Y	Foreign Affairs
State Counsellors	Xiao Jie				Y	Finance
State Counsellors	Zhao Kezhi				Y	Public Security
Secretary	Xiao Jie (concurrent)				Y	Finance

Notes: The State Council was elected at the Thirteenth National People's Congress held in March 2018.

Source: State Council website; http://www.gov.cn/guowuyuan/index.htm.

The National People's Congress (NPC) is the highest organ of national state power, the equivalent to China's parliament, which is composed of deputies elected by the provinces and the military. These number around 3,000 delegates, who are elected every five years and meet annually in Beijing (CSY 2020: table 24.1). They oversee the State Council but in practice are a rubber stamp. At provincial and lower levels there are corresponding people's congresses (PC). The constitution vests a wide range of powers in the NPC including the power to amend the constitution, make laws, approve the appointments to the State Council and review economic plans. In practice, the major decisions and appointments are made by the CPC's CC and passed to the NPC for their consideration (Saich 2015: 126–8). Also, meeting annually at the same time as the NPC, is the Chinese People's Political Consultative Conference (CPPCC), with about 2,200 delegates, of whom about 40 per cent are party members (CSY 2020: table 24.2). It is a consultative body, the largest of the party's united front organizations, and a forum for prominent non-party people to debate policy. It is headed by a member of the Politburo SC – currently Wang Yang. The CPPCC provides the party and the NPC with input to policy making and can help to head off potential criticism before a proposal goes to the NPC. Membership of the provincial and lower level PC and PPCC are keenly sought after by Chinese entrepreneurs as a way to influence party-state formulation of business and economic policy (Zhao & Morgan 2019).

The "dual hierarchy" that combines party and state roles enables the CPC to exercise control over government agencies. Authority is concentrated at the top, but the power of senior party leaders does not come merely from their organizational pre-eminence but from their control over sources of patronage. This was the basis of elite power under the command economy before 1978. During the reform period the party needed "to protect and recreate a system of patronage" to ensure its survival in a new world governed by markets (Naughton 2008: 91). A capacity to award coveted posts is the most valuable source of patronage. The party leadership through the Central Organization Department controls appointments to higher-level provincial, municipal and other important government and party posts as well as the senior executives of SOEs, state banks and the associated regulatory agencies. These appointees in turn dispense rewards to their clients through appointments and promotions. Despite the appearance of a modern and accountable organizational structure, the party-state is mired in a patron–client web of personal and particularistic relations. These make it firstly unstable in the event of an individual crashing out for political reasons, such as the downfall in 2012 of Bo Xilai, and secondly inherently prone to peculation and malfeasance in its ranks as top leaders look after their subordinates at all levels.[8]

Without checks and balances other than the leaders watching one another, corruption is endemic to the system. Market reforms offered huge opportunities to reward subordinates as well as family and friends. Family members of senior leaders were frequently appointed to coveted roles. Corruption was rife and increasingly venal before Xi Jinping acted in 2013. Many thousands of party members have been swept up in his campaign, purged from the party and imprisoned for corruption, along with non-party accomplices. There is little likelihood of Xi succeeding in the long term – others have tried in the past and failed because of the systemic roots of corruption in the patron–client networks that underpin party control. This, however, is never acknowledged and corruption is explained away as a moral and discipline failing of the individual party member or state official.

For Xi Jinping the scale and venality of corruption was more than a simple moral story.[9] It struck at the heart of the efficiency and credibility of the party to lead. In that sense corruption for the party differs from typical Western views of corruption as the misuse of public office for private gain. Corruption is intensely political. And, unsurprisingly, there is suspicion the campaign since 2013 has targeted Xi's enemies. Past leaders did exactly that: in 1998, Beijing party secretary Chen Xitong, an opponent of Jiang Zemin, was sentenced to 16 years in prison for corruption, and in 2008, Shanghai party secretary Chen Liangyu, an opponent of Hu Jintao, was sentenced to 18 years. The downfall of Chen Liangyu in 2007 opened the way for Xi to move from party secretary of Zhejiang to a brief stint in Shanghai as party secretary before his promotion to central roles in Beijing at the Seventeenth Party Congress (Saich 2015: 69, 71). And the charge of corruption can be used viciously against critics, such as the 18-year sentence handed out to Ren Zhiqiang after a one-day trial in September 2020.[10]

Whatever the motivations of Xi's anti-corruption campaign, it has raised the bar, curtailed many abuses and brought down corrupt officials from petty ones to those at the top of the power structure. The CDIC has been strengthened and expanded. Xi deeply fears that unless corruption is tackled the party will lose its moral authority to lead China, undermining its rule and vision. Such is his fear that he broke an unspoken rule of not prosecuting serving and retired top leaders. The most spectacular was bringing down Zhou Yongkang, who had served in the Politburo SC until 2012. Zhou, the much-feared former head of public security, had built a network of patronage based on his former role in the petroleum sector stretching back decades to his later control of state security and the People's Armed Police, linking old comrades, their clients and families in a gigantic web of corruption. After he was detained investigators seized $14.5 billion of assets (there are many news reports, but for a concise account see Brown 2014: 192–7; 2017: 44, 172–5; McMahon 2018: 150–51).

Between 2013 and 2015, the CDIC investigated all the central SOEs under SASAC, resulting in major cases against 28 board-level personnel including chairmen, presidents, vice-presidents, and party secretaries. Those dismissed and imprisoned ran companies listed on the Fortune Global 500 such as China National Petroleum Corporation, China Telecom, Dongfeng Motor Corporations, among others. The deputy party secretary of SASAC itself and former chairman of China National Petroleum Corporation, Jiang Jiemin, was among those caught (Li 2016: 940–42).

Throughout the party-state, corruption reaches from the lofty heights of the Politburo to village-level party secretaries and state officials. It ultimately flows from the patron–client deals that secures the party's standing. Corruption in the PLA, the ultimate guarantor of party power, has reached epidemic proportions too. Two senior commanders, former Politburo members and vice-chairmen of the Central Military Affairs Commission, Guo Boxiong and Xu Caihou, were arrested in 2014–15 for accepting bribes to promote subordinates. Xu was reported to have hoarded tons of cash (about ¥100 million), gold bars, rare jade and artworks that needed many trucks to carry away from his 2,000m² Beijing residence (SCMP 2015a, 2015b; Pei 2016: 6, 262). Another general, Gu Junshan, the former deputy head of logistics for the PLA who owed his position to Xu, was found to have among his loot a gold statue of Chairman Mao (SCMP 2015c). Historically, there is little that is new in the corruption and cronyism at play here. Favours, gifts and patronage are part of the cultural fabric of social relations in China that too easily can lead into corrupt behaviour.

CULTURE, NETWORKS AND FAMILY FIRMS

Asian firms are networked firms; their growth is grounded on personal and particularistic relationships. In China, the social connections between individuals is called *guanxi*, the foundations of the personal networks on which business, political and societal relationships are built. These social relations structure the network ties among firms and between firms and government. In the popular imagination business cannot be done without building *guanxi* with partners, suppliers and government officials. There is much truth in such kinds of thinking – indeed, personal relationships are important for business everywhere – but much is also obscured in a fog of cultural exceptionalism that sometimes drifts over descriptions of doing business in China. *Guanxi*, however, I would argue is an entirely rational economic response to a business environment in which historically there has been high levels of uncertainty, low trust and very imperfect institutions for merchants. It serves to reduce high transaction costs in the market arising from imperfect information and improves access to scarce resources. We shall now look at how *guanxi* is formed, its role in business, and the way it structures business relations and networks.

Defined simply, *guanxi* is an intricate web of social reciprocities that bind people via obligations, debts and responsibilities. These reciprocities bond an individual into a social and economic contract in their business dealings in ways that differ from those in the West.[11] It implies mutual interests and benefits: "Once *guanxi* is established between two people, each can ask a favour of the other with the expectation that the debt incurred will be repaid sometime in the future" (Yang 1994: 1). These networks of personal relationships are the foundational pillar of social intercourse. Chung & Hamilton (2001: 332, 334) argue "The basic operative logic of *guanxi* is the logic of reciprocity. … [which] implies a society that is structured primarily in terms of relationships".

The reciprocity of obligations in *guanxi* rests on personal trust (*xinyong*, a word which also means credit, integrity and reliability), demonstrated affection (*ganqing*), which often involves ritual gift giving, and the exchange of personal favours (*renqing*). *Guanxi* is contextual, procedural and particularistic; it varies between individuals, their place in society and the specific attributes of the tie between any two individuals. The concept of face (*mianzi*) or reputation is integral to *guanxi* networks; an individual can "give face" to another, enhancing the other's reputation and their own, thereby strengthening the relationship. Relationship networks are therefore embedded in public rituals that express status, respect and bonding in Chinese society. The rules of *guanxi* rituals place interpersonal business relations within a prescriptive social framework that improves "economic calculability" in the market and can be viewed as a substitute for a legal framework that governs economic practices in Western societies (Chung & Hamilton 2001).

The increase in economic certainty that flows from *guanxi* has several effects that are well observed in the operation of social networks, and business networks in particular. Social networks enable those within to discover information about the character, reliability and performance of firms within the network. Ties between firms, their owners and managers that come from iterated business dealings increases the level of trust between firms, improves the flow of information and reduces uncertainty, which lessens the transaction cost of doing business. Cheating is reduced because it betrays the bonds among members; it is also more easily discoverable when everyone is closely linked together. Importantly, members learn about others and their capabilities. This can lead to new business opportunities, the sharing of resources or the capture of the resources of another. Often in a Chinese business relationship a formal contract is less important than the history of past relationships; a contract is thus an expression of sincerity, of the intention to cooperate in business, rather than a prescription of what will actually be done.

Economic action in China accordingly is embedded in a network of relations (cultural, political and societal), which can be both formal (legal ties) and informal (social ties). Even among Western firms, network relationships have become more important in many industries where complex contracting, and strategic alliances are common: "[I]ndustries can no longer be meaningful analyzed without considering the strategic networks that bind" (Gulati *et al.* 2000: 204).[12] Network structures within industries influence how participant firms compete and cooperate, and engage in alliances and partnerships, while the social ties among managers and between managers and employees structure behaviour in the workplace and influence the performance of the firm.

Social networks and *guanxi* relationships manifest themselves in various ways in the evolution and operation of family firms, the private sector and state firms. The basic business unit for many centuries in China is the family. It is telling that the Chinese language classifier for a firm or business is "*jia*", the root meaning of which is family.[13] The Chinese family business (CFB) is the basis of almost all private sector firms in China or outside, including the conglomerates that have played a big role in the life of Southeast Asian economies over the past century (Redding 1990).

The CFB begin as family businesses do everywhere, drawing on the resources of the individual, family members and friends to grow. But the CFB is distinguished by familism, which in the past prescribed a unique development path. Wong (1985) identified four stages. The "emergent" firm beyond a sole proprietor was based on a partnership, the pooling of resources to overcome capital constraints of the individual in building a business. Classic examples include the Rong family businesses in Wuxi in the early twentieth century and the Li & Fung company in Hong Kong.[14]

Partnerships are inherently unstable. One partner will usually ascend, take over, and establish the "centralized" firm. Ownership in the centralized CFB is concentrated in the immediate family and control in the entrepreneurial founder. There is a low degree of delegation. At this stage the firm expands by horizontal replication of business units (Figure 4.1), which creates business units for family members to run, especially the sons of the founder. Replication permits new businesses to emerge with new social networks distinct from one another in contrast to growing a firm by creating new business divisions within a unified single company. The aim of the firm is to maximize the welfare of the family rather than maximize profits. Capital is retained and reinvested in *jia*-related businesses. Likewise, there is a reluctance to sell off poor-performing businesses as the founder conceives of his role as the trustee of the family's (*jia*) assets. Over time there is a tendency for the CFB to become less entrepreneurial and innovative than when the founder was young (Wong 1985).

Figure 4.1 Growth of Chinese family businesses through firm replication

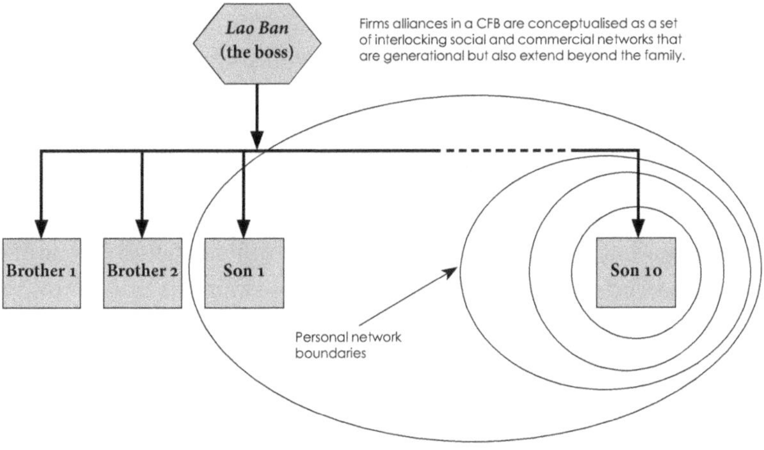

Note: This schematic model of the organic growth of CFB into large groups via the proliferation of discrete firms was inspired by Wong (1985), Redding (1990) and Chung & Hamilton (2001).

In the third phase, the CFB begins to "segment" as the founder's sons take over the running of the firm. Management of the firm is divided between the founder's sons in contrast to the division of land assets into roughly equal shares between sons because the scale, efficiency and intangibles of the business is indivisible. Usually one son will assume the mantle of the founder's leadership of the business and the others support in specialist roles. Some children might leave the business. Professional managers might even join to run some of the business units, but as Kilduff and Tsai (2003: 26–7) show for a large Taiwan multi-unit firm, the family run units are at the centre of information networks, receiving information from family and non-family units, while the non-family units are in general peripheral in the flow of information within the business group.

The fourth phase leads to "disintegration", the collapse of a family business that occurs frequently when the third generation takes control of the firm. Different sons produce different numbers of heirs, which translates into intra-family disputes over claims to the collective assets of the CFB. First cousins (the sons and daughters of the founder's sons) find it more difficult to cooperate and they identify less with the CFB as the embodiment of the extended *jia* and more with their immediate family. But collapse is not inevitable. Wong (1985) identified situations where the son who had taken the lead in the segmentation phase recentralizes the CFB and begins a new centralized phase, which prolongs the life of the firm.

Among CFBs outside China and the private sector entrepreneurial founders in China today there are processes at work that modify the observations of Wong, which was based on a study of family-run textile businesses in Hong Kong in the late 1970s whose founders had come from Shanghai around 1948–51. Economic development leads to smaller families, demographic change which was accelerated in China by the one-child policy. Succession is difficult when there are fewer children who are willing or capable to lead the business. These changes have motivated a search for corporate structures to preserve and pass on the value of the firm to heirs. Delegation of authority in the CFB let alone the use of professional managers was uncommon in the past. Restructuring into shareholding vehicles that can be "dismembered" with the family holding a "golden share" is one option, which might transform the firm from individual or family control to a hybrid of family ownership and professional managers (Chen 2001). More typically the use of holding companies with prior rights over the group companies is often found in larger Chinese firms. Such organizational practices have been long used as the vehicle to control listed conglomerates, such as the CK (Cheung Kong) Group in Hong Kong, the CP (Chaoren Pokphand) Group in Thailand, among many others. Their strengths rest in a combination of kin and personal network ties.

Most Chinese family firms are small and local in their operation. When they enter into business with others and especially at a distance social networks come into play. Outside of China, ethnic Chinese businesses will prefer to do business with other Chinese, which is similar to ethnic-based networks found among immigrants, such as the Jewish, South Asian and Vietnamese diaspora in many countries. In China, they prefer to do business with firms whose principals have a similar geographical origin or native place (*jiguan*) and speak the same dialect of Chinese. In recent decades ties based on school, army service, or a particular party school cohort are also important for social networks. There is a distinction between insiders and outsiders, between those who are close and alike and those who are more distant and dissimilar. There are gradations of outsider-ness. Social networks based on such personal affinities become coalitions of similar others or, to put it another way, clubs of fictive siblings, people who can be trusted and from whom favours can be asked.

Insiders and outsiders are like the layers of an onion, with the ties and degree of affinity weakening from the inner-most kin and friends, to fellow villagers and provincials, and finally to non-Chinese in the outer-most layer. Social networks in China today are more fluid than the onion metaphor might suggest. Still, these degrees of network affinity or closeness have implications for business as discussed above in describing the economic logic of *guanxi*. A nice example of the costs of network affinities is an account of Hokkien [Fujian] Chinese rubber traders in colonial Malaya. The transaction costs between individual traders would increase with the number of the business partners within the same affinity group. However, trading with partners outside of the immediate Hokkien group incurred an incremental jump in costs due to network distance (hetero-geneity). Instead of credit-based transactions, the trader might resort to transact in cash with the outsider, which is an opportunity cost because the cash is unavailable for other uses (Landa 1994). In short, the trader uses cash to compensate for doubts about the trustworthiness of the outsider to observe the insider rules.

In contemporary China, we can observe the above *guanxi*-based networks and clubs in the organizational behaviour among both private and state sector managers, and within party-state organizations. Chinese business networks are a mix of horizontal and vertical ties. Horizontal networks are business-to-business ties. These link suppliers and buyers in an industry or across industries. Their purpose is to improve information flows, increase sales and enhance the monitoring of contracts between parties. Vertical networks are business-to-government ties, links with government or regulatory agencies.[15] Their role is to minimize shocks that might arise from changes in government policy and regulations or to tap scarce resources controlled by the state, in particular access to land, technology and capital. This type of *guanxi* network with party-state actors is more instrumentalist compared with those among businesspeople. It is highly goal oriented in which businesspersons seek specific resources from their ties to state officials.

Many different factors can influence the structuring of these Chinese business networks. The use of *guanxi* networks is contingent on institutional factors (firm ownership and location; the political and legal system), environmental factors (industry growth and competitive intensity), organizational factors (firm size, firm age, technological and managerial capabilities), and the strategic outlook of the firm (Xin & Pearce 1996; Park & Luo 2001; Li 2005). Network strategies also evolve over time: a decrease in state interference and a stronger legal environment, for example, might lessen the need for network building (Guthrie 1999; Peng & Zhou 2005).

Managers of non-state firms, for example, are more likely to form *guanxi* networks with officials than state-owned firms, which are already insiders to the party-state. Firms in less open economic areas are more likely to develop *guanxi* networks with other businesses and with government agencies because the institutional environment is far weaker than in developed regions, which increases uncertainty, raises transaction costs and makes access to scarce resources dependent on personal ties to those who control them. Firms which are smaller, younger, and possess poor technology and poor management capabilities are more likely to network with other firms to compensate for their weaknesses, hoping to partner with the better endowed or the older and more experienced players in the market (Park & Luo 2001; Luo 2003). Both managers of state firms and private firms will alike seek to exploit opportunities in their networks, although their behavior and motivation differ in many ways because of the network ties and the opportunities these allow.

THE RE-MAKING OF SOES: CAPITALISM FROM ABOVE

State firms are unrecognizable in their organization to what they had been. At the start of the reform period, SOEs were hardly firms in the conventional sense. They were administrative units whose purpose was to execute the state plan, produce goods and distribute them. Today the central state enterprises (*yangqi*) that come directly under the State Council's SASAC are among the largest firms in the world and some are very profitable. Still, many SOEs are inefficient, with a negative return on capital in some instances. They benefit as always from the party commitment to the public sector as the cornerstone of the "socialist market economy", which is enshrined in the constitution. Growing awareness in the mid-1990s of the need to raise the performance of SOEs and the risk to the financial system of their non-performing loans motivated the policy of "grasp the large, let go the small" (*zhuada fangxiao*). Many firms were merged, others were allowed to go out of business, and millions of state workers were laid off as China prepared to join the WTO.

State firms from 1952 to 1983 served the production plans of state agencies. Some of the SOEs can be traced back to state firms of the 1930s and 40s (Chapter 2). These pre-reform SOEs engaged in production and distribution according to the plan as directed by officials in Beijing and the provinces but were not fit for the market economy. An urban reform package in late 1984 set out to revitalize SOEs through the use of contracts much as the rural sector had been, along with a dual-track price system that allowed state-controlled prices to co-exist with market prices. Power was devolved to managers who were responsible for profit and loss, required to share profits with the state, and allowed control over retained profits. These reforms failed to raise efficiency or profits of SOEs. Managers engaged in profiteering while the SOE's soft budget constraints increasingly exposed the state banks to bad loans (Chapter 3). SOEs were still controlled by a complex network of vertical ties to the central ministries responsible for the particular industry and horizontal ties to the local government bureau that oversaw operations in a province or municipality. From the mid-1980s SOEs were restructured into enterprise groups (*qiyetuan*) with their operating units (*danwei*) reorganized as subsidiary companies of the larger group (Tang & Ward 2003: 49–51, 65–8).

The Chinese Company Law of 1994 introduced on paper a modern corporate model. SOEs became just one of many corporate forms. Larger SOEs were "corporatized" (*qiyehua*) and listed their better performing assets on local stock markets while warehousing other assets and liabilities such as employee pensions into non-listed vehicles, all controlled by a non-listed holding company. Soon after the state began to sell or close poor performing and small SOEs, the bankruptcy law was given teeth to reshuffle assets back into play and state banks were reorganized, their NPLs stripped out, and recapitalized (Chapter 3). In 1995, the Bank of China and Sinochem Corporation were the first SOEs to appear on the Fortune Global 500 List, which ranks the largest companies in the world by their revenue.

Property rights over SOEs remain vague and contested. SOEs are defined formally as national owned (*guoyou*) enterprises "owned by all the people" (*quanmin suoyouzhi*), which in effect made them property of the party-state and its agents. In 2003, the party-state sought tighter control over the largest state firms through establishing the Central SASAC. At the time it supervised 183 non-financial central SOEs. SASAC was in effect the world's largest holding company and the central SOEs were characterized as "national champions", which dominated vital sectors such as telecommunications, petroleum, transportation and power generation (Lin & Milhaupt 2013; Leutert 2016). Other SOEs numbering more than 200,000 were put under provincial SASAC and lower-level counterparts.

By 2019, the central SOEs had been reduced to 96 industrial groups (SASAC website), of which nearly half were included in the Fortune Global 500. They contain many thousands of subsidiaries. According to Lin & Milhaupt (2013), these massive state groups are organized into two interlocking structures comprising an internal network hierarchy of top-down governance and network bridges that institutionally link the SOE group and the party-state. Each central SOE group contains a parent or holding company wholly owned by SASAC; one or more publicly traded subsidiaries, the global face of the group; a finance company that serves the financing needs of the group in a way similar to the central bank in the Japanese *keiretsu* (industrial groups) of the 1960s–90s; and a research institute to coordinate innovation. Networks of firms joined together the group, while the networks of their managers bridged into the institutions of the party-state, as shown in Figure 4.2.

Figure 4.2 Network hierarchy and party control of central SOEs

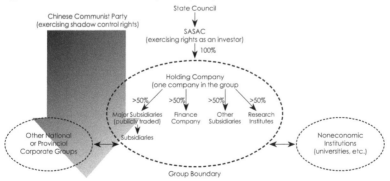

Source: Adapted from Lin & Milhaupt (2013: figure 1). Reproduced with permission.

Each of the SOE groups, as well as their senior managers, are tied to larger industry clusters. Although the groups are legally distinct, they form joint ventures, strategic alliances and equity holdings with one another. They are also joined through SASAC and the Central Organization Department of the CPC, which decides senior appointments. Intergroup networks are formed to take advantage of complementarities between groups and to support each other overseas. The three national steel groups Baosteel, Wuhan Iron and Steel, and Anshan Iron and Steel in the late 2000s had established equity linkages with First Auto Works, China State Shipbuilding, China Shipping Group and the province-level Hebei Iron and Steel Group.[16] They often also entered into contractual relationships with the same groups (Lin & Milhaupt 2013: 723–6). Such interlocks and related-party transactions would raise the anti-trust eyebrows of many regulators in market economies.

Each group has a dense network of ties involving equity and control as well as information flows. The China Datang Corporation, which is a Fortune Global 500 member and one of the five largest power generation companies in China, illustrates the inter-firm and inter-group networks (Figure 4.3).[17] Around 2009 the corporation had 143 separate companies, three of which were publicly listed and one finance company. Beyond the group boundaries, China Datang had extensive links with other companies through equity ties and strategic alliances. These included JVs with three power generation groups, Guodian, Huadian and Huaneng, as well as with the China Three Gorges Corporation, which is also involved in power generation. All five major power generators were therefore linked not only through their common controlling shareholder, SASAC, but also through these equity tie ups and the intra-party groups that the senior executives were a part (Lin & Milhaupt 2013: 731–4).

All of the above mentioned SOE groups are members of the Fortune Global 500. China first joined the list in 1995. By 2000, the list had grown to ten companies, of which three were in the top-100: China Petrochemical Corporation (ranked 68), State Grid (77, then known as the State Power Corporation of China) and the China National Petroleum Corporation

Figure 4.3 China Datang Corporation intra- and inter-group networks

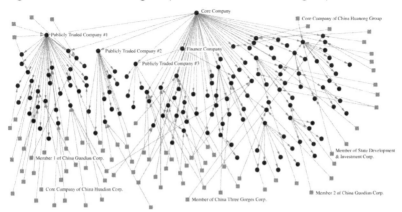

Notes: The black, round nodes indicate member companies of China Datang; the grey square nodes indicate non-member companies. There are 143 member companies and 84 non-member companies in the figure. The grey arrows indicate ownership direction of the 248 ownership connections shown.

Source: Adapted from Lin & Milhaupt (2013: figure 5). Reproduced with permission.

(83). Four of the ten were the major state banks: ICBC (208), BoC (255), CCB (411) and ABC (448). In 2007, the computer manufacturer Lenovo was the first nominally private firm to enter the list at 499. Two years earlier Lenovo had acquired IBM's personal computer business.[18] The other 26 firms in the list that year were state owned led by China Petro-chemical Corporation (then ranked 16) and included state banks, state insurers, telecom companies, power generators, steel producers, and auto-motive companies. From 2008 to 2019, as Figure 4.4 shows, the PRC firms in the list rose quickly as China's economy grew strongly in spite of the GFC.

In the early 2010s there was a remarkable increase in Chinese trans-port, energy and infrastructure firms in the Global 500 list. This seemingly reflected the economic growth that accompanied the stimulus package in 2008–09 to shield China from the impact of the GFC and the ensuring growth of both state and private firms. These firms rode the infrastructure and urban building boom of the early 2010s. The other notable feature was

Figure 4.4 PRC firms in the Fortune Global 500

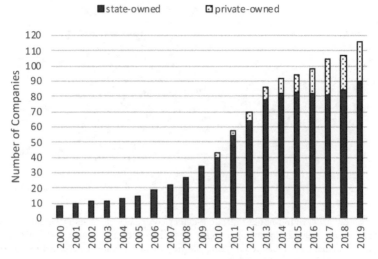

Note: The year is the list year, which reports rankings based on the revenue for the previous calendar year.

Source: *Fortune* magazine; www.fortune.com/global500.

the increase in private-owned enterprises from ten firms in the 2014 list to 26 firms in the 2019 list.

The 2019 Fortune Global 500 list had 119 Chinese firms including those in Hong Kong, but those controlled by PRC interests numbered 116.[19] The *China Daily* (24 July 2019) crowed the list was 129 if the ten Taiwan firms were included, so that for the first time in the history of the list another country had eclipsed the United States with its 121 firms. Ranked second on the 2019 list after the US giant Walmart was the Sinopec Group with revenues of $414.65 billion. Two others in the top-10 were the China National Petroleum Corp. (fourth; revenues of $392.98 billion) and State Grid (fifth; revenues of $387.06 billion). The top private-owned firm was Ping An Insurance, (29th; revenues of $163.60 billion) and another two were in the top-100 list: Huawei Holdings (61st; revenues of $109.03 billion) and Pacific Construction (97th; revenues of $86.62 billion). The leading headquarter locations for the 116 listed enterprises were Beijing

(55), Shanghai (eight), Shenzhen (eight), and Guangzhou and Hangzhou (three each).

Table 4.3 lists the top-ten state-owned enterprises on the Fortune Global 500, which comprised both industrial and financial enterprises. The industrial ones were all central SOEs directly under the State Council's SASAC. The big four state-owned commercial banks were similarly controlled by the State Council through the Central Huijin Holding Company, the financial sector counterpart to SASAC. All but one of the top-10, the Shanghai-based automobile producer SAIC Motor, had their headquarters in Beijing. Of the 90 SOEs, 50 are headquartered in Beijing and nearly all are central SOEs. The strategic importance of these SOEs is evident in their industry sector: 22 are in the broad energy sector, which includes power generation, petroleum and coal mining; 16 in the financial sector, mostly banks and insurance firms; 12 in materials, which includes steel and non-ferrous metals; eight in wholesaling (distribution); seven in construction and engineering; six in aerospace and defence; five in motor vehicles and the three monopoly state telecom providers.

China's private firms, which will be discussed in the next section, differ markedly from SOEs in the Global 500. In 2017, private firms on the list jumped from 16 to 24, the new entrants including the internet giants Alibaba and Tencent, the electronics retailer Suning.com, the real estate developer Country Garden and Anbang Insurance, which crashed out the next year after the arrest of its CEO and the state takeover of the company (see Chapter 3). Private firms have been the driver of the recent rise of PRC firms on the Fortune Global 500 (Figure 4.5). A notable new entrant in 2019 was Xiaomi, a mobile phone and appliance producer that is known as "China's Apple Inc". Coming in at 468, Xiaomi was two notches below Finland's Nokia and two notches above Japan's NEC.

Comparison of Table 4.3 for listed SOEs and Table 4.4 for private firms highlight the differences between the state and private sectors. Half of the top-10 Chinese private firms are headquartered in Shenzhen, the technology and innovation hub that borders Hong Kong, which was the leading SEZ in the 1980s. Shenzhen is home to Ping An Insurance and Huawei,

Table 4.3 Top-10 Chinese state-owned enterprises in the Fortune Global 500, 2019

China rank	G500 Rank	Company Name	Sector	HQ Location	Employees ('ooos)	Revenues ($millions)	Profits ($millions)	ROA (%)*
1	2	Sinopec Group	Energy	Beijing	619	$414,650	$5,845	1.8
2	4	China National Petroleum	Energy	Beijing	1,382	$392,977	$2,271	0.4
3	5	State Grid	Energy	Beijing	917	$387,056	$8,175	1.4
4	21	China State Construction Engineering	Engineering & Construction	Beijing	302	$181,525	$3,160	1.2
5	26	Industrial & Commercial Bank of China	Financials (Banking)	Beijing	449	$168,979	$45,002	1.1
7	31	China Construction Bank	Financials (Banking)	Beijing	366	$151,111	$38,498	1.1
8	36	Agricultural Bank of China	Financials (Banking)	Beijing	477	$139,524	$30,657	0.9
9	39	SAIC Motor	Motor Vehicles & Parts	Shanghai	147	$136,393	$5,444	4.8
10	44	Bank of China	Financials (Banking)	Beijing	310	$127,714	$27,225	0.9
11	51	China Life Insurance	Financials (Insurance)	Beijing	175	$116,172	–$2,567	–0.4

Notes: The list is based on reported revenue for 2018. ROA, the return on assets, is the profits to assets ratio, an indicator of relative performance.

Source: Fortune magazine; www.fortune.com/global500.

Table 4.4 Chinese private enterprises in the Fortune Global 500, 2019

China rank	G500 Rank	Company Name	Sector	HQ Location	Employees ('000s)	Revenues ($millions)	Profits ($millions)	ROA (%)*
6	29	Ping An Insurance	Financials (Insurance)	Shenzhen	376	$163,597	$16,237	1.6
15	61	Huawei Investment & Holding	Network & Other Comms Equipment	Shenzhen	188	$109,030	$8,954	9.2
23	97	Pacific Construction Group	Engineering & Construction	Ürümqi	387	$86,623	$3,391	5.8
28	119	Amer International Group	Industrials	Shenzhen	16	$76,363	$1,483	7.0
33	138	China Evergrande Group	Real Estate	Shenzhen	131	$70,479	$5,653	2.1
34	139	JD.com	Internet Services & Retailing	Beijing	178	$69,848	–$377	–1.2
43	177	Country Garden Holdings	Real Estate	Shenzhen	131	$57,309	$5,234	2.2
44	181	Hengli Group	Textiles	Suzhou	81	$56,199	$583	2.6
45	182	Alibaba Group Holding	Internet Services & Retailing	Hangzhou	101	$56,147	$13,094	9.1
52	212	Lenovo Group	Technology	Hong Kong	57	$51,038	$596	2.0

Notes: The list is based on reported revenue for 2018. ROA, the return on assets, is the profits to assets ratio, an indicator of relative performance. The extent of "privateness" of some of firms could be debated (see the next section).

Source: Fortune magazine; www.fortune.com/global500.

which are in the Global 500 Top-100 firms, as well as the industrial enterprise Amer International, the three largest private sector real estate developers (only two in the top-10) and Tencent (not in the top-10), and unlisted firms such as ZTE (telecoms), BYD (electric vehicles) and BGI (biopharma). The two China giants of e-commerce, JD.com and Alibaba, both in the top-10 of Chinese private firms, come from Beijing – home to another four private firms on the list – and Hangzhou respectively. Coming in at tenth among the top-10 private firms on the list is Lenovo, the computer and technology group headquartered in Hong Kong.

For the most part, SOEs and private sector firms do not compete in the same sector. The dominance of big financial, heavy industry and strategic sector firms on the Global 500 list compared with consumer-oriented firms point in a general way to the underdevelopment of the consumer sector still in China, despite four decades of enormous change in consumption, and the reluctance of the state to open some sectors to non-state competitors. Most of the firms listed are focused on China's large domestic market and their international operations are a sideshow, as they are for many of the largest American firms too, with most sales and most of the workforce at home. Despite the increase in outward foreign investment of Chinese firms, very few have an international focus, and even fewer have the capabilities to succeed outside China.

Many studies have paid attention to the ownership and structure of the SOEs, but fewer to the management culture and career of managers. As might be expected from the role of personal networks, communications between managers is mostly verbal, in meetings or on the phone. There is a reluctance to commit to writing or even keeping diaries. Authority is exercised directly, which reflects a cultural preference to avoid delegation and which leads to managers often micromanaging operations and attending an inordinate number of meetings (Tang & Ward 2003: 85–6).

The career paths of the CEOs of industrial SOEs share similarities with those in state banks. But there are differences too. They both shun outsiders. At the central SOEs and banks, Lin (2017: 16, 19) reports that among her sample of leading state firms only one bank and one industrial

SOE had a CEO with non-state sector experience. The CEOs of industrial SOEs spent their entire careers within a single business group or multiple groups in the same industry sector, or in a supervisory agency related to the industry. Bank CEOs developed their careers across multiple banks within the industry: "Virtually none of the CEOs has any work experience outside the state system, despite partial privatization through public listing in domestic and international capital markets, the mass-scale internationalization through the 'going out' policy since the late 1990s, and executive recruitment reform over the past decade" (Lin 2017: 19).

This limited career experience of managers handicaps state firms abroad. Since the early 2000s, China has encouraged firms to internationalize or "go out" (*zou chuqu*), which accelerated after the GFC to peak at \$196.2 billion in 2016 (see Chapter 3). The preferred mode for internationalization has been merger and acquisition (M&A), which reduces the level of scrutiny by regulatory agencies in the target host country. The lack of international experience and weak brands also make M&A a faster route to an overseas presence than a greenfield wholly-owned subsidiary (Shambaugh 2013: 179–80).

Whether through acquisitions or greenfield ventures, China's state firms have struggled to build MNEs with Chinese characteristics. Many acquisitions fail or lose value.[20] State companies struggle to deploy globally their resources and build brand presence. Their managers prefer interpersonal to institutionalized relationships, overlook regulatory and legal environments in the host country, and do not build strategic alliances with local partners. Instead of being global oriented and attuned to foreign practices, Shambaugh (2013: 187) argues "Chinese companies and their management display an inability to escape their own national corporate culture and business practices". Some Chinese firms are also seen as an arm of the state. There are exceptions that operate successfully abroad, but these are mostly private sector firms, such as Lenovo, the white goods manufacturer Haier, the automotive firm Geely and the telecoms and phone manufacturer Huawei. However, there are questions over whether any of these firms are truly private and increasingly so under Xi Jinping.[21]

In September 2020, the CPC's General Office issued instructions to strengthen oversight of the private sector (*minying jingji*) and encourage private firms and entrepreneurs to implement Xi's thoughts and better serve the party's goal for national rejuvenation (CPC General Office, 15 September 2020).

PRIVATE FIRMS AND ENTREPRENEURISM: CAPITALISM FROM BELOW

Of the many extraordinary developments in China since 1980 none is more contradictory in a country ruled by the world's largest communist party than the re-emergence of the once prohibited private sector. In the space of two decades the private sector became the leading contributor to China's economic growth and employment. It took root first in the countryside among rural households who established non-farm activities, running sole proprietor businesses (*getihu*) or joint-household partnerships (*liantihu*). These spread to the cities, mostly engaging urban residents who were marginalized in the informal sector, unemployed youth and rural migrants. In the more developed provinces such as Jiangsu the commune and brigade enterprises, through which the state had promoted rural industries to serve agriculture during the planned economy were transformed into township and village enterprises (*xiangzhen quiye*; TVEs). These were formally collective owned enterprises and overseen by the local government TVE bureau (Morgan 1994). TVEs increasingly absorbed surplus rural labour, diversified into consumer goods and grew rapidly during the 1980s, and some became major exporters in the 1990s.

By the mid-1990s, some of these many diverse ventures had become large, generating big profits and employing increasing numbers of urban residents as well as those in rural towns. They prospered paradoxically in an institutional void of few rules or laws. In a formal sense, their business activities were more often than not illegal. They hid their private character under a "red hat" (*hong maozi*), often registering as a collective owned business (Dickson 2008). But their success brought recognition and with recognition there followed formal institutional change as the state scrambled to legitimize the dynamic private sector (Nee & Opper 2012).

Private sector growth had exposed the inefficiencies of the state sector, and as discussed in Chapter 3, motivated the then Premier Zhu Rongji to restructure SOEs in the 1990s, laying off 50 million workers and reorganizing the state banks. The private sector at the time struggled to find a voice, win acceptance and raise finance. Officials pretended they did not exist, openly discriminated and ruthlessly extracted fees and taxes. Capital was scarce since the state banks only made loans to SOEs. Along with the economic change that brought these private firms to the fore and paved the way for the rapid growth after 2000, came changes to the PRC constitution, the regulatory framework and party rules that allowed the private sector to come out of the shadows. Each change to the constitution chronicled the begrudging acceptance of the private sector by the party-state.

The first constitutional amendment favourable to the private sector came nearly ten years after the start of reform in 1988: "… the state permits the private sector of the economy to exist and develop within the limits prescribed by law. The private sector of the economy is a *complement* to the socialist public economy. The state protects the lawful rights and interests of the private sector of the economy, and exercises guidance, supervision and control over the private sector of the economy" (emphasis added). This amendment made private enterprise once again a legal activity in the PRC.

The 1999 amendment raised the status of the private sector a notch but tellingly used the term "non-public" (*feigong*): "The non-public sectors of the economy such as the individual and private sectors of the economy, operating within the limits prescribed by law, constitute an *important component* of the socialist market economy" (emphasis added). And in 2004, the party having agreed in 2002 to accept entrepreneurs into its ranks as bona fide members, amended the constitution once again to state: "The state *encourages, supports and guides* the development of the non-public sectors of the economy, and exercises supervision and control over the non-public sectors according to law" (emphasis added). After a quarter of a century of economic reform, the private sector had advanced from the precarity of an illegal outcast to become a sector whose development the party-state encouraged.

Still, the "liability of private-ness" makes life tough for the private sector. As China's entrepreneurs have done throughout the ages, they turn to building networks to overcome their disadvantages, tap capital, open markets, access technology and build their reputation. Private sector firms use business-to-business networks within an industry sector or a region to acquire information that is not readily available about suppliers, customers and competitors. Many of these firms are joined in local industry associations. Information flows are diverse: from suppliers they learn about the reliability of other firms in the industry they might do business with; from buyers they acquire market intelligence; and from competitors they learn about industry trends that can influence their strategies (Zhao & Morgan 2016).

Private sector business-to-government networks are a later day version of the "red hat" strategy of the past to gain legitimacy, especially the acceptance of officials. They use these vertical networks to help acquire scarce resources controlled by the local party-state, such as urban land, and to build relationships with public institutions to access technology and form private–state partnerships. Close ties with government officials enable private firms to avoid or at least mitigate the effects of regulatory shocks arising from local party-state policies that might impact their business. These ties to the state help strengthen their legitimacy in the eyes of both officials and the public. Many private entrepreneurs have joined the CPC, which institutionally links them to the party-state and permits the building of *guanxi* ties with officials. Interestingly, entrepreneurs in Guangdong province believe membership of the local level PC and PPCC are stronger channels for building legitimacy than membership of the party. Membership of the local PC and PPCC allow the entrepreneurs direct input to government policy formulation and decision making that does not come from party membership alone (Zhao & Morgan 2019).

Without doubt the revival of the private sector has delivered huge benefits to China's economy, which Lardy (2014) captured in the title of his book *Markets Over Mao* on the rise of the private sector. Across China there are tens of thousands of small private businesses with a handful of employees, along with partnerships and sole proprietors or self-employed, which account for 56.2 per cent of the urban workforce and 38.1 per cent of the non-farm rural workforce (see Chapter 3, Table 3.5). But the provincial distribution of the larger private-owned enterprises (POEs) is highly skewed. Four provinces over the past decade have accounted for about half of all the firms above a designated size (annual revenue of ¥20 million, $2.8 million) and a similar share of employment: Zhejiang, Jiangsu, Shandong and Guangdong. Table 4.5 summarizes the data for selected provinces. Just 11 provinces account for 80 per cent of all these enterprises and their employment (CSY 2019: table 13.7). The distribution is much the same for the top-500 POEs in the All-China Federation of Industry and Commerce annual list. Zhejiang and Jiangsu, the Yangzi Delta provinces, which are home to some of the most prosperous private firms, were centres of commerce and industry before 1949. Although Shanghai had many of the largest private firms in China before 1949 – it was then part of Jiangsu – SOEs have dominated the economy since and crowded out the private firms in many sectors.

Analysis of the ACFIC Top-500 POEs over the past decade shows interesting shifts in the distribution of industry activity. Five sectors account for the lion's share of private firm activity. In 2017, these were manufacturing 56.6 per cent, construction 10 per cent, wholesale and retail 8.8 per cent, which collectively have declined 10 percentage points since 2010, conglomerates 7.8 per cent, and real estate 7.4 per cent (ACFIC). Finance, transport and information technologies have been growth areas for POEs, increasing collectively five-fold since 2010. Among the top-20 firms on the 2019 ACFIC list, shown in Table 4.6, which was headed by the mobile phone giant Huawei, four were in real estate and another four in metals, three in retail, three in electronics-electrical manufacturing broadly, and two conglomerates (each with extensive real estate portfolios). The ACFIC classification of sectors differs from the Fortune Global 500 list of leading Chinese POEs (Table 4.4), but in general the sectoral distribution is broadly similar. Meanwhile, the Hurun list (2020) of the 500 most valuable private firms in China for 2019 were Alibaba ($545 billion), Tencent Holdings ($408 billion), Ping An Insurance ($215 billion) and Huawei ($172 billion).

Table 4.5 Selected provincial distribution of private-owned enterprises

	Top-500 POEs (2017)		POEs above designated size (2018)		
	Number of firms	% Share	Number of firms	% Share	Employees ('ooos)
Zhejiang	120	24.0	28,745	13.0	3,496
Jiangsu	82	16.4	28,747	13.0	3,792
Shandong	57	11.4	25,512	11.6	2,732
Guangdong	60	12.0	20,061	9.1	3,212
Shanghai	13	2.6	3,551	1.6	445
Beijing	14	2.8	1,022	0.5	125
Others	154	30.8	112990	51.2	14607
TOTAL	500	100.0	220,628	100.0	28,409

Notes: The ACFIC list does not include Alibaba and Tencent because these are listed offshore using a "variable interest entity" registered in the Cayman Islands (see text). Industrial enterprises above a designated size are state (*guoyou*) and non-state (*fei guoyou*) firms that since 2011 had an annual revenue from their principal business of over ¥20 million.

Source: ACFIC (http://www.acfic.org.cn/); CSY (2019: table 13.7).

CORPORATE GOVERNANCE IN CHINA

In a collectivist-oriented and networked society, the development of a modern corporate governance regime has proved difficult for both private and state firms. The difficulty for state firms is pretty obvious: the government as the dominant shareholder is both owner and regulator, and the lack of clarity in property rights over SOEs in China makes ownership

Table 4.6 Top-20 private-owned enterprises in China, 2019

Rank	Company	Province	Industry	Revenue (CNY bllns)
1	Huawei Investment Holdings Limited	Guangdong	Computer, communications etc manufacturing	721.2
2	HNA Group Co., Ltd.	Hainan	Comprehensive (Diversified conglomerate)	618.3
3	Suning Holding Group	Jiangsu	Retail	602.5
4	Zhengwei International Group Co., Ltd.	Guangdong	Nonferrous metal smelting and rolling	505.1
5	Evergrande Group Co., Ltd.	Guangdong	Real estate	466.2
6	JD Group	Beijing	Internet and related services	462.0
7	Country Garden Holdings Limited	Guangdong	Real estate	379.1
8	Hengli Group Co., Ltd.	Jiangsu	Chemical raw materials and products manufacturing	371.7
9	Lenovo Holdings	Beijing	Computer, communications etc manufacturing	358.9
10	Gome Holding Group Co., Ltd.	Beijing	Retail	334.1
11	Zhejiang Geely Holding Group Co., Ltd.	Zhejiang	Automotive Manufacturing	328.5
12	Dashang Group Co., Ltd.	Liaoning	Retail	300.3
13	Vanke Enterprise Co., Ltd.	Guangdong	Real estate	297.7
14	Shandong Weiqiao Venture Group Co., Ltd.	Shandong	Nonferrous metal smelting and rolling	284.5
15	Cedar Holding Group Co., Ltd.	Guangdong	Business services	268.8
16	Midea Group Co., Ltd.	Guangdong	Electrical machinery and equipment manufacturing	261.8
17	Jiangsu Shagang Group Co., Ltd.	Jiangsu	Ferrous metal smelting and rolling	241.0
18	Qingshan Holding Group Co., Ltd.	Zhejiang	Ferrous metal smelting and rolling	226.5
19	Zhongnan Holding Group Co., Ltd.	Jiangsu	Real estate	222.5
20	Sunshine Longjing Group Co., Ltd.	Fujian	Comprehensive (Diversified conglomerate)	220.9

Note: These are firms with domestic registration and listing and therefore excludes several large firms that use overseas domiciles when listed abroad, such as the New York traded shares of Alibaba and Tencent, which are listed via a variable interest entity registered in the Cayman Islands.

Source: ACFIC via Sina.com news; http://finance.sina.com.cn/zt_d/2019_mq500qbd/.

murky at best and are often simply the prior rights which accrue to a party-state manager who holds the reigns at any moment. In the private sector, the challenge in implementing modern corporate governance rests in the personal and particularistic ways of business in China that makes it difficult, if not nigh on impossible, for directors on a company board to truly challenge a CEO, who is most likely the entrepreneurial founder and principal shareholder.

Corporate governance differs widely around the world and no one model is better than another, but for convenience sake we can classify simplistically public companies into two broad ideal types, the Anglo-American model and German-Japanese model. The Anglo-American model – also known as the outsider or capital market model – is premised on shareholder sovereignty, widely held shares and raises capital for expansion via the issue of shares or debt (bonds and warrants). The goal of corporate governance is to enable the "suppliers of finance [to] assure themselves of getting a return on investment" (Shleifer & Vishny 1997). In other words, to align the interests of the managers (agents) and the shareholders (principal owners), especially minority shareholders. In the German-Japanese model – also known as the insider or bank/finance-centred model – ownership and control are in the hands of a group of insiders and capital is raised internally or quasi-internally through group-linked banks or allied firms. Outside shareholders get less of a look-in and related parties influence outcomes, but there is also a broader stakeholder perspective in theory that is evident in the presence of a supervisory board as found in Germany in addition to the main board, which includes stakeholders such as representatives of the workforce.

Chinese companies began to issue shares in the 1980s, which were traded on an over-the-counter market before stock exchanges were established in Shenzhen and Shanghai (Green 2004). Laws and regulations were rudimentary. The dominant model for corporate governance was the German-Japanese one including a supervisory board. During the 1990s interest in corporate governance grew. Jiang Zemin told the Fifteenth Party Congress in 1997 that shareholding companies were not only good for capitalism but also for the socialist market economy (CPC web). This was part of his championing of "scientific management" (*kexue guanli*). After the 2001 dotcom bubble, the Enron scandal in the United States and the subsequent legislative change, China moved to adopt the formal structure of the Anglo-American model. This included mandating the appointment of independent directors on the main boards, which the US and other regulators had strengthened after 2001, and quarterly reporting of results. But still missing in China is the empowerment of civil society actors so important for corporate governance elsewhere, such as the press, professional associations of directors and company secretaries, and independent corporate lawyers (Yang & Morgan 2011: 172).

Up to the 2000s, whether the state firm was listed or not, the CPC and the supervisory ministries determined the appointment of not only the chief executive and senior management but also the board and the supervisory board: "There is little sign of the board of directors and the supervisory board serving as an effective form of internal review in companies where the state remains the principal shareholder" (Tang & Ward 2003: 56). Since the formation of the SASAC in 2003, there has been a decline in the average proportion of shares the state holds and independent directors are now required. But these changes have been more form than substance. The CPC still makes the major appointments and often will arbitrarily swap the senior executive teams. In 2015, for example, the vice minister of industry and information technology, Shang Bin, was installed as the new chairman of China Mobile, the world's largest telecom by subscribers, while the chairman and CEO of the second largest firm China Unicom, Chang Xiaobing, was transferred to China Telecom and Wang Xiaochu moved in the opposite direction (Reuters 2015). It is not unusual for the senior-most executive to wear not two but three hats: the CEO, the chairman of the board and the party secretary.

Independent directors are a difficult call for Chinese firms. They can be "troublesome", as Yanzhou Coal Mining discovered at its Australian subsidiary, Yancoal Australia, the largest pure coal miner in the country (Yancoal website). The chairman Li Xiyong engineered the resignation in 2015 of a "bossy" independent director: "Yancoal had an independent director who was very difficult and always speaking up for minority share-holders … [he] didn't consider the position of the major shareholder", Li is reported to have said (AFR 2015). Foreign independent directors are valued by some Chinese firms, as James Stent recounts of his experience on the board of China Minsheng Bank (Stent 2017). Their foreignness makes them unbeholden to the *guanxi* networks of the business and government, unlike Chinese who are unlikely to be appointed unless they are connected in some way to the firm's founder or others involved in the company. Stent's experience was a notable exception from all accounts.

In 2018, China's code of corporate governance was revised to empha-size environmental, social and governance disclosure, to improve the accountability of board directors and their skills, and to require the formal incorporation of the party committees, although more clarity is needed in how this will work (Allen 2018). Too often firms have leveraged rela-tionships and manipulated the books to rise rapidly, only to collapse even more quickly. The crash of Anbang Insurance the year after it joined the Fortune Global 500 at number 136 in 2016 was mentioned in Chapter 3. It is far from alone. Tycoons often use their control of local banks to bankroll their investments. Chairman of the Tomorrow Group, Xiao Jianhua, had used more than 200 shell companies to borrow ¥156 billion ($22.5 billion) from Baoshang, which led to the bank being taken over and liquidated (*Financial Times* 2020f, 2020g, 2020h).

The Luckin Coffee chain, the wannabe rival to Starbucks that was launched in 2017, out-performed even Anbang in boasting its value. It disclosed nearly half the revenue reported in the three quarters to April 2020, or ¥2.2 billion ($310 million), was falsified, which sent shockwaves through Wall Street. The company had been listed on the Nasdaq less than a year earlier in 2019 (*Financial Times* 2020a). It was delisted in June 2020 and its chairman Charles Zhengyao Liu was ousted in July (*Financial Times* 2020f). Chinese corporate authorities were also very unhappy. The scandal led the US Congress to pass legislation to require foreign firms to disclose their ties to governments and submit to audits by the Public

Company Oversight Board. This might debar Chinese firms from listing and even force the exit of such giants as Alibaba and Baidu. Up to $1 trillion of Chinese listings in the US could be affected, forcing many to consider second listings in Hong Kong. Between late 2019 and June 2020, there were second listings in Hong Kong by Alibaba (raising $13 billion), NetEase ($2.7 billion) and JD.com ($4 billion) (*Financial Times* 2020e).

At issue in the Luckin Coffee debacle is more than simply fraud, but the refusal of the Chinese government to allow American corporate watchdogs to audit Chinese firms and a perception that all Chinese firms are hostage to the whims of PRC policy. None are more vulnerable than the internet giants, which have used variable interest entities (VIEs) to circumvent China's ban on foreigners owning shares in Chinese internet and media companies. Alibaba, Tencent, Baidu, JD.com and as many as 100 PRC internet and media firms use VIEs. Light was shone on VIEs when Alibaba listed in New York in 2014, the world's then largest-ever IPO. The buyers of Alibaba shares (or any VIE) do not have title to the underlying assets, but instead to share in the profits of a Cayman Island-registered entity. There are two clear risks: the PRC government could declare VIEs illegal and from time to time MofCom has hinted it might; VIE owners might appropriate the assets and Chinese courts may be unwilling to enforce the contracts held by investors (*The Economist* 2017). As one lawyer in 2014 was quoted saying: "You can't afford not to invest in these things. But if something goes wrong, you are left with nothing" (*Financial Times* 2014).

State action against Chinese firms and entrepreneurs suspected of crimes have an extra-judicial character in their execution. Anbang Insurance was seized, and its chairman Wu Xiaohui arrested, quickly tried and imprisoned for economic crimes. Tomorrow Group chairman, Xiao Jianhua, whose corporate plays bankrupted Baoshang Bank, was abducted from his hotel room in Hong Kong in early 2017 about the same time as Wu Xiaohui was detained, but Xiao has not been seen, charged or put on trial since. Xiao was once the broker to the Chinese elite and one of China's wealthiest businessmen (*Financial Times* 2020d).

Similarly disappeared was Ye Jianming, the chairman of CEFC China

Energy, once China's largest private energy conglomerate; he was detained in March 2018 for economic crimes reportedly on the direct orders of Xi Jinping (SCMP 2018b; Reuters 2018). Ye had often paid bribes along the way to build his oil and gas trading company. CEFC joined the Fortune Global 500 in 2014 and in 2017 was ranked 222 with revenues of $43.74 billion (Fortune Global 500). In 2016, Ye went on a buying spree with finance from the China Development Bank, including paying $9.1 billion for a stake in Rosneft, Russia's state-backed oil company. After his detention an investment agency of the Shanghai municipal government took control. In March 2020, CEFC was declared bankrupt (Caixin Global 2020).

None of the flamboyant business deals or recent governance issues are new. They are just bigger in scale. For example, in the mid-1990s a few dozen PRC state firms obtained backdoor listings on the Hong Kong Stock Exchange through buying shelf or dormant companies, renaming them and pumping in mainland assets. They became known as "Red Chips" and have their own special "H Index" (de Trenck 1998). Next, they raised more capital in Hong Kong, advised by the big-named investment bankers who took hefty fees with glee, despite the lack of transparency. The H-share brewer Tsingdao Beer's capital raising around this time, which was intended for expansion to combat the inroad of international brewers, was recycled as loans to affiliated firms. An investor in Tsingdao had not bought an interest in a brewery so much as one in a loan shark.[22] Similar issues confront international investors today keen to get a share of China's domestic yuan-issued green bond market, which has soared from $1.2 billion in 2015 to $33.2 billion in 2019, leading the world. China does not have agreed standards for green bonds which adhere to international standards. The bonds might fund wind or solar projects. Then again, they might not, instead used for refurbishing a coal plant or for the working capital of a state firm. The latter two would disqualify the China bond for international investors targeting environment friendly projects (*Financial Times* 2020c).

In summary, what are the ongoing issues for corporate governance? Ownership of public state firms is concentrated in state-linked parties, which disadvantages minority mum and dad shareholders and foreign investors. This leads to the lack of a market for corporate control as state-linked parties can block hostile acquisition bids. That in turn reduces the competitive pressure on state firms – the average return on assets of state firms is below private firms – and disincentivize managers to lift performance. Transparency and disclosure are poor. A cursory glance of any listed state firm website compared with a similar firm in a Western market reveals how scant information is, from operating details through to the background of directors and senior executives. There is a lack of accountability for boards and directors; the supervisory board and independent directors are rarely independent in practice; the observance of regulatory codes is at best weak. And the idiosyncratic party control over executives of leading state firms, the patron–client and other personal ties, severely limit the scope to discipline senior personnel and improve their performance. Lastly, many Chinese investors assume the state will bail out poor performers in the interest of maintaining financial stability.

Chen (2015) argued the current weakness of corporate governance practices in China can be ascribed, to a great extent, to the incompleteness and weakness of the enforcement of the law. But the weakness is more than that, in my view. It is systemic, on the one hand rooted in the way the party-state governs the economy, and on the other in the broader network dynamics of Chinese society where the rights of the individuals are subordinated to the group, a hierarchy of privileges determines an individual's share, and relationships may appear as both a set of resources and a means to access those resources held by the group. Corporate governance in China cannot escape these institutional constraints and cultural boundedness. Whether that is a bad thing or not for firm performance is an open question, since some firms perform well, but it is not something with which foreign investors or global capital markets are comfortable.

CONCLUSION: WITHER THE STATE?

Business and government are entwined in China much as they are in many countries in Asia where a statist economic ideology bestows on the state responsibility to guide economic and social development. Japan, Korea, Taiwan and others during the second half of the twentieth century were able to discipline the market by the means of state policies and guiding agencies (Wade 1990; Chowdhury & Islam 1993; World Bank 1993). There is a lot of variation in Asia to this broad characterization, of course, with Southeast Asia open to FDI while Northeast Asia was not, except for China. At all times China has followed its own path. And, increasingly in recent years, the party-state has bent the market to its will and vision for China's future and safeguarded the state sector despite the overwhelming importance of the private sector to economic growth and employment. Business is subordinated to national development goals articulated by the CPC, and especially the goals espoused by Xi Jinping.

Paradoxically, however, the world's largest communist party has overseen the abandonment of the planned economy for a vibrant and at times raw capitalism that in its organizational form is clearly a hybrid mix of capitalism and socialism. This makes for an extreme tension between the role of the state versus the market in the economic development of China. The CPC uses a dual hierarchy to control state organs, whose senior leaders are invariably party members and appointed by the CPC to both party and state roles, including the senior executives of SOEs. Such blurring of the separation between party, state and business is a breeding ground for recurring corruption that reaches to the very top of the political elite. At all times the party has the upper hand whatever the constitution of China might say in making economic policy and running the government and will all too readily intervene to force changes in the market and in firms whatever their ownership. Overlaid on this political economy is what many would call a collectivist or group-oriented culture. In particular, the deep-seated customs of interpersonal relationships that mould the connections and practices of daily life in both business and government. The business of government in China ultimately is ensuring business serves the interest of the party-state and its goals.

5

Rich China, poor China:
disparities and inequalities

There are some inescapable truths about the transformation of Chinese lives over the past four decades. Hundreds of millions lifted themselves out of poverty, tens of millions became well off to affluent, and many millions are now rich, even super rich. The Chinese are indeed richer than they have ever been; they are also on average taller, healthier and fatter; they are better educated and more productive; and they have previously undreamed-of opportunities to travel within China and abroad. Materially, the Chinese live in a world of abundance compared with even the very recent past. But inequalities are starker too. These have the potential to destabilize and rip apart society. This chapter will explore these aspects of the social and material change that have accompanied four decades of rapid economic growth.

Every week in China in 2017 and 2018 four new dollar-denominated billionaires were minted (Hurun 2018, 2019). China had 819 billionaires in early 2018, 210 more than the previous year, and pulled further ahead of the United States's tally of 571. The US is still home to the richest in the world: Jeff Bezos, Warren Buffet, and Bill Gates head the global rich list. But Beijing is the world's billionaire capital. In 2018, the capital and seat of power for the Communist Party of China was home to 131 billionaires, 39 more than in New York; 10 cities in Greater China had 15 or more billionaires.[1] Little would the 1980s reform leader Deng Xiaoping have imagined his fellow Chinese would embrace with such lust his call to get rich. Even less so, would he have imagined how his party comrades and their families would likewise enrich themselves at the expense of the state and citizenry. Looting of state assets by officials in collusion with private business was covered in the previous chapter. China is truly a country of peculiar dissonance and phenomenal disparities.

More detail on the life, careers and fortunes of the super-rich will follow next, but most of the chapter is devoted to the less extraordinary, focused on the disparities in income, education and health status that are the lived experience of ordinary Chinese. At the start of economic reform inequality was low. Everyone was poor, often chronically hungry and with few opportunities to change their circumstances. Per capita availability of grain in 1978 was no more than in 1958 and in between often much lower in the worse years (Lardy 1983). The biggest difference in the standard of living was between urban and rural residents, as it still is today. Even the materially best-off urban residents had only an income a few multiples of the poorest. Access to scarce goods and services was a privilege of party rank that could not be bought but could be bartered for with favours. For a country that proclaimed to have liberated its peasant farmers from exploitation of landlords the persistence of high urban–rural disparities was extraordinary and at variance with the image of socialist equality.

China's great economic transformation in the late twentieth century changed the country from one of the reputedly most equal in the world to one of the most unequal (Riskin, Zhao & Li 2001), of which its tally of millionaires and billionaires is but an extreme indicator. Economic reform has nevertheless created opportunities that earlier generations could not have imagined: international travel, higher education for their children, salaries that reward investment in education and training rather than privilege, and higher levels of consumption generally. In the midst of a new plenty in China to focus on inequalities is not to disparage the achievements but to bring to the fore the real challenges to create a more equitable and fair society that economic modernization has the potential to yield for all Chinese, be they a resident of an affluent suburb in Shanghai, a remote village in the mountains of Guizhou or a hamlet on the fringe of the Gansu deserts in western China.

BECOMING RICH IN CHINA

Jack Ma (Ma Yun) is to the current generation of Chinese like Hong Kong's Li Ka-shing was to two or more generations of Chinese in the past.[2] Founder of the e-commerce giant Alibaba, the one-time English teacher Ma from Hangzhou has created an internet behemoth that in its reach to Chinese consumers exceeds the impact of Jeff Bezos's Amazon. Bezos turned a book-selling portal from the 1990s into an internet shopfront for everything and became the world's richest man. Ma similarly began modestly with a site for English translation and a listing of businesses that wanted to make connections in China or globally. Alibaba.com is the world's largest business-to-business trading platform but is dwarfed by the consumer-oriented website Taobao, launched in 2003, and sister site Tmall. These sites comprise in effect China's largest retailer. In China "to *tao*" is to search online for a product. The 2014 float of Alibaba on the New York Stock Exchange was then the largest ever IPO at $25 billion.[3] The company made Ma the richest man in China with a net worth of $34 billion in 2019 (Fortune China Rich List).[4] To put that in perspective, Table 5.1 shows his wealth as a percentage of his home province and of equivalent country GDP, along with the wealth of the next three richest entrepreneurs, Ma Huateng, Hui Kayan and Wang Jianlin.

Many of China's richest are self-made entrepreneurs who had great intuition and built companies with products and services, which if not original were at least novel to China. Jack Ma's success has come from extremely nimble opportunism, launching the Alibaba business-to-business marketplace site in 1999 and the online shopping portal Taobao in 2003 to stymie the entry of eBay to China. Jack Ma in effect married China's huge population to the model borrowed from eBay and Amazon to create an online consumer powerhouse. That was innovation, of a sort.

169

Table 5.1 China's Top-4 billionaires, wealth compared with home province and country equivalent size

Name	Rank	Net Worth ($b)	Industry	Home province	Net worth % province GDP	Net worth country GDP equivalent
Jack Ma	1	34.6	e-commerce	Zhejiang	4.5	Cameroon
Pony Ma	2	32.8	internet media	Guangdong	2.4	Yemen, Rep.
Hui Kayan	3	30.8	real estate	Guangdong	2.3	Latvia
Wang Jianlin	4	22.7	real estate	Beijing	5.4	Honduras

Note: The wealth of any individual and their respective rank can fluctuate depending on the change in the market value of the listed companies they control.

Source: Forbes China Rich List 2018, https://www.forbes.com/china-billionaires/list/; World Bank WDI Database. Data are for calendar 2018.

Pony Ma (Ma Huateng), owner of Tencent and the second richest in China in 2018, is best known outside of China for his social media app WeChat (*weixin*), which is a social media ecosystem of apps within apps that is used by more than one billion people. It allows users to do everything from sending friends messages and pictures, through making payments in shops and restaurants, to ordering a taxi, paying utility bills and many other things. This app in its original form around 2010 bears an uncanny resemblance to an app in Japan. But the basis of Pony Ma's wealth is not WeChat, but from Tencent's production of popular online games. China's eighth richest entrepreneur in 2018, Robin Li, captured the web search market with his Baidu search engine, but he benefited from the de facto protectionism following the withdraw and exclusion of Google from China in the 2000s. Foreigners are banned from running internet, media and telecommunications firms in China. As can be seen from Table 5.2, the top-20 entrepreneurs made their fortunes in a range of sectors, although internet-related new media activities account for about one-third.

Many entrepreneurs have also gained their wealth through cosy relationships with the party-state. Even where they have resisted the

Table 5.2 Top-20 billionaires in China in 2018 and the corporate source of their wealth

Name	Net worth 2018 ($b)	China Rich List 2018	Global Rich List 2019	Industry	Company name
Jack Ma	34.6	1	21	e-commerce	Alibaba
Ma Huateng	32.8	2	20	internet media	Tencent
Hui Kayan	30.8	3	22	real estate	Evergrande
Wang Jianlin	22.7	4	36	real estate	Wanda
He Xiangjian	19.5	5	50	home appliances	Midea
Yang Huiyan	17.1	6	42	real estate	Country Garden
Wang Wei	14.9	7	110	package delivery	SF Express
Robin Li	14.6	8	143	internet search	Baidu
Li Shufu	14.2	9	91	automobiles	Geely Automobile
William Ding	13.5	10	81	online games	Netease
Lei Jun	11.9	11	143	smart phones	Xiaomi
Colin Huang	11.3	12	94	e-commerce	Pinduoduo
Wang Wenyin	11.2	13	127	mining, copper	Amer
Zhang Zhidong	11.2	14	98	internet media	Tencent
Sun Piaoyang	10.4	15	174	pharmaceuticals	Jiangsu Hengrui
Xu Shihui	9.1	16	153	snacks, beverages	Dali
Pang Kang	8.8	17	162	soy sauce maker	Foshan Haitian Flavoring & Food
Zong Qinghou	8.5	18	174	beverages	Wahaha
Zhang Yong	7.7	19	224	restaurants	Haidilao
Gong Hongjia	7.4	20	171	video surveillance	Hikvision

Source: Forbes China Rich List 2018, https://www.forbes.com/china-billionaires/list/.

party-state's intrusion into their firm, such as requiring the establishment of party branches, they recognize the need to be on good terms with the state, both central and local. In fact, very good terms, such that entrepreneurs often seek membership of the party and of local and national political bodies (Zhao 2016; Zhao & Morgan 2019). The decentralization of control rights over state assets in the early 1990s to the local state without clarification of ownership rights gave local party officials huge discretionary power, and in particular over urban land and local SOEs' assets. Entrepreneurs grew rich exploiting the ambiguities in property rights, which persist and seem unlikely to be remedied (Pei 2016; McMahon 2018). They did deals with the local state that enabled them to buy state-controlled assets at below-market prices, which they flipped quickly for huge profits. In no sector has this been more evident than real estate. Quite a few industrial firms are subsidized by their property operations (McMahon 2018: 131–2, 189–90). Access to land is a "gift" of the local state. Many corruption cases involving local party secretaries and mayors revolve around land scams (Pei 2016, cites numerous cases).

Not all real estate development is crooked. Rapid institutional and social change created big opportunities for fortunes to be made. The privatization of urban housing between 1998 and 2002 was an historically large transfer of wealth from the state to urban citizens who were fortunate enough to be in possession of state-supplied housing at the time. And that was nearly everyone employed by a state-run entity such as an SOE, government office, research institute or university. They were allowed to purchase their state units at prices well below the market and with loans from their employers. Overnight they became homeowners. Many resold their units to trade up to better quality apartments. Within four years 80 per cent of urban public housing was sold to occupiers (Li, Sicular & Tarp 2018: 11).

This process fuelled the development of the urban property market that has been a hallmark of China's economic growth the past two decades. Urban real estate including malls and offices as well as apartments became a critical component of the Chinese economy, even "the engine of China's growth" (McMahon 2018: 89). Price rises in tier-1 cities like Beijing and Shanghai have averaged double digits a year most years since the early 2000s. This has made real estate a magnet for investment from which many firms earn more than from their primary business operations (McMahon 2018: 131–2). Table 5.3 shows that real estate is the main source of wealth of one-fifth of China top-100 richest people in 2018, followed by the internet and new media businesses.

Table 5.3 China's Top-100 billionaires by industry source of net worth, 2018

Number	Industry/sector	Total worth ($b)	% share
20	real estate	145.9	22.7
15	manufacturing	78.1	12.1
5	media	64.7	10.1
4	e-commerce	57.2	8.9
7	retail	44.0	6.8
10	hospitals, pharmaceuticals, biotech	43.5	6.8
7	food, beverage, restaurant	43.3	6.7
10	mining, metal products, gas, oil	42.7	6.6
4	IT, security	33.3	5.2
6	conglomerate, diversified	31.8	4.9
3	package delivery	21.4	3.3
4	chemicals, petrochemicals	17.6	2.7
2	agriculture, pork industry	7.3	1.1
1	logistics	4.4	0.7
1	education	4.1	0.6
1	finance	4.0	0.6

Source: Forbes China Rich List 2018.

Ownership of real estate is the largest single source of disparities in income and wealth in China today. Many younger urbanites are priced out of the market. Those employed in the informal sector and migrants to the city are even more disadvantaged in acquiring property. The rapid rise in urban property values has also contributed greatly to rural–urban inequalities in general and within-urban inequality in particular where income direct or inputted from property assets have becoming increasingly important compared with income from wages (Li, Sicular & Tarp 2018; McMahon 2018: 74–96 *passim*).

INCOME INEQUALITIES AND POVERTY

The Chinese are richer, healthier and better educated than at any time in the historical past. Incomes have risen for all, although faster for some than others; pervasive poverty in the 1970s and 1980s has dwindled, although there remain vulnerable low-income populations in poorer areas who live slightly above the poverty line; and investment in education and health has improved well-being and raised the quality of human capital. One of the most striking aspects of China's economic transformation has been the rapid increase in inequality along many different dimensions.

In the space of less than two decades after economic reform began the distribution of income in China changed from being one of the most equal in the world to one of the most unequal. "Seldom has the world witnessed so sharp and fast a rise in inequality as has occurred in China" (Riskin, Zhao & Li 2001: 6). The measure of inequality used here is the Gini coefficient and the ratio between rural and urban household consumption. The Gini coefficient ranges from zero, which represents perfect equality, to one, which represents perfect inequality. Typically, the Gini coefficients range from 0.20 to 0.70 (some authors will multiply the coefficient by 100 and write in terms of percentage). Figure 5.1 shows estimates of the Gini coefficient for China over the period 1978 to 2019.

At the start of economic reform, the overall national Gini coefficient was about 0.30, which is low by international standards. The urban Gini

Figure 5.1 Change in estimates of Gini coefficient, 1978–2019

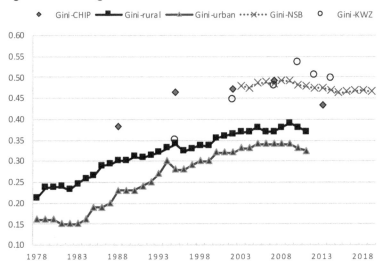

Notes: The rural and urban Gini for 1978–96 are estimates using official household data without adjustment for subsidies from Zhao (2001) and Li & Sicular (2014). The Gini-KWZ 2007–12 is a combined CHIP and CFPS estimate with adjustment of each data set to ensure data consistency from Kanbur *et al.* (2017).

Sources: Zhao (2001); Li & Sicular (2014); Li *et al.* (2018); Luo *et al.* (2018); Kanbur *et al.* (2017); CSY 2014–2020, table 1.4.

coefficient was an extraordinarily low 0.16 and even declined slightly at the start of the 1980s. Low urban inequality reflected the high compression of urban wages during the planned economy and the common level of food, housing and welfare subsidies the state supplied to urban residents. The rural Gini coefficient was higher, around 0.22 and remained below 0.25 until the mid-1980s. In rural China, the differences in inequality at the start of the reform period reflected the natural endowments of the land, the main determinant of farm incomes; later, opportunities for off-farm employment in rural business or in nearby towns became more important for the inequality in farm household incomes (Griffin & Zhao 1993).

From the late 1980s into the 2000s, structural reforms in finance, foreign trade and investment, and urban enterprises fuelled rapid economic

175

growth and an accompanying increase in inequality, as shown in Figure 5.1. Estimates from the China Household Income Project (CHIP), which corrects the incomes of households for subsidies, transfers and income from assets, show the national Gini coefficient rose from 0.381 in 1988 to 0.462 in 1995, 0.471 in 2002 and 0.490 in 2007 and then declined to 0.433.[5] Another estimate shows the Gini coefficient peaked at 0.533 in 2010.[6] The official NSB estimates show the Gini in the 0.479–0.490 range from 2003 to 2009 before it began to decline to a low of 0.462 in 2015, and has since remained in the 0.46–0.47 range.[7]

Household consumption data (Figure 5.2), suggest inequality between rural and urban households peaked during the mid-2000s and has since declined. However, the NSB switch in 2013 to a new sampling approach for the household survey makes it difficult to determine exactly by how much the rural–urban gap has declined in recent years.

Figure 5.2 Urban–rural household consumption ratio, 1978–2019 (rural = 1)

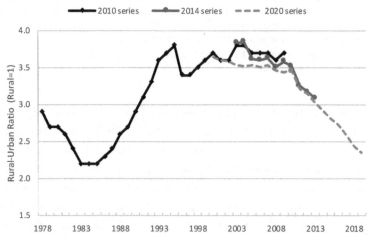

Notes: The ratio is the household consumption of rural households divided into that of urban households based on the NSB annual household surveys in current RMB. It is unadjusted for subsidies received by urban households in the 1980s and 1990s. Change in the survey method since 2013 mean that recent data lack comparability with the series before 2013.

Sources: CSY (2010, 2014, 2020).

The level of inequality conveyed by these estimates are relatively high, well above the average for OECD countries and many developing countries and similar in level to the more unequal societies in Latin America. In 2010, the Gini coefficient for the EU averaged 0.33, North America 0.37, and Latin America 0.49 (Han *et al*. 2016: 26). Increasing concern about inequality in the early 2000s motivated the then party General Secretary Hu Jintao to advance the idea of making China a "harmonious society" (*hexie shehui*) and "moderately well off society" (*xiaokang shehui*). New measures were introduced to reduce disparities and protect the vulnerable. These included agricultural support policies, social welfare transfers, targeted reductions of rural taxes and fees, and poverty alleviation programmes.

To an extent the high degree of pre-reform equality is "illusionary", according to Zhao (2001: 26–7), because the official estimates ignored the in-kind supply of goods and services to urban residents that made the rural–urban income gap larger than in money alone. Most income in kind went to the better off urban residents, so the real income inequality was higher. Consumption data without adjustment for urban subsidies show the rural–urban gap has remained high since 1978, except for the early 1980s (Figure 5.2). Urban household consumption in monetary terms was 2.9 times that of rural households in 1978, higher than elsewhere in Asia. World Bank data for 1983 showed the average ratio in low-income countries in Asia was 1.5 and in middle-income countries 2.2 during the same period (cited in Zhao 2001: 26).

In the early 1980s, the rural–urban ratio declined sharply as institutional change and the increase in agricultural prices raised rural incomes quickly while urban residents experienced slower income growth. From the mid-1980s, structural reform of the urban economy along with an inflow of foreign direct investment led to increasingly differential rates of growth between coastal and interior provinces. Incomes began to rise in the cities and especially those in eastern China. Over the reform period the increase in urban incomes has been steadily consistent, but rural incomes have passed through three phases: 1978–85, rapid growth; 1985–2009, much lower growth and below that of urban residents; and from 2009, an acceleration with rates exceeding those in urban area (Naughton 2018: 218–19). As a consequence, in 2019 the rural–urban ratio reached a low of 2.3 (Figure 5.2), a level not seen since the mid-1980s (CSY 2020: table 3.13).

What factors have driven the increase in inequality? China's three-decade increase in inequality and the recent apparent reversal fits the inverted U model of Simon Kuznets (1955). In the early stages of economic development inequality rises as the workforce shifts out of low-productivity activities into higher ones, raising the incomes of those in the more advanced sectors and leaving others behind, which widens the income gap until at a higher level of income catch-up begins in the poorer areas and inequality starts to decline. Millions of Chinese rural workers who were surplus to agriculture from the 1980s moved to the city for jobs in export-oriented manufacturing, new industries or building infrastructure. Others moved from farming into off-farm private business. They and their left-behind families, who received remittances from migrant workers, benefited from such economic growth.

This development process exacerbated spatial inequality; the coastal provinces, which attracted the lion's share of FDI and government support, grew faster. The east–west ratio in income increased from 1.7 in 1988 to an average of 2.2 between 1995 and 2007 before declining to 1.6 in 2013 (Li, Sicular & Tarp 2018: 3). Eventually the surplus labour dwindles and rural to urban migration slows. This produces the downward shift in the inverted-U and the associated "Lewis Turning Point", an inflection in the labour supply which leads to tighter labour markets and a rise in wages. As a consequence, the rural–urban income gap begins to narrow. In China this turning point appears to have occurred around 2010 when the workforce peaked, or even a few years earlier because labour shortages began to appear in the mid-2000s in the southern China export-oriented manufacturing zones.

Increased inequality, however, was not simply a product of economic growth and rising incomes, nor was it a product of declining incomes among the poorer population. There was robust growth in incomes for rural households as well as in the interior provinces. Still, income increased more rapidly for those in coastal provinces and cities. Regional and sectoral differences contributed to the increase too. Education became more important for earnings as the economy modernized; the better educated lived in the already more developed and richer parts of China. There were changes to the sources of household income and its distribution. An increasing share of income came from very unequally distributed sources of income, such as housing and other assets, but also state transfers, such as pensions and medical benefits that are higher for urban residents than rural. Nearly a quarter of household income growth from 2007 to 2013 derived from increases in income from property (Li, Sicular & Tarp 2018: 13). And not a little increase in inequality came from what Zhao called "disorder changes", the institutional voids and the unequal access to opportunities thrown up by rapid change that allowed for gross rent-seeking, monopolistic behaviour, and corruption and collusion between vested interests (Zhao 2001: 37–9).

The recent decline in China's inequality is the subject of debate and public incredulity. Government health and pension policies since the late 2000s have contributed to reduce inequality and alleviate poverty. Yet, we are constrained by available data. Household survey samples in China – and elsewhere, for that matter – do not fully capture data for the poorest and the richest segments of the populations. Data collected recently on the income and wealth of the super-rich to augment the household survey sample found the Gini coefficient for China in 2016 increased from 0.464 to 0.646, an increase of 39 per cent in the severity of inequality, while similar corrections have reported results even as high as 0.739 (Li, Li & Wan 2020). Missing data on the rich matter for measuring inequality: the decline in inequality might be more apparent than real.

In May 2020, the Premier Li Keqiang made the startling statement that 600 million Chinese, some 40 per cent of the population, lived on an income of less than ¥1,000 ($140) a month or about $4.60 a day (SCMP 2020a). China is officially a middle-income country with a per capita GDP slightly short of $10,000. The PBoC reckons urban households on average had assets of ¥3.2 million in 2019, while the NSB reports the median disposable household income was ¥26,523 ($3,715), with urban households having ¥42,359 and rural households ¥16,021 (SCMP 2020a; NSB 2020b). A former senior official subsequently called on the government to postpone the 2021 centenary goal for achieving a well-off society when many clearly are not (SCMP 2020b). And the 2020 coronavirus pandemic pushed incomes lower, dropping many into poverty again.

Poverty has diminished rapidly over the past four decades and so large have been the numbers that it has reduced overall global poverty hugely. Exactly how many have escaped poverty and at what speed depends on the choice of the poverty line by which the population is classified. In 1978, 250 million people lived in poverty based on the then official poverty line. These were rural residents; urban poverty was not recognized and is still ignored in official statistics. A more generous World Bank poverty line for the same year implied about 800 million were in poverty, more than 80 per cent of the then population of 963 million. Recent official estimates using the 2010 poverty line report just 1.7 per cent of rural Chinese lived in poverty in 2018 and 0.6 per cent in 2019; the same poverty line applied to 1978 produces an estimate of 97.5 per cent in poverty (CSY 2019, 2020: tables 1.4 and 6.35). Figure 5.3 shows this decline in the rural population living in poverty along with the poverty incidence based on the poverty lines for 1978, 2008 and 2010.[8]

The historical reduction in poverty is impressive. Since the mid-2000s new or improved programmes have been introduced to reduce inequality and alleviate poverty. China's development policy is broadly pro-poor. The government aspired to rid China of poverty by 2020. But as with similar official goals around the world the likelihood appeared at best a political dream. Despite the pandemic disruption of the economy, Xi Jinping in December 2020 declared victory in the party's target to end "absolute poverty". He told a meeting of the Politburo SC that all rural poor had shaken free of poverty and that China had removed all poor counties from its poverty list (Xinhua 2020). Impressive as the outcome is, unevenness

Figure 5.3 Population and poverty incidence (headcount %) in rural China, 1978–2019

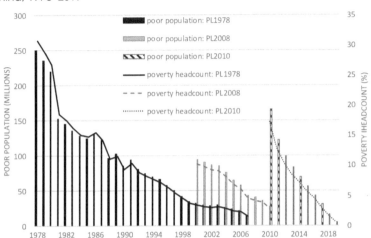

Notes: The population are those classified as rural. Missing data for 1979, 1993 and 1996 are interpolated. The poverty line (PL) was 100 yuan in 1978, 1195 yuan in 2008 and 2300 yuan in 2010. See Luo *et al* (2018) and Li & Sicular (2014).

Source: CSY (2020: table 6.35); NSB (2020b).

in implementation of poverty alleviation is widespread, often due to the capacity of the local state to carry out the programmes, which suggest the reported achievement rests on a fragile base.

The major components of the social welfare system are pensions, health insurance, and cash transfers to the poor. Pensions were once the privilege of the employees of SOEs. In 2009, the government launched the New Rural Pension Scheme. By 2012, the scheme reputedly covered 100 per cent of China's rural counties. The benefits are low and regional variation is big: residents of Beijing's rural districts in 2015 received ¥475 a month but those in Gansu received just ¥85. In 2011, China extended pensions in cities with a new basic pension scheme for all and in 2014 merged it with the rural scheme. Health insurance also had previously been limited to employees of the urban formal sector. A New Rural Cooperative Medical Scheme from 2009 had over 95 per cent coverage by the mid-2010s.

In 2007, the government initiated the Urban Resident Basic Medical Insurance to cover those without insurance through their employers. Enrolment is voluntary but numbered nearly 400 million by 2015. These schemes have increased the affordability of healthcare, reduced the use of household savings, and have had a positive impact on household incomes. Contributions and reimbursements, however, vary widely from region to region (Li, Sicular & Tarp 2018: 14–15).

EDUCATION, HEALTH AND WELFARE

Human capital at the start of the economic reforms was impressive for a country as poor as China. Investment in education and health during the Mao years had delivered significant gains, with levels well above countries of similar per capita income. Literacy had improved across the nation; illiteracy among those 15 years or older was less than 20 per cent by 1980s according to the official data and declined to 15.9 per cent in 1990, 6.7 per cent in 2000 and 4.6 per cent in 2019 (CSY, various years). Average years of schooling of the workforce 15 years and older had increased from less than one year in the 1940s to 1.8 years in 1960 and to 5.2 years by 1980, though well behind others in East Asia (Morrisson & Murtin 2009; Gao 2015). Communicative diseases had been reduced or nearly eradicated and basic public health provision vastly expanded, which raised average life expectancy at birth from below 40 years in the early twentieth century to 50–60 years in the 1950s, to 67 years in 1982 and to 76 years by 2015 (CSY 1984: 95; CSY 2020: table 2.4). National averages like these conceal rural–urban and provincial disparities. Economic growth since the 1980s has made the Chinese healthier and better educated on average, and the challenges are now akin to those of an advanced economy rather a developing one.

The Chinese education system comprises three tiers: primary education (six years), secondary education (middle school three years and high school three years) and a post-secondary sector of universities and vocational colleges primarily delivered by the state. Nine years of compulsory education has been required since 1986 but local governments have discretion to adjust to local conditions. Attainment levels vary between provinces and rural and urban areas. The quality of rural schools is often dismal, with few resources. Enrolment rates in primary school has increased from 97.8 per cent in 1990 to 99.9 per cent by 2015, with progression to junior high school rising from 74.6 per cent to 98.2 per cent over the same period (CSY 2018: table 21.13).

Since the late 1990s the government has poured money into higher education to support industrial policies to raise scientific and technological capabilities. First-degree university graduates increased from 147,000 in 1980 to 950,000 in 2000 and then accelerated to reach 7.6 million in 2019 (CSY 2020: table 21.9). Postgraduates have risen from a mere 476 graduates in 1980 to 639,666 graduates in 2019 and about the same number studying higher degrees abroad (CSY 2020: table 21.10). By the 2010 census, 48 per cent of 16–24-year-olds had attained a high school diploma or post-secondary qualification (Figure 5.4) compared to 1982 when about 20 per cent had completed high school and barely any post-secondary. In many East China cities in the late 2010s there is nearly 100 per cent completion of middle school (to year nine) and more than 90 per cent might also complete high school to year 12.

Despite big strides in education and the large numbers of graduates turned out each year, China still lags behind the level of educational attainment in advanced economies along several measures. Illiteracy remains stubbornly prevalent in many provinces, although it affects mostly older people. Although the national average has declined to 4.6 per cent by the late 2010s, gender and regional disparities remain high. Figure 5.5 plots the illiteracy rates for men and women older than 15 years against regional per capita income. Illiteracy is lowest in the rich metropolitan cities of Beijing, Tianjin and Shanghai, and highest in the low-income provinces of Guizhou and Yunnan in the southwest and Gansu in the northwest (excluding Tibet, a big outlier, where average illiteracy is 35 per cent). There is a large middle group with a per capita regional income between ¥40,000 and ¥110,000 where illiteracy for men ranges over 0.9–3.5 per

Figure 5.4 Completed education in years by age group, 1982–2010

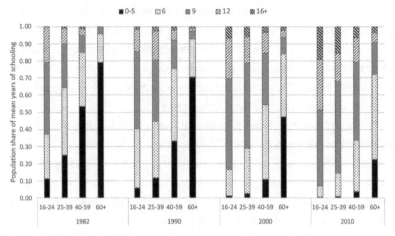

Source: National Population Census 1982, 1990, 2000 and 2010.

Figure 5.5 Percentage of illiterate population relative to provincial per capita GDP, 2017

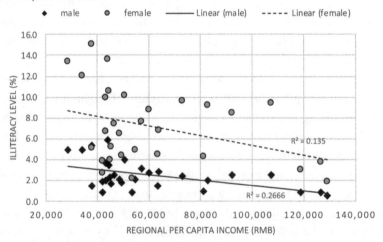

Note: The NSB define the illiterate population as the percentage of those 15 years or older who cannot read or have difficulty reading and the data are from the 2017 National Sample Survey of Population Changes (sample size, 0.824%). Tibet is excluded as an extreme outlier (average illiteracy 35%).

Source: CSY (2018: tables 2.15, 3–9).

cent and women 4–10 per cent, with a couple of exceptions. Some of the richer coastal provinces have surprisingly high levels of female illiteracy, including Shandong, Jiangsu, Zhejiang and Fujian.[9] Illiteracy among women on average is 3.1 times that of men, ranging from a low of 1.8 times for Xinjiang to a high of 4.7 times for Fujian.

Education of the workforce in China in 2010 was on average 50 years behind Japan and Europe. Table 5.4 compares the average years of schooling of the workforce in China with Britain, the United States, France, Germany and Japan. In 2010, China's workforce on average had 8.8 years of schooling, equivalent to Europe and Japan in 1960 and about 3.8–4.8 years behind contemporary Europe, Japan and the United States. Averages conceal much. In Beijing the average years of schooling is about 12 years while in Guizhou it is only a little above seven. To put this in perspective using American popular language, the data reported in Figure 5.4 means that half the new entrants to the workforce (16–24-year-olds) in 2010 were high school dropouts; in addition, many older workers had not graduated from middle school.

Table 5.4 Average years of schooling of the workforce, 1960–2010

	1960	1970	1980	1990	2000	2010
Britain	8.5	10.3	11.6	12.3	13.1	13.3
USA	10.3	11.1	12.0	12.8	13.0	13.6
France	8.6	10.4	11.3	11.6	12.0	12.6
Germany	8.9	11.1	12.7	13.2	13.0	12.7
Japan	8.9	10.4	11.2	11.9	12.6	13.1
China	1.8	3.2	5.2	6.3	7.6	8.8

Sources: Morrisson & Murtin (2009); PRC Census (1982, 1990, 2000, 2010); Gao (2015).

Vital to raising human capital in China is equipping workers with the skills to participate in an advanced economy. A big weakness in China is the low share of the workforce that has attained at least some level of upper secondary education. This might well be a far bigger obstacle to further economic growth than poorly trained university graduates. In 2010, just 24 per cent of the population aged 25–64 years had upper secondary attainment (Table 5.5). This had increased to 30 per cent in 2015, but that level was still just 40 per cent of the OECD average and less than half the level of the G20 Group. High school attainment was much higher in urban areas than rural areas, and among the youngest segment of 25–34 years.

Table 5.5 Percentage of workforce that has attained some upper secondary schooling by age

Country/Country Group	25–64	25–34	35–44	45–54	55–64
China, average 2010	24	36	23	12	12
urban	37	53	37	28	21
rural	8	14	7	10	4
China, average 2015	30	47	31	22	16
OECD average, 2015	76	83	80	74	66
EU 21	78	85	83	77	68
G20 average, 2015	64	73	66	60	51

Source: Khor et al. (2016); Wang et al. (2018); Bai et al. (2019).

China between 2005 and 2015 has done a fantastic job of increasing high school attainment of 15–17-year-olds from 53 per cent to, depending on the source, between 80 per cent (2015, 1 per cent national sample) and 87 per cent (Ministry of Education). Still, the 13–20 per cent missing out on high school translates into the need to find places for and retain at school some 8–12 million children a year if China is to realize its goal for universal high school attainment (Wang et al. 2018; Bai et al. 2019).

The PISA education attainment rankings show China's children lead the world in reading, mathematics and science (OECD 2019). These misrepresent, however, not only the general level of attainment in China but also the attainment level in the four test sites of Beijing, Shanghai, Jiangsu and Zhejiang because the schools selected for the PISA tests are elite schools in the best-endowed and wealthiest of China's provinces (see Table 3.2). And, as detailed in this chapter, the PISA rankings completely ignore that more than 60 per cent of 25–34-year-olds in the workforce have not attained upper secondary education and many rural students barely make it into junior high school, which gives a false impression of the average level of school attainment in China (OECD 2018; Wang *et al.* 2018; Bai *et al.* 2019).

These data on literacy and education underscore the challenge for China in developing a workforce who are able to participate in a high-skills economy and who can deliver the productivity gains China needs to catch up with the rich economies. According to Khor *et al* (2016) the defining characteristics of countries that are trapped in the middle-income group of economies is the insufficient development of their human capital. In China's countryside and poorer provinces, the problem is not just the number of years of schooling, but also the quality across the school system.

Factors other than the quantity and quality of education are important for development of human capital. Attainment alone is insufficient if children have not acquired during their growing years the cognitive skills to participate in high-skills employment. Early childhood development, poor parenting, and poor child health and nutrition combine to influence later performance in schools. Many children in rural areas are behind in health status and cognitive development before they begin school. Even in the 1980s a World Bank study had observed that stunted (short for age) children were up to nine months behind their peers in cognitive development and at higher risk of dropping out (Jamison 1986). These health and developmental delays hold them back and increase the rate at which they dropout (Bai *et al.* 2019; Wang *et al.* 2018; Yue *et al.* 2017).

Health is an important but often under-recognized contributor to the wealth of nations. Over the past four decades the growth of the economy has come not from the huge investment in industry and infrastructure alone, but also from the improved education and health of the Chinese. A large share of the productivity growth since 1980 can be attributed to higher levels of human capital, that is, a better educated and healthier workforce (Liu *et al.* 2008; Heckman & Yi 2012). As the Chinese become richer – and increasingly older on average – demand is rising for better quality and new health services in the face of an epidemiological transition. The health problems that confront China are now similar to developed countries. Chronic diseases have replaced infectious diseases. Cancer, stroke, heart attacks, respiratory diseases and external trauma (road accidents and suicide) account for the top five causes of death (Table 5.6). The most frequent infectious diseases are viral hepatitis, pulmonary tuberculosis, syphilis, gonorrhoea and dysentery, and the major causes of death attributed to infectious diseases are from AIDS, pulmonary tuberculosis, viral hepatitis and rabies (CSY 2020: table 22.15).

Health reform since the late 2000s has recognized the failings of the highly bureaucratic system inherited from the planned economy that focused resources on large public hospitals. In August 2016, Xi Jinping told a health sector conference: "If we cannot ensure the people's health, we cannot achieve moderate prosperity in all respects. We should prioritize public health, popularizing a healthy lifestyle, improving health services and security, building a healthy environment and developing health industries, promoting the building of a healthy China …" (Xi 2016: 399).

Delivering on that promise is a gigantic challenge for China. The health system is highly bureaucratic and centralized in which more than 90 per cent of services from outpatient to advanced surgery are delivered in large public hospitals (Liu *et al.* 2017). Most of these are tertiary-level hospitals with more than 500 beds. With inadequate primary care clinics in the community and no referral system, doctors in these large hospitals see 60–100 patients in a morning in addition to their specialist practice. They are overwhelmed with patients who do not need their level of specialist service. General practice medicine is underdeveloped and looked

Table 5.6 Ten leading causes of death in China, 2019

Type of Disease	Rural		Urban	
	Crude mortality (1/100,000)	Rank	Crude mortality (1/100,000)	Rank
Heart diseases	164.66	1	148.51	2
Malignant tumour	160.96	2	161.56	1
Cerebrovascular disease	158.63	3	129.41	3
Diseases of the respiratory system	74.61	4	65.02	4
External causes of injury and poison	51.08	5	36.06	5
Endocrine, nutritional & metabolic diseases	17.80	6	21.44	6
Diseases of the digestive system	14.49	7	14.86	7
Diseases of the nervous system	8.60	8	9.14	8
Diseases of the genitourinary system	7.28	9	6.60	9
Infectious disease (including respiratory tuberculosis)	6.94	10	6.01	10

Notes: The data are based on 605 monitoring sites. The rural data include county-level cities.

Source: CSY (2020: tables 22.16 and 22.17).

on unfavourably compared with specialization, although training programmes at elite medical schools are bringing in change. Many Chinese think they will find the best medical professionals at the best hospitals in their area, and with good reason they are mostly right. This leads to long queues at tertiary-level hospitals, overcrowding and patient–doctor interaction that engenders misdiagnosis, miscommunication, distrust and even violent conflict. Doctors have been murdered by patients or their relatives (Cai *et al.* 2019; *The Lancet* 2020).

In 2009 the government introduced a new wave of health reforms. This has focused on universal basic medical insurance coverage, the essential drug system, primary healthcare service provision, equitable public health services, and public hospital improvements. The three health insurance schemes covering urban workers in the formal sector, other urban residents and rural residents have delivered universal health coverage in a little over a decade. In 2002, less than 10 per cent of the population was covered by health insurance; in the late 2010s this had reached more than 95 per cent (Liu *et al.* 2017). Everyone is issued with a medical treatment card that is scanned when a service is booked, linked to an individual health record and account in the place of residence. Once the allowance is used, out-of-pocket medical expenses can become considerable, often causing hardship, but the level of out-of-pocket expenses varies by location. The new essential drug list introduced in the 2009 reform has put an end to the perverse practice of hospitals meeting the shortfall in their state-supplied budget by selling medicines at a hefty mark-up, which resulted in unnecessary services and over prescription. While the government still exercises close control over hospital budgets and personnel, an element of competition has emerged with the proliferation of private-run hospitals and clinics that offer choice for those able to pay the premium (Liu *et al.* 2017).

At the end of the 1970s China suffered from chronic hunger. Per capita consumption of rice and protein was barely different from 20 years earlier. The improvement since in the net nutrition of the population has translated into big increases in the average height and weight of children (Morgan 2000, 2014; Morgan & Su 2011). An individual's height is a complex trade-off between inherited genetics and the environment, but the average height of a population or subgroup is largely a function of the net nutrition available for human growth from *in utero* through childhood to adulthood and not genetics (Floud *et al.* 2011).[10] It is strikingly obvious to a frequent visitor that today the Chinese are taller on average, and fatter too, although regional and gender variations remain. A seven-year-old Beijing boy in 2014 was 129.6 cm tall, compared with 123.2 cm in 1979 and 118.8 cm in 1955, while a girl was 127.1 cm, compared with 123 cm in 1979 and 117.9 cm in 1955. By 2014, a 17-year-old boy on average had attained a height of 176.4 cm, similar to the average for boys in the United States, and a girl 163.6 cm (Morgan 2014; Student Survey 2014).

All Chinese children are on average taller today whichever region they come from. Figure 5.6 summarizes the national increase in average height-for-age of Chinese urban and rural boys between 1979 and 2014. The height of urban boys increased 1.2 cm per decade and rural boys about 2 cm per decade. Such secular change is very fast compared with the average increase of 1cm/decade in stature for Western Europe over the century from the 1850s (Floud *et al.* 2011). The magnitude of these changes underscores the chronic levels of malnutrition that impaired the growth of Chinese children before the 1980s.[11]

Figure 5.6   Increase in average height of Chinese boys aged 7–22, 1979–2014

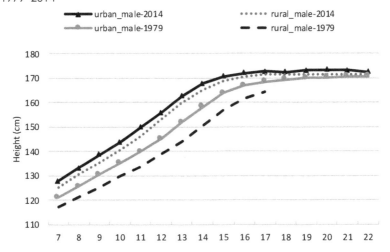

Note: There were insufficient youth of rural-origin older than 17 years in full-time education in 1979 for sampling purposes.

Source: Student Survey (1979, 2014).

Rural–urban and regional variations in height and weight are large, despite the narrowing of the rural–urban gap in nutrition shown in Figure 5.6. Historically the northern Chinese were taller and heavier than the southern Chinese. The difference in the past was related largely to diets – the northern diet was a wheat staple with more meat whereas the southern was rice with vegetables and fish protein – but some scientists have suggested there may be genetic differences (Morgan 2000, 2008). These days regional differences mostly reflect the relative level of economic development. Those in the less developed provinces are on average shorter and lighter.

In the 1990s, overweight and obesity began to emerge among children in the richest cities and has also become common among adults, even in rural areas. For sure, that Chinese children are better fed, taller and heavier is welcomed, but the increased incidence of overweight and obesity will impose long-term health costs on individuals and the public health budget from the rise in preventable chronic diseases such as type-2 diabetes (French 2010; Ji & Cheng 2008, 2009; Morgan 2014). A government report in late 2020 said China faced severe levels of obesity and chronic illness with more than half of its adults overweight (SCMP 2020c).

Our common measure for body weight is the body mass index (BMI). The increase in overweight in China shows big gender and regional differences. In the mid-1980s, there were few overweight and obese children, ranging from 1.4 per cent for urban boys to 4.1 per cent for rural boys. By 2005, a quarter of urban boys were overweight or obese, as were 14 per cent of urban girls, 13 per cent of rural boys and 7 per cent rural girls. The incidence of overweight and obesity on average doubled for boys and girls between 1995 and 2005. The rising trend plateaued in the 2010s, yet underweight persists. In 2005, 34 per cent of urban girls and 33 per cent of rural girls were relatively or severely underweight, a decrease of only three percentage points over 20 years, whereas the proportion of underweight urban boys had declined from 33 per cent to 22 per cent and rural boys from 29 per cent to 26 per cent (Morgan 2014).

Provincial variations in the BMI for 12-year-olds in 2005 show the disparities between rural and urban areas. The average BMI of 12-year-old urban boys in Beijing was above the WHO cut off for overweight, as shown in Figure 5.7, while those in rural Anhui, Guangxi and Qinghai were on the threshold for underweight or below. The majority of rural boys were below the WHO recommended mean weight as were most rural girls. Twelve-year-old urban girls were usually within the WHO recommended range (Morgan 2014).

Figure 5.7   Regional mean BMI of 12-year-old urban and rural boys, 2005

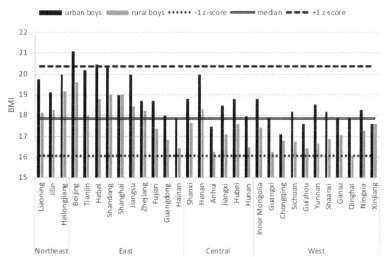

Note: The BMI age z-score is for boys aged 150 months (12.5 years). The WHO (2007) growth reference recommended median BMI is 17.87, with the −1 z-score of 16.06 and +1 z-score of 20.38.

Source: Adapted from Morgan (2014: figure 6); WHO (2007).

While the average height and weight of Chinese children has improved markedly since the 1980s, analysis of the change in distribution of BMI shows that disparities in nutritional status have increased. This is unsurprising in view of the increase in income inequality described above and the positive correlation between income and height and weight. The dispersion in BMI between minimum and maximum around the mean has increased for all ages, with a doubling of the coefficient of variation for provincial BMI means (Morgan 2014).

INTER-ETHNIC DISPARITIES

China is a multi-ethnic country (*duo minzu guojia*). There are 55 non-Han Chinese ethnicities or national minorities (*shaoshu minzu*). The 2010 census reported the Han Chinese comprised 91.5 per cent of the population and the ethnic minorities 8.5 per cent. Many of the minorities are artificial constructs. According to Mullaney (2010), in the early 1950s when China undertook an initial classification of minorities more than 400 groups thought themselves ethnically distinct. Ethnic self-identification is fluid in the border regions of China (Harrell 1995). Minorities such as the Hui live throughout China, while others reside in particular regions, such as the Uighurs, Kazakhs and Tajiks who live in Xinjiang, the Bouyei in Guizhou, and the Hani in Yunnan. The Zhuang, who are widely distributed in southern China are the largest non-Han group, numbering about 17 million, followed by the Hui, Manchu and Uighur with around 10 million each, and the Miao with 9.4 million found in Hunan, Guizhou, Guangxi, Sichuan and Yunnan. Others are tiny, such as Lhoba in Tibet, who numbered just 3,682 people in the 2010 census.

Most of China's non-Han ethnicities live in the poor southwestern and northwestern provinces. Both Han and minorities in these areas are likely to be disadvantaged compared with the Han in developed areas. One of the few studies of the income inequality between ethnic minorities and the Han majority in rural China found the increase in the income was slower for the minorities than the Han from 1988 and 1995, and the gap widened (Gustafsson & Li 2003). However, in rural Guizhou and Yunnan the "income levels of minority persons actually increased more rapidly than those of the [Han] majority population" (Gustafsson & Li 2003: 820). For this reason, comparison between the income and nutritional status of the Han and ethnic minorities need to take into account location factors and the local economy.

The nutritional status of the ethnic minorities on average has improved, but the change overall has been slower than for the Han and the gap has not narrowed, which suggests they have not shared to the same degree in the recent economic growth of China. Table 5.7 reports the change in height for minority boys and girls aged seven and 17 years and Han children overall in East and West China between 1985 and 2014. Minority children were on average shorter in absolute terms than Han children at seven years of age. The relative change in height over the period measured in z-scores was also greater, implying gains in nutritional status were greater for Han children.[12] For 17-year-olds, the absolute difference in height between Han and ethnic minority population was about 4 cm compared with East China and 2 cm compared with West China, but the difference in relative change was smaller. The implication is that the 17-year-old ethnic minority children growing up during the late 1990s and 2000s had a similar net nutritional gain to Han children.

Controlling for location produces mixed effects. The relative and even absolute gains in height of some minorities have been greater than their Han counterparts. In Ningxia, shown in Table 5.8, Han boys and girls of the selected ages were taller than the Hui minority children in 1985. After 30 years that was no longer so. For most age groups the height of the Hui children had increased faster than the Han, closing the gap and even surpassing the Han. Hui girls have become taller than their rural and urban Han sisters. The right-most column (M-H diff) of Table 5.8 shows the difference in height between the Hui and Han is positive for most reported ages. The likely explanation for the height advantage is that the rural Hui in Ningxia engaged in short-term employment migration that increased their income, with positive effects for nutrition compared with the rural Han, who otherwise have higher farm income on average than the rural Hui (Gustaffson & Ding 2014).

In Yunnan, the impact of residence and access to market-based economic opportunities has had similar differential consequences for nutritional status. The nutritional status of the lowland Bai people is on average better than the rural Han. In 1985, both seven- and 17-year-olds were taller

Table 5.7 Summary change in the stature of ethnic minority and Han children, 1985–2014

	1985		2014		Change 1985–2014	
	cm	z-score	cm	z-score	cm	z-score
Minority girls 7	116.38	–0.811	121.31	0.092	4.9	0.903
Han National 7	118.42	–0.438	125.13	0.789	6.7	1.227
Han girls 7 East	119.01	–0.330	125.83	0.918	6.8	1.248
Han girls 7 West	117.36	–0.631	123.91	0.568	6.6	1.199
Minority girls 17	154.62	–1.231	156.68	0.092	2.1	0.308
Han National 17	156.97	–0.880	159.83	0.789	2.9	0.427
Han girls 17 East	157.26	–0.837	160.44	0.918	3.2	0.476
Han girls 17 West	156.45	–0.957	158.77	0.568	2.3	0.347
Minority boys 7	117.25	–0.849	122.14	0.077	4.9	0.926
Han National 7	119.51	–0.420	126.63	0.925	7.1	1.346
Han boys 7 East	120.11	–0.306	127.35	1.063	7.2	1.369
Han boys 7 West	118.43	–0.625	125.37	0.688	6.9	1.313
Minority boys 17	163.87	–1.477	168.34	–0.892	4.5	0.585
Han National 17	167.55	–0.996	172.05	–0.407	4.5	0.589
Han boys 17 East	168.06	–0.929	172.84	–0.303	4.8	0.626
Han boys 17 West	166.63	–1.116	170.68	–0.586	4.1	0.530

Source: Student Survey (1985, 2014); Morgan (2018).

than the Han and the gap had even widened for some ages in 2014. The Dai children were shorter than Bai and Han in 1985. While their average height has increased, the gap with the Han and Bai has widened. The Hani, who live in remote upland regions, were the shortest of the four minorities with the least improvement in average height. Hani seven-year-old girls in 2014 were just 118.8 cm tall, up 5.1 cm from 1985, but 2.4 cm shorter than

Table 5.8 Change in average height of Han and ethnic Hui children in Ningxia province, ages 7, 12 and 17 years, 1985–2014 (cm)

Location	Age	Han Boys			Min Boys			M-H Diff*
		1985	2014	change	1985	2014	change	
urban	7	120.7	128.5	7.8	119.9	129.3	9.4	1.5
	12	144.7	155.1	10.3	143.0	158.3	15.3	5.0
	17	169.3	174.2	4.9	168.0	174.6	6.6	1.7
rural	7	118.4	125.7	7.3	118.8	125.7	6.9	−0.3
	12	140.8	153.2	12.4	139.9	153.9	14.0	1.6
	17	167.3	173.2	5.9	165.7	172.7	7.1	1.1

Location	Age	Han Girls			Min Girls			M-H Diff*
		1985	2014	change	1985	2014	change	
urban	7	119.3	126.7	7.3	119.1	127.0	7.9	0.6
	12	146.9	154.8	7.9	145.7	155.9	10.2	2.3
	17	158.3	161.2	2.9	157.9	162.5	4.6	1.7
rural	7	117.3	124.7	7.4	118.8	125.6	6.8	−0.5
	12	142.7	153.9	11.2	142.9	155.3	12.4	1.2
	17	156.9	159.4	2.5	155.2	160.9	5.7	3.2

Note: M-H diff = minority-Han difference.

Source: Student Survey (1985, 2014); Morgan (2018).

rural Han in Yunnan; the average height of 17-year-old girls had increased to 153.4 cm, up 1.1 cm compared with 1985, but 2.2 cm shorter than rural Han (Morgan 2018).

GENDER INEQUALITIES

Gender inequality in income, welfare and nutrition has been mentioned several times in this chapter, but the scale of the change over recent years in not only economic dimensions but also ideologically is breathtaking. Equality between the sexes was fundamental to the early communist revolutionaries. Mao summed it up in his aphorism that women hold up half the sky. The Marriage Law of 1950, one of the earliest pieces of legislation by the infant PRC, was a bold strike for the equality of women. Much of that has now been undone the past two decades through the retreat of the state from childcare and the impact of marketization, although it could be seen to have begun at least in 1980 with the one-child policy that robbed women of control over their bodies in the interests of state deemed desirable reproductive outcomes.

The story of increased gender inequalities in contemporary China is more than about the impact of marketization, although these are striking. Under the command economy women were to play their role in China's industrialization. Participation in paid urban work increased because rural–urban migration was closed off, which raised urban household incomes in real terms despite near static urban wages during the 1960s and 1970s. China as a result had one of the highest female participation rates in the world. Despite the provision of nurseries and other welfare in state work units, women still bore the double burden of work and responsibility for the caring and raising of the future workforce (Ji *et al.* 2017). Over the past two decades the participation of urban women in paid employment has fallen; egalitarian values and firm-provided welfare have been reduced; and the state has shifted responsibility for care and nurture to the family and individual along with a reassertion of a Confucian patriarchal ethos that subordinates women.

Hong Fincher (2014, 2018) exposed how rising gender equality robs China's women of the benefits of recent economic growth. In 2007, the party-state media and women's organization began a campaign to pressure educated middle-class women into marriage and child rearing, labelling those who had not committed to home, hearth and children by 27 years of age to be "leftover women" (*shengnü*). This has had severe economic consequences and especially for gender equality in wealth, such as ownership of property. Hong Fincher reckons Chinese urban women have been shut out of "the biggest accumulation of residential real estate wealth in history", with urban real estate valued at about three times China's GDP in 2013 (2014: 43, 47; Chapter 2). As recounted above, the privatization of urban housing led to a real estate boom and rising property prices, which turned urban Chinese into homeowners with rapidly appreciating wealth, and which exacerbated inequalities within urban China and between urban and rural China, but also between genders.

Most urban residential property titles are in the name of the husband and in the event of a divorce the registered owner has sole entitlement. That is a direct outcome of a Supreme Court re-interpretation in 2011 of the Marriage Law and property distribution in the event of divorce, which produced a "stunning reversal of women's property rights in China" (Hong Fincher 2014: 48). Data are not transparent, but surveys point to the disparities women face in entitlement to China's real estate wealth. A survey in Beijing, Shanghai, Guangzhou and Shenzhen found the man's name appeared on 80 per cent of the property titles and the woman's name on 30 per cent; a national social survey found 52 per cent of married men had sole ownership compared with just 13 per cent of married women, while only a quarter of the titles were in joint names (Hong Fincher 2014: 46, 70).

In the workplace, the decline in participation rates and the gender wage gap is the other dimension of growing inequities for women. The workforce participation rate for urban women fell from 77.4 per cent to 60.2 per cent between the 1990 and 2010 census, some 20 percentage points lower than urban men (Hong Fincher 2014: 36). Participation declined quickly for older urban women. According to the 2010 census, about 75 per cent of urban women aged 25–45 years were in employment, but just 15 per cent of urban women 55–59 years were in work, compared with 55 per cent of urban men and 75 per cent of rural women (Naughton 2018: 211). Marriage and motherhood penalties have increased, with many women unable to return to a similar level of employment after bearing a child and forced into the informal sector, especially lower middle- and working-class women (Ji et al. 2017).

In 1990 the average salary of urban women was 78 per cent of men, but by 2010 it had declined to about 67 per cent (Hong Fincher 2014: 35–6). Naughton (2018: 227–8) reports that studies have shown the gender gap in wages has widened from between 8 and 12 per cent in 1988 to more than 20 per cent by the mid-2000s. Differences in gender earnings in the Chinese labour market have increased across the earnings distribution, with the increase greatest among the lower paid. This is a "sticky floor" effect, where poorly educated women in low-skilled low-pay employment are more disadvantaged than better educated women in occupations at the upper end of the wage distribution, despite a "glass ceiling" that results in pay lower than their male counterparts (Chi & Li 2008). The size of the gender gap, however, may be underestimated because low-wage women are more likely to drop out of the workforce (Chi & Li 2014).

Lastly, ideological and political factors figure in gender inequalities. Not one woman has ever served on the Standing Committee of the Politburo of the CPC's Central Committee, the ultimate source of political power in China, which currently comprises seven men headed by Xi Jinping. Only one woman, Sun Chunlan, is on the 24-person Politburo for the 2017–22 term and just ten women on the 204-person Central Committee.[13] Hong Fincher (2018: 162) argues the subordination of Chinese women is "a fundamental element" of the CPC's rule and its focus on "stability maintenance" (*weiwen*), which in party thinking is pivotal to regime survival, and includes an almost Confucian obsession with the proper ordering of familial relationships. This has produced a "patriarchal authoritarianism", a marriage between the party-state's vision of socialism and revived Confucian social values. Xi Jinping, speaking at a ceremony to honour family values and virtues, said Chinese society should promote "socialist family values" as "an important foundation" for national development (*Global Times* 2016). In this world women are to serve the communist state through reproducing the family: "The Chinese government wants women to be the reproductive tools of the state, obedient wives and mothers in the home, to help maintain political stability, have babies and rear the workforce of the future" (Hong Fincher 2018: 170).

The social clock has been seemingly turned back to a time before the New Culture and May Fourth movements of the 1910–20s, whose idealistic youth – many of whom became leading communists – sought to rid China of conservative Confucian values, symbolized for them in the oppression of marriage and family in China.

CONCLUSION

Richer, better educated and healthier than they ever were, the Chinese today nevertheless live in a society that is far more unequal than it was even in the recent past. Across all measures of inequality – income, wealth, education, healthcare and nutritional status – we see stark differences between rural and urban populations, between those who live in the coastal provinces and those inland, between ethnic groups, and between the genders. For Chinese with physical and other disabilities, the inequalities in access and even recognition as citizens, their existence hidden behind closed doors and unrecorded in official statistics is a stark reminder of the social stigma and exclusions in Chinese society (Dauncey, 2020). Most Chinese, however, have benefited from the phenomenal economic growth of the past four decades, but clearly some groups have enjoyed greater gains than others.

China has a class of super-rich now whose income and wealth too often escape measure and the tax authorities. Many Chinese in well-off urban areas might think of themselves as having made it, with an apartment (or two), a car and occasional overseas holidays, but they grumble on social media when the state media announce new per capita GDP data. They do not feel that their personal income lives up to these averages. More than half the population lives on a tiny fraction of the much-touted official data. Still, the chapter has shown incomes, education and health have improved, and poverty has vastly shrunk. China's economic growth has delivered much for many, and hugely so for the well-connected elites. The transformation in lives, well-being and opportunities whatever the disparities probably does deserve the "miracle" label, however overworked the word is to describe East Asian economic development since the 1950s. Income inequality in China might have peaked, but this is a contested space, because the data on the upper and lower tail of the income distribution are subject to large errors. Meanwhile, inequalities among and between ethnicities and along gender lines are far from diminishing and may well be worsening.

6

A sustainable future?

China's future will be an urban one, but there are big challenges in building liveable cities and providing work for their inhabitants in the advanced economy of tomorrow. Today China is not so much at a crossroads as at an intersection with many forks. There is no single path that will lead China assuredly to become a wealthy and strong country by 2049, the centenary of the founding of the PRC. Many Chinese would like to see realized this dream of Xi Jinping, but far from all would agree with him and the party leaders on how to build a prosperous and sustainable future. This chapter will look at three challenges that will be crucial: making Chinese cities liveable, reducing energy use without reducing growth and incomes, and becoming a global innovator. These are inter-connected. Indeed, innovation in one form or another is at the centre of all paths to a sustainable future. China will need to develop the capabilities to deliver the science, the technologies and the processes that distinguish a high-income economy from the rest if it is to grow and sustain the living standards of the predominantly urban population.

Cities in China have long been among the largest in the world, yet only 40 years ago 82 per cent of Chinese lived in rural settlements. In 2020, 61 per cent of the population was urban. Rapid economic growth and massive migration swelled existing cities and created vast new urban settlements. Unbridled economic growth has had big environmental consequences, poisoning air, water and land in many parts of the country. China is para-doxically the world's largest emitter of greenhouse gases and the largest producer of renewable energy. Massive investment has created modern urban spaces and efficient intra- and inter-urban transport. The residents of these cities are ardent consumers of Chinese and international brands. Buying a car to get around the new urban areas is a must for the swelling middle class. China is not only the world's largest automobile market for conventional-powered vehicles, but also has more electrical vehicles on its roads than the rest of the world combined.

Making Chinese cities liveable is also about transforming how energy is produced and consumed. Households and transport account for about one-third of total energy used, but industry is the major user. Over the past two or more decades China has successfully reduced energy intensity – industries have become far more energy efficient. But these efficiency gains have been swamped by the sheer size of the growth in China's econ-omy, which has pushed up the absolute amount of greenhouse gases pumped into the air. Higher incomes also mean higher per capita energy consumption. All of today's rich and advanced economies have high per capita energy use. Limiting the growth in energy use is necessary for China and for the world to lessen the adverse effects of climate change but doing so without inflicting big costs on its economic future and the livelihoods of its people is tricky. China is not alone in this challenge. And, the rich world has not been helpful, seeking to impose limits on the con-sumption of the Chinese they would not impose on their own people. That is hardly an acceptable outcome for leaders in Beijing.

Innovation is central to building liveable cities for the many millions of new urbanites, reducing greenhouse gases and other pollutants, and producing economic growth and rising living standards. In the face of an ageing and a shrinking workforce and the environmental challenges of increased energy use, China needs to stimulate innovation that will increase productivity and supply solutions for sustaining growth. Without raising the productivity of its workforce – making its workers cleverer, if you want, and able to produce more with fewer energy inputs – China will struggle to increase living standards, which has been the litmus test of the party-state's legitimacy over the past three decades. Huge investment has been poured into higher education, science and technology (S&T), and research and development (R&D) since the late 1990s. Yet, as discussed in Chapters 3 and 5, China lags far behind the advanced economies of the world in the average level of education attainment. Shifting from an export-oriented manufacturing economy to a service-based economy that can deploy human capital effectively is not simply an economic challenge, but a political one, and one which I will argue the CPC is not well equipped or willing to implement.

CITIES AND URBANIZATION

At the start of the reform period only 18 per cent of Chinese lived in cities. In 2011, the level of urbanization officially passed 50 per cent and in 2019 it reached 60.6 per cent, with 848 million Chinese living in designated urban places (CSY 2020: table 2.1). The populations of these urban centres range from rural towns with tens of thousands of residents to the megacities of East China, such as the Beijing-Tianjin-Hebei conurbation and the Yangzi River Delta region with Shanghai at the apex. Over the next 20 years the government plans to move another 200 million people into cities, making China a country with more than one billion city dwellers. These cities are the wealth producers of China's economy, home to an increasingly richer middle class, the major consumers of energy and as a result huge emitters of greenhouse gases. Making these cities sustainable and liveable will be no mean feat.

The transformation of the grey and poor cities of the past into the vibrant modern urban centres of the twenty-first century is quite astonishing. Many of the cities in the early 1980s looked as if they had not had a coat of paint since 1949. Looking at the vista of the Shanghai Bund along the Huangpu River from my room in the art deco Shanghai Mansions in 1982, the only big difference compared with photographs from 1950 was that the electric trams had been replaced with electric trolley buses.

Opposite the Bund on the Pudong side of the river were low-rise factories and warehouses reached by ferries. Today, Pudong is the heart of the Shanghai new financial district, connected to the districts across the river by metro lines, tunnels and bridges. The skyscrapers are some of the tallest in the world. Many are architecturally arresting, such as the futuristic Pearl of the Orient tower that resembles a giant space vehicle ready for launch. The data on urban growth barely captures the magnitude of the change and certainly not the experience.

The 1982 census reported 75 million Chinese or just 7.3 per cent of the population lived in 38 cities with a population of 1–2 million or more (see Table 6.1). There were no cities larger than 10 million inhabitants. By the 2010 census, there were 381 million Chinese – 28.6 per cent of all Chinese – residing in 136 cities with populations greater than 1 million people. China had six cities with more than 10 million people and another ten cities with populations between 5 and 10 million. Urbanization has created megacities at the apex of large agglomerations that join dozens of urban centres, from small towns to large cities, into city-regions where the distinction between rural and urban has almost disappeared.[1]

Below the central government, China is organized into a four-tier spatial administrative hierarchy of provinces, prefectures, counties, and towns and townships. Restructuring of this spatial administration since 1980 has been motivated by an urban growth-pole type of strategy in which cities (towns) lead the surrounding urban (rural) areas. Table 6.2 shows the change in the administrative hierarchy between 1982 and 2019. Many prefectures in the 1980s and 1990s were reclassified as cities despite the sum of their widely dispersed townships having less than 20 per cent of the prefecture population. This policy was known as "cities governing counties" (Zhang *et al.* 2016: 103–04). Urbanization was more a product of administrative change than true urban growth. Since 2000 the main thrust of restructuring has been abolishing counties and county-level cities, turning these into urban districts under the local central city. Major cities such as Hangzhou, Guangzhou, Ningbo, Suzhou and others have replaced counties with urban districts and forged large city-regions.

Table 6.1 Number and population of China million-plus cities, 1982–2010

City size (millions)	1982	1990	2000	2010
A. Number of cities				
10 +	0	0	2	6
5–10	3	3	7	10
2–5	10	14	19	35
1–2	25	42	65	85
TOTAL	38	59	93	136
B. Population (millions)				
10 +	0.0	0.0	25.9	89.4
5–10	17.1	21.4	52.8	70.0
2–5	26.7	40.7	54.7	106.9
1–2	31.6	55.3	92.4	114.9
TOTAL	75.4	117.3	225.7	381.2
C. Share of national population (%)				
10 +	0.0	0.0	2.1	6.7
5–10	1.7	1.9	4.3	5.3
2–5	2.6	3.6	4.4	8.0
1–2	3.1	4.9	7.4	8.6
TOTAL	7.3	10.4	18.2	28.6

Note: City size refers to the population in the city districts (*shixiaqu*). These may contain people who are rural and engaged in agriculture, especially in the 1990s when many prefectures were reclassified into cities without having any large towns. This was a driver of the 1990 census jump in the number of 1–2 million class cities.

Source: Population census data; Zhang (2019: 144).

·

Table 6.2 China's administrative system, 1982, 2000 and 2019

	Prefecture Level		County Level			Town Level	
	Prefectures	Prefecture-level cities	Counties	County-level cities	Urban districts	Rural towns (*zhen*)	Townships (*xiang*)
1982	210	109	2,133	133	527	2,660	54,352
2000	74	259	1,674	400	787	20,312	23,199
2019	40	293	1,430	387	965	21,013	9,221

Notes: Counties include autonomous counties associated with a particular ethnic minority. The county-level urban districts refer to counties that are administratively subordinated to larger adjoining cities. The township data for 1982 refers to people's communes which were converted to townships between 1982 and 1984.

Sources: Zhang *et al.* (2016: 102); CSY (2020: table 1.1).

The development of large agglomerations and city-regions is the most marked change to the spatial organization of China over the past four decades (Wu 2015; Zhang *et al.* 2016). This is in stark contrast to the command economy period when the main strategy was to contain urbanization. From 1979 to 1999 promotion of urban growth was unbalanced and favoured economic development in East China. In general, small and medium-sized cities were favoured over large cities. Since 2000, the urban growth strategy has been more balanced and has strived to coordinate development from large cities to small towns to form integrated regions (Wu 2016: 121; Xu 2019: 141–3). As a result, urban agglomeration has increased. The population in cities larger than one million has swollen about 70 per cent between the census of 2000 and 2010 (Table 6.1), a rate of growth continued the past decade. Rapid urbanization is obvious even in the less developed provinces. In Guizhou, the growth of county-level towns is closely associated with the poverty alleviation programmes that relocate people from remote villages to towns where better services are available and new housing is built for them.[2]

Recent development policies have aided urban agglomerations. The 20 largest of these cover about 28 per cent of China's land area, contain 68 per cent of the population, produce about 82 per cent of economic output, and receive 90 per cent of FDI (Xu 2019: 145). The major city region agglomerations include the Beijing-Tianjin-Hebei Region, which is part of the broader Bohai Gulf Zone; the Yangzi River Delta Zone centred on Shanghai; the Pearl River Zone centred on Guangzhou and Shenzhen but with cross-border ties to Hong Kong and Macau; the Wuhan-Hubei Zone in central China, and the Chengdu-Chongqing Zone in southwest Sichuan. The Yangzi Delta Zone is the largest with a GDP more than the combined GDP of the Beijing-Tianjin-Hebei and Pearl River Delta zones (Xu 2019: 147). These megacity regions are shown in Figure 6.1 along with a simplified map of the interconnecting high-speed rail network.

What is most remarkable about these new city-regions in China is the "spatial logic" differs from larger cities of the past. Although the economics of agglomeration is important, there is a "de-concentration" occurring in which activities that were once centralized in the inner core of the central city are distributed within the "polycentric" urban system of lower-level cities surrounding the core city (Xu 2019: 139). The Yangzi Delta shows the interconnection of multiple city-regions within the larger agglomerated regional zone.

The main axes of the Yangzi Delta region are the Shanghai-Nanjing and Shanghai-Hangzhou corridors, which are almost a continuous urban strip, and the spur Hangzhou-Ningbo corridor, which together forms a gigantic "Z" pattern of cities, Nanjing-Shanghai-Hangzhou-Ningbo. This is far from just a recent phenomenon. These cities were joined in the early twentieth century by the Shanghai-Nanjing and Shanghai-Hangzhou-Ningbo railways, and in earlier times by canal, river and coastal shipping. A new high-speed rail line now connects Hangzhou and Nanjing, bypassing Shanghai, which allows direct trains from Ningbo to Beijing via Hangzhou and Nanjing in less than seven hours. Ningbo was also the primary port for international exports of East China for centuries until overtaken by Shanghai in the nineteenth century. The Ningbo-Zhoushan port is the fourth largest container port in the world after Shanghai, Singapore and

Figure 6.1   Megacity agglomerations and high-speed rail network, 2020

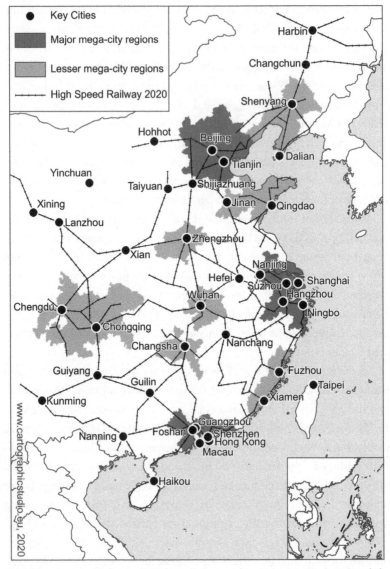

Note: The megacity agglomerations have drawn on descriptions in Xu (2019) and the core high-speed rail network from the official railway map (http://cnrail.geogv.org/enus/about).

Shenzhen (WSC 2019); eight of the largest 20 ports are in China (including Hong Kong makes nine).

Not only has the physical topography of China's cities changed – the growth in numbers, population and urban infrastructure – but also the social geography. Up to the late 1970s, urban growth was restricted by the household registration (*hukou*) system, which began in 1958. The system made it almost impossible for rural residents to migrate to cities. The basic division was between agricultural (*nongye*) *hukou* and non-agricultural (*fei nongye*) *hukou*, loosely interpreted as urban. A person's *hukou* was not strictly related to residence or birthplace: officials, teachers and others in rural areas had an urban *hukou*. In addition to the rural–urban *hukou* distinction, each person was classified by their residential location (city, town or village), which might not be their birthplace, and which defined a person's rights and eligibility for government services in a location. *Hukou* status is passed on via the mother's *hukou*.

Although the *hukou* system has been relaxed in recent years and the distinction between rural and urban even abolished in lower-level urban centres, it still impedes permanent settlement of migrants in larger cities and has many pernicious social and economic effects. Local government officials are reluctant to change the *hukou* status of migrants. Those who have moved to a city are classified as "non-*hukou* population" and they are unable to enjoy the benefits of citizenship afforded *hukou* holders. In effect, rural migrants are guest workers in their own country and reported in statistics as the floating population (*liudong renkou*), which peaked at 253 million in 2014 (SCY 2019: table 2.3). The floating population accounts for most of the discrepancy between the urban resident population and the lower urban *hukou*-registered population. As Chan (2019: 69) observed, "they are 'in the city but not of the city', lacking legal and social claims to their residency".

Since rural migrants are legally in limbo in the city, they can be readily deported to their home village or town and sacked from their jobs without the right to claim support. A major consequence is labour market segmentation and discrimination, which contributes to within-urban inequality.

Their wages have been held down to the benefit of urban residents and the export-oriented industries that have fuelled China's growth as an economic power (Chan 2019: 69; Roberts 2020). They and their dependents are also denied social benefits. Education for migrant children is poor. For this reason, migrants "leave behind" their children with grandparents or other relatives who are often ill-equipped to raise and educate them (Yue *et al.* 2017).

Even for those with urban *hukou* the benefits depend on where they reside in the spatial administrative hierarchy; resources and benefits are far better for those in higher-order cities. Urban residents in Shanghai, for example, receive larger health insurance reimbursements than those in small towns in western provinces. As Chan (2019: 72) noted, "Chinese citizens do not possess equal citizenship and equal access to welfare and services. This inequality has created two separate 'peoples' in China (agricultural versus non-agricultural *hukou*), each of which is further located within specific administrative unit (that is, a neighbourhood) within the hierarchy." Lack of entitlements in the city and opportunities to settle permanently mean rural migrants are reluctant to give up their rights to home-village land, which hinders the reallocation and more efficient use of farmland. Migrants hang onto their land-use entitlements as a safety net in case they are expelled from the city or retrenched from their job.

Urban landscape and infrastructure have been vastly transformed over the past two decades. New urban districts have been built on former rural land, with large high-rise estates, huge shopping malls and wide boulevards, and interspersed with big landscaped parks. In the early 1980s urban residents lived in state-supplied housing, usually tiny and poor in quality. SOE reforms and the privatization of housing fuelled a property boom. The one-off asset windfall for residents is a growing component of income and wealth inequality in China, within urban areas and between urban and rural residents (see Chapter 5). In 2018, most urban *hukou* residents own their apartment – sometimes multiple apartments – and enjoy an average housing floor space many times that of the past.

Urban malls in China at first glance are similar to elsewhere, filled with outlets selling international brands and Chinese brands, coffee shops run by Starbucks, Costa Coffee and local rip-off brands, and many restaurants catering to a variety of Chinese cuisine as well as Japanese, Korean, Thai and Western. All the major franchise food operators are present in China with thousands of restaurants: McDonalds, Burger King, KFC, Pizza Hut, Subway and others. Eating out in the food courts or at the discrete restaurants in malls is a frequent activity for urban residents. The brand mix in malls, however, is an indicator of the relative affluence and sophistication of consumers. Inland malls will host more local brands than those in the richer cities of East China.

Consumption levels were extremely low in the early 1980s and the products aspired to very different from today. Annual average urban wage income in 1983 was ¥826 ($418 at the time) and average rural income was only ¥310, with a range ¥213–563 (CSY 1984: 453, 475). Big ticket consumer purchases then were sewing machines, bicycles, watches and televisions. In 1983, every 100 urban (rural) households owned 76 (38) sewing machines, 160 (63) bicycles, 268 (91) watches and 83 (4) black and white televisions (CSY 1984: 14). A ration ticket issued by the work unit (*danwei*) was needed to buy the preferred brands recognized for their better quality.

In 2018, China's urban residents had an average of ¥39,251 ($5,931) in disposable income (CSY 2019: table 6.6). Their consumption of durables is very different, of course, not only because of increased purchasing power but also the change in the products available. Every 100 urban households in 2018 owned on average 41 automobiles, 55 electric bikes (scooters), 98 washing machines, 101 refrigerators, 121 colour televisions, 142 air conditioners and 243 mobile phones (CSY 2019: table 6.10). Rural household ownership of consumer durables is lower for most items – 22 automobiles per 100 households, 96 refrigerators and 117 colour televisions – but higher for some, such as 65 electric bikes and 257 mobile phones (CSY 2019: table 6.15).

China's urban consumers are mobile and wired consumers. They find and pay for goods on their mobile phones. Alibaba's Taobao is the go-to app for buying goods, but it is not alone. They buy-in food on delivery apps like Meituan. Payment is executed using the Alipay or WeChat mobile payment services.[3] And the goods and food are delivered to their home or office by a legion of electric-scooter riders. The Alipay and WeChat apps are an ecology of apps-within-apps, mobile communications platforms which allow residents in China to use their phones to book taxis, trains, flights, and hotels; transfer money between friends and others, such as landlords; pay their utility bills; and even engage in investments. Cash in most of the cities of East China is going extinct and often will not even be accepted. Taxi drivers want to be paid using Alipay or WeChat, restaurants and big shops prefer the same mobile payments, as do fruit, vegetable and convenience food stalls, and even beggars will offer their phone (or a card with a QR code) for alms from pedestrians who deign to give them money.

Interconnecting China's cities and urban agglomerations are networks of expressways and high-speed trains; within the cities networks of new metro lines have been built in many cities since the 2000s and electric-powered bus services are replacing conventional powered vehicles. At the start of the 1980s inter-city transport infrastructure was poor other than the trains, hauled by coal-fired or diesel locomotives. Railway route length has increased 2.5 times since 1980, while the proportion of electrified lines has increased from 3 per cent to 70 per cent, with a nine-fold increase since 2000 (Table 6.3). High-speed rail, which in 2008 had only 672 km of dedicated track, by 2018 accounted for nearly a quarter of the rail network and carried 61 per cent of all rail passengers (CSY 2019: table 16.19). Total route length of highways has increased 5.5 times and expressways, which did not exist in 1980, totalled 142,600 km in 2018 (Table 6.3).

Urban Chinese have fallen in love with the automobile and today road holidays on the vastly expanded highway networks are as common for them as for the middle class in America, Australia or Britain. Chinese urbanites who own a car use them primarily for commuting to work from the new suburban estates and for weekend recreation (Khan & Zheng 2016: 112–13). Highway exits from the cities become incredibly congested on public holidays as residents embark on their travels. Private vehicle ownership is part of this story, but public-owned vehicles have similarly increased. The growth in automobiles has followed at a faster rate than the extraordinary growth of the economy since the late 1990s (Figure 6.1).

Table 6.3 Expansion of China's inter-city transport network, 1980–2018

	1980	2000	2018
Railway route length (km)	53,300	68,700	131,700
Electrified routes (km)	1,700	14,900	92,200
Highway route length (km)	888,300	1,679,800	4,846,500
Expressways (km)		16,300	142,600

Source: CSY (2019: table 16.3).

In 1985, the first year for which we have data for private vehicles, there were just 19,300 privately owned passenger vehicles on the road (CSY 2019: table 16.21). There were 1.1 million private vehicles a decade later and 3.7 million vehicles by 2000, after which the swelling middle class's rush to car ownership pushed up numbers to 189.3 million by 2018. China was by then the world's largest automobile market, having overtaken the United States as the world's largest market for cars in 2011. At the same time, cars operated by state firms and party-state agencies followed a similar growth path (Figure 6.2).

China is not only the largest market for conventional vehicles, but also the largest market for new energy vehicles. Government industrial policies have supported the development of electric vehicles (EVs) since 2002, which were one of the ten strategic industries identified in the "Made in China 2025" programme (Li *et al.* 2016; State Council 2012; Helvestona *et al.* 2019). In 2019, about 1.2 million pure battery or plug-in hybrid EVs were sold, comprising 53 per cent of the global deliveries of 2.3 million electric vehicles, well ahead of Europe with sales of 504,000 and US sales of 318,000 (EVvolume.com 2020). Growth in sales slumped in late 2019

Figure 6.2 Rapid growth in passenger and goods vehicles, 1997–2018

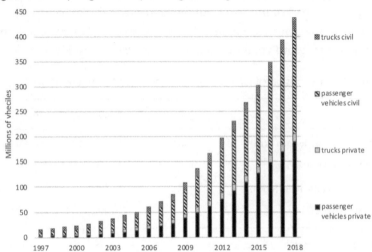

Note: Public owned are listed as "civil" in Chinese statistics, which refer to non-military vehicles used by state and party entities.

Sources: CSY (2019: tables 16.20 and 16.21).

after the Chinese government had cut generous subsides, but that has hardly put a dent in Tesla CEO Elon Musk's ambitions to capture a large slice of the China EV market by building a huge factory in Shanghai (ABC 2019).

Trucks had once dominated road traffic. In 1985, passenger vehicles comprised just 7 per cent of private vehicles and 25 per cent of public-owned vehicles. By 2018, the share was 92 per cent and 88 per cent respectively. This rapid growth in passenger vehicles, inter-city passenger traffic and new city-regions with their shopping malls and high-rise residential estates have brought to China the symbols of affluence, but also high environmental cost. China's cities in the early 2010s were often shrouded in health-threatening clouds of smog, while its waterways were badly polluted and the soil in many areas contaminated. These "negative externalities" of China's growth directly relate to the structure of its economy and its energy use, to which we now turn.

ENERGY AND THE ENVIRONMENT

The economic growth that turned China into the second-largest economy came at the price of increased pollution and adverse health effects which may not be fully realized for years to come. Growth means increased energy consumption and with it a rise in greenhouse gas (GHG) emissions and other pollutants. In 2006, China surpassed the United States to become the world's leading emitter of carbon dioxide and other GHG. China has a lot of people and a large industrial sector, so high energy use and emissions in aggregate is not surprising. The more important questions are the level relative to its population and economic weight, the structure of energy production and consumption, and the efficiency of its use. How China produces and consumes energy – the size, fuel type and efficiency – is vital not only for the sustainability of China's future economic growth and living standards, but also in the face of worsening effects of climate change for the sustainability of the planet.

China is an energy giant. It is the world's largest producer and consumer of coal, and accounts for nearly half of all coal mined. China is the largest generator of hydroelectricity, the largest producer of solar and wind power, and the largest importer of oil (Naughton 2018: 554–5). In 2018, China burned 3,273.5 million tonnes of oil equivalent (MTOE), which accounted for nearly one quarter of global energy consumption (Table 6.4), compared with 16.6 per cent for the United States and 12.2 per cent for the EU, and many multiples the consumption in India, Japan and Russia. Coal is king. It is the main source of energy and accounted for 59 per cent of energy used, which is down on the 1990–2010 period when it hovered around 72–76 per cent (CSY 2019: table 9.2; BP 2019, reports coal at 58.2 per cent in 2018). As shown in Table 6.4, China's consumption of coal in its energy mix is more than twice the world average and more than four times the average in Europe and the United States.

While in total China is the world's largest energy user, its per capita energy consumption is below the level of advanced economies. In 2018, as shown in Table 6.4, China consumed 2,350 kilograms of oil equivalent

Table 6.4 Energy consumption by type, 2018

	Total consumption		Per capita	Percentage consumption of energy						
	MTOE*	%world	Kg OE**	Oil	Natural Gas	Coal	Nuclear	Hydro	Renewables
China	3,273.5	23.6	2,350	19.6	7.4	58.2	2.0	8.3	4.4
India	809.2	5.8	598	29.5	6.2	55.9	1.1	3.9	3.4
Japan	454.1	3.3	3,589	40.2	21.9	25.9	2.4	4.0	5.6
Brazil	297.6	2.1	1,421	45.7	10.4	5.3	1.2	29.5	7.9
Russian Federation	720.7	5.2	4,989	21.1	54.2	12.2	6.4	6.0	0.0
European Union	242.6	12.2	3,290	38.3	23.4	13.2	11.1	4.6	9.5
France	323.9	1.7	3,622	32.5	15.1	3.5	38.5	6.0	4.4
Germany	192.3	2.3	3,906	34.9	23.4	20.5	5.3	1.2	14.6
United Kingdom	1,688.2	1.4	2,892	40.1	35.3	3.9	7.7	0.6	12.4
United States	2,300.6	16.6	7,032	40.0	30.5	13.8	8.4	2.8	4.5
WORLD	13,864.9	100.0	1,826	33.6	23.9	27.2	4.4	6.8	4.0

Note: *Million tonnes of oil equivalent. **Kilograms of oil equivalent. One tonne of standard coal equivalent (SCE), which is the unit China uses for domestic statistical reporting, is equal to about 0.7 tonnes of standard oil equivalent or 4.79 barrels of oil. The per capita energy consumption is calculated using the population data from the World Bank's WDI database.

Source: BP Statistical Review (2019), "Primary Energy: Consumption by Fuel"; World Bank, WDI, March 2020 update.

per capita, which was one-third of the US level, about half of the Russian Federation, slightly less than about two-thirds of Germany, 71 per cent of the EU level and 81 per cent of the UK level.

China's energy efficiency is simply dismal. It is by a wide margin the world's most energy intensive economy, although efficiency is superior to in the past (Rock & Toman 2015). In 2018, China burned 303 kg of oil equivalent for every $1,000 of GDP (constant 2010 US$) produced, which was 2.5 times more than the United States, 3.5 times more than the EU and 4.1 times more than Japan. This, still, is a big advance on energy efficiency four decades ago when China consumed 1,224 kg of oil equivalent for every $1,000 of GDP compared with the US level of 273 kg. By 1990, this was more than halved and in 2018 was just one-quarter of the 1980 level (calculated from BP 2019; WDI GDP at constant 2010 US$).

The evolution of energy use over the past four decades is not simply about scale but also changing composition. China's energy consumption has increased from 628 million tonnes standard coal equivalent (SCE) in 1978 to 4,655 million tonnes SCE in 2018, which came from both domestic and imported sources. Figure 6.3 shows energy consumption from domestic production (above the horizontal axis) and from net imports (below the axis) from 1990. The sum of the stacked columns in absolute terms (total distance) is the consumption of domestic produced and imported energy. Coal's dominance is starkly evident, despite its recent decline in the energy mix. Domestic production of coal peaked in 2013 at 2,705 million tonnes SCE, declined to 2016, before turning upwards again, although it remains below the 2013 peak.

The downward shift in domestic produced fossil-fuel energy from 2013 was offset by the rise in coal imports to 2016 and the rise in imports of coal, oil and natural gas.[4] Oil imports have doubled over the past decade and natural gas imports have increased 48 times, with sea-borne supplies from Australia and Indonesia and pipeline deliveries from Myanmar, Central Asia and Russia. China and Japan are the world's largest importers of liquified natural gas, accounting for 17 per cent and 26 per cent respectively of global imports (BP 2019). Rapid growth in renewable sources is

Figure 6.3 Composition of energy consumption, domestic and imported sources, 1990–2018

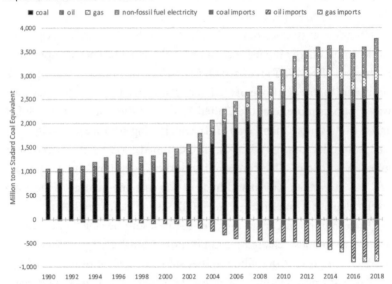

Note: Imports are calculated as the difference between domestic energy production and domestic energy consumption for each broad fuel type. The negative values are net imports.

Source: CSY (2019: tables 9.1 and 9.2).

Table 6.5 Electricity output by fuel source, 1990–2018 (thousand GWh)

	1990	2000	2010	2018
Total Generation	621.2	1,355.6	4,207.2	7,166.1
Hydropower	126.7	222.4	722.2	1,231.8
Thermal Power	494.5	1,114.2	3,331.9	5,096.3
Nuclear Power		16.7	73.9	294.4
Wind Power			44.6	366.0

Source: CSY (2020: table 9.6).

reflected in the data for primary electricity generation, power from non-fossil-fuel sources such as hydropower, wind and solar. It has doubled since 2010 and accounts for about 18 per cent of domestic produced energy.

Electricity generation is still dominated by coal, shown in Table 6.5 as thermal (includes a small amount of gas generation), but the growth in renewable sources is faster than the increase in total generation. Thermal generated electricity has declined 11 percentage points since 2000, from 82.2 per cent to 71.1 per cent. Total renewables – hydropower and wind reported here – have increased from 16.4 per cent to 22.3 per cent between 2000 and 2018. China accounts for 29 per cent of the world's hydroelectricity capacity (BP 2019). Output from wind is up seven times since 2010 and accounts for 5.1 per cent of generation; there was no reported installed capacity even as late as 2005 (CSY 2020: table 9.6). China has the world's largest installed capacity of renewables accounting for 25.6 per cent, ahead of the US 18.5 per cent, Germany 8.4 per cent, India 4.9 per cent and Japan 4.5 per cent (BP 2019). The country is also the largest producer of wind turbines. In 2015, Goldwind, which is owned by the Xinjiang government and uses German technology, surpassed Denmark's Vesta to become the world's leading supplier of wind turbines (Jiang 2017).

Pollution levels by the 2000s began to prompt change in energy and environmental policies. In the later-2000s the government introduced policies to curb pollution and reduce energy use, which recognized a "new normal" (*xin changtai*) of lower economic growth would require radical economic readjustment. Premier Wen Jiabao declared China was "unstable, unbalanced, uncoordinated and unsustainable" (cited in Shambaugh 2016: 1). Progress has occurred on the environment – the State Environment Agency was promoted to ministerial level and given more teeth – but the GFC 2008–9 and the ensuing stimulus has muted the shift to a lower energy-intensive economy. China's environmental wake-up call was the "airpocolypse" in the winters of 2012–13 and 2013–14 when many cities were smothered in asphyxiating smog. In mid-January 2013, the PM2.5 air pollution index for particulates of 2.5 microns in diameter in Beijing passed 900 and approached 1,000 microgram per cubic metre, or nearly

40 times the WHO interim target-2 for PM2.5 (Ma 2017: 1). This endangered the health of more than 600 million people across East China. Since then, the air of many cities has become visibly cleaner, although China is on average far from meeting the WHO interim target-2. There are still horrid days, and especially so in northern China during the winters.

Press reporting, social media posts and even citizens' protests about the environment are widespread. Numerous studies have estimated the economic and health costs of pollution in China. Below is a short list of selected studies that have estimated economic and health costs of pollution in China (Ma 2017: 4–6; Khan & Zheng 2016: 27; Naughton 2018: 560):

- For every 10 micrograms increase in PM2.5 level the mortality rate for cardiovascular diseases rises 0.53 per cent and that for respiratory diseases 1.42 per cent.
- In 2010, PM2.5 pollution in Beijing, Shanghai, Guangzhou and Xian resulted in 7,777 premature deaths and economic losses of ¥6.2 billion ($1 billion).
- A 2007 World Bank study estimated that in 2003 air pollution cost China ¥520 billion or 3.8 per cent of GDP and water pollution another 2 per cent of GDP.
- Based on a study of economic losses from air pollution in 2010 in East Asia, the cost to China was about ¥700 billion.
- A 2013 study estimated the 500 million people living north of the Huai River, who receive winter-time heating distributed from municipal-run coal-fired boilers, had a combined loss of 2.5 billion years of life expectancy (about five years per person).
- An OECD study estimated the loss to GDP in 2014 was a whopping $1.4 trillion from health costs alone in addition to the efficiency losses.
- A 2016 World Bank study estimated air pollution in China caused 1.6 million premature deaths, equal to one third of world premature deaths due to air pollution.

Although the estimates vary depending on the methods used, there is little doubt the human and economic cost of pollution from China's rapid economic growth is staggering. Shifting to a less energy-intensive structure of production is necessary. It is not just about the energy used per unit output, but also about the total of the average per capita output of carbon emissions in a country of China's size and the increasing standard of living. This is a challenge for China and also for the world confronted with the accumulated impact of fossil fuel use from industrialization over the past three centuries.

What is to be done? Ma (2017) argues that most approaches to reduce GHG emissions have focused on "end-of-the-pipe" actions, but these at best are unlikely to realize even half of Beijing's reduction targets. There needs to be more comprehensive efforts to address the deep-seated economic structural factors, such as the dependence on heavy industry, the low share of clean energy in total energy use and the over reliance on road transport.

Despite the rapid growth in China's economy since 2000 and change in the mix of products produced and exported, such as high-tech manufactured exports, the structure of energy use has barely changed, regardless of the government's often repeated desire to lower energy intensity. Industry dominates energy consumption, as shown in Table 6.6, and heavy industry in particular. Secondary industry accounts for two-thirds of all energy consumed. The most energy-intensive subsectors have increased their share of total energy consumption between 1999 and 2018, including the chemical industry and the smelting and processing of ferrous and non-ferrous metals. Manufacturing industry's share of total energy consumption was almost unchanged, yet its contribution to GDP and employment has fallen in recent years. Compared with other countries, the reported end-consumption for transportation and households is unusually low, only 9.2 per cent and 12.8 per cent respectively in 2018.

Transportation consumes about 25 per cent of energy used globally and contributes 20–25 per cent of GHG, although in China the contribution of transportation to pollution appears to be lower, which according

Table 6.6 Energy consumption by sectors, 1999 and 2018

Sectors and selected subsectors	1999		2018	
	Million tonnes*	%share	Million tonnes	%share
Total Consumption	1,301	100.0	4,719	100.0
A. Primary Industry	58	4.5	88	1.9
B. Secondary Industry **	908	69.8	3,112	65.9
1. Mining and Quarrying		7.1		4.0
2. Manufacturing	707	54.4	2,586	54.8
Processing Petroleum, Coke, Nuclear Fuel		5.4		6.1
Chemical Materials and Chemical Products		9.9		10.9
Non-metallic Mineral Products		8.4		6.9
Smelting and Pressing Ferrous Metals		13.0		13.2
Smelting and Pressing Non-ferrous Metals		2.7		5.2
3. Electricity, Gas, Water and Heating	108	8.3	336	7.1
C. Construction	14	1.1	87	1.8
D. Transport, Storage and Post	92	7.1	436	9.2
E. Wholesale, Retail, Hotel and Restaurants	28	2.2	130	2.8
F. Others	55	4.2	263	5.6
G. Residential Consumption	146	11.2	604	12.8

Note: *SCE = standard coal equivalent. **Within the three broad industry classes under Secondary Industry, only selected high energy-intensive subsectors are listed to show their share of total energy consumption.

Sources: CSY (2020: table 9.9; 2001: table 7.9).

to Ma (2017) is due to data availability. Changes in passenger and freight traffic and volume over the past four decades has large implications for energy consumption. The big story is the relative decline in passengers and freight carried by rail for most of the past four decades and the increase in road transportation, and in recent years the shift to private transport. Passenger numbers on public transport increased from 2.5 billion in 1978 to 38.0 billion in 2012 but had about halved to 17.9 billion by 2018 as travellers abandoned highway buses for high-speed rail or private cars (CSY 2019: table 16.6).

From the start of the reform period, the share of passengers carried on railways declined startlingly, as shown in Figure 6.4 left panel, from 32.1 per cent in 1978 to reach an all-time low of 5 per cent in 2012 before a rapid upturn to 18.8 per cent by in 2018. Highways in 1978 already accounted for more than half of all passenger traffic and rapidly increased to peak at 93 per cent for the years 2008–12 before declining to 76.2 per cent by 2018. Waterways carriage of passengers rapidly dwindled after 1978. Air travel share rose from 0.1 per cent to 3.4 per cent of all passengers, or about 612 million. Since the late 1990s there has been a boom in airport construction to cater for the emerging Chinese middle-class travellers as well as the growth of the economy.

Passenger volume (passenger-km) data shows the growth in transport traffic in terms of not only the number of passengers but also how far they travelled. Increased volume has come with a marked shift in the modal share since the late 2000s. Railway passenger volume increased 10 percentage points to 41 per cent between 2012 and 2018, air passenger volume more than doubled to 31 per cent and highway passenger volume halved to 27 per cent (Figure 6.4 right panel). This is a fantastic story about long-distance travellers' embrace of high-speed rail as new routes have been added (Table 6.3). But it is also a story about the Chinese embrace of the private automobile. The net effect of these changes on GHG emissions is unknown. While more people use rail for long trips, we do not have data for trips and distances in private vehicles. The horrendous highway congestion of any holiday period suggests the Chinese have got off buses

Figure 6.4 Change in the composition of passenger and freight by mode, 1978–2018

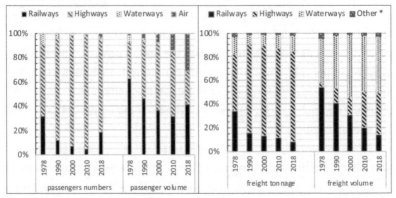

Notes: Passenger volume is in billion passenger-km and freight volume is billion tonne-km. Other joins air freight and pipelines, with the latter accounting for most of freight.

Source: CSY (2019: tables 16.6–16.9).

and into private cars, at least for shorter trips and family outings. There would appear still room for more high-speed rail. Despite their high cost, high-speed rail is a viable alternative to air travel for distances less than a 1,000 km and far preferable to highway buses.

A similar transformation has occurred in freight tonnage and volume (tonne-km). Gross freight tonnage has increased many folds with the growth of the economy since 1978 for all transport modes, and totalled 51.53 billion tonnes in 2018 (CSY 2019: table 16.8). Road transport has accounted for three-quarters of freight tonnage moved in China since 1990 and overshadows all other modes, as shown in Figure 6.5 right panel, while rail has shrunk from about one-third to just 7.8 per cent. Freight volume (tonne-km) shows that rail's share, which was 54 per cent in 1978 was overtaken in the 2000s by highway freight movement, a modal shift brought about by the rapid increase in high-quality inter-city highways discussed above. Internal waterways appear to have regained share of long-distance freight in recent years. But if reduced emission targets are to be met China will need to find a cleaner alternative to diesel hauled trucks and ways to curtail increased carbon emissions as living standards continue to rise.

China has higher emissions intensity – the ratio of per capita emissions to per capita income – than that of any highly industrialized high-income country. China emitted 0.9 tonnes of carbon for every $1,000 of per capita GDP (2005 PPP$), according to Stanton (2011: 120), compared with the US's 0.6 tonnes, and 0.3 tonnes for Japan, Germany and Singapore. The global median was 0.3 tonnes. PPP-adjusted GDP per capita explains about two-thirds of international variations in carbon emission intensity. As economies grow richer so do the total emissions, irrespective of efficiency gains.

All high-income countries have relatively high energy use and thus carbon emissions, and efficiency gains and emission reduction targets over the past four decades have done little to bring these down. There is no evidence from today's high-income countries to suggest that a country can become rich and yet have low emissions. Since 1980, the United States has edged down from about 7.8 tonnes of oil equivalent per capita to 7 tonnes, although it peaked at 8 tonnes around 2000, while the EU and Japan have hovered within the 3–4 tonnes range. Meanwhile, China's per capita use rose slowly from 0.4 tonnes in 1980 to 0.8 tonnes in 2000 and has since nearly tripled to 2.3 tonnes (BP 2019; Table 6.4). The conundrum is that countries with higher emissions per capita also have higher living standards, not only in terms of personal consumption (or PPP-adjusted GDP) but also in life expectancy, literacy and health. High-income countries with the lowest emission levels have a high proportion of renewable energy in use and very low if any use of coal. This conclusion has far reaching implications for economic development: low emissions are associated with low incomes and the cost of reducing emissions for developing countries will be high. For middle-income economies such as China, "these costs could be devastating to the maintenance of current standards of living and could even cause a reversal in the level of development" (Stanton 2011: 118).

Such a scenario is politically unpalatable for Xi Jinping and CPC leaders. Avoiding that scenario drives China's search for innovative solutions, including big investment in R&D, the support for new energy vehicles, green technologies and low carbon cities, and a focus on an across-the-board raising of productivity to enable continued economic growth and increased living standards. Is such a sustainable future achievable? What might be the obstacles in China's pathway?

INNOVATION AND GROWTH

Innovation is "pivotal" to China's future economic growth and central to the dream of Xi Jinping to make China a rich powerful country by 2049, the centenary of the founding of the PRC (Xi 2014: 131). China needs to become a clever country. Or to be more precise, a global innovator. No longer content with being the world's second-largest economy and leading exporter of manufactured goods, China wants to be an international leader in the new and emerging technologies that mark out an advanced economy from an also-ran middle-income economy. It is a shift from "Made in China" to "Invented in China", which has profound implications for almost everything from how China approaches the support of R&D, promotion of industrial and S&T policies, and scientific collaboration, through to China's role in the international trading system, the setting of product and process standards, and the institutions of global governance.

Of course, China is clever in many ways. No country or people have an exclusive gift of cleverness. Ingenuity is found around the world. But marshalling it for economic, scientific and technological advancement is one of the biggest challenges for the modern nation state (Taylor 2016), especially one such as China that aims to catch up with the frontier advance economies of the world. The focus in this section is on the challenges confronting China in developing its innovative capacity to grow the economy and sustain rising living standards, and thereby achieve the 2049 dream of wealth and power. Demographic and political constraints are likely to thwart realization of the dream vision. China is at a fork in its development. One path leads towards innovative economic growth and

higher living standards. The other to stagnation and lower living standards. And in between, a number of middle pathways, something akin to
the muddling through as China did in the 1980s, but unlike in the past
such pathways are ill-equipped to deliver the future that China's leaders
have mapped out. Politics, not economics, is in my view central to which
path will be taken.

The constraints on future economic growth have been laid out in the
previous chapters. The first is demographic. In Chapter 3 we saw that the
workforce peaked around 2010 and is now shrinking, the population is
rapidly ageing and the dependency ratio (the supported population as a
share of those who work) is rising; during the 2020s, China's population
will peak and thereafter shrink. China banked its demographic dividend
early: the fertility level reached a far lower level at a much lower relative
per capita GDP than any of the East Asian "miracle economies" of the
second half of the twentieth century (see Figure 3.7).

Not in modern times have economies such as China and others faced
the dilemma of how to grow with a declining workforce in a society of
older and increasingly even fewer people. Growth accounting makes this
stark. Economic growth (Y) is a product of capital (K), labour (L), land
or natural resource (N) inputs, which in resource-poor East Asia usually
comes from imports, and a residual factor (A), known as total factor productivity (TFP), a catch-all residual that captures the effects of technology,
institutions, culture, social organization and other factors that influence
economic growth.[5] In this framework, growth comes primarily from an
increase in capital stock and the labour force plus TFP, which translates
into better technology to allow capital and labour to be used with more
effect and greater efficiency. Institutions, state policies and societal organizations that raise productivity are therefore the vital factors influencing
growth rates.

What does this growth framework mean for China? Future economic
growth in the face of a shrinking workforce and ageing population will
depend on raising productivity (TFP). We cannot assume capital stock
(K) will be positively augmented because the state sector is inefficient

if not destructive in its use of capital, and the likelihood of reforms succeeding slim (Chapter 4). Natural resources (N) are in net terms limited,
with a high level of dependence on imports for energy, food and raw
materials. And the population (L) is going backwards. In this scenario,
sustaining future growth in China therefore entails raising the output of
the shrinking workforce. Fewer workers must produce more with greater
efficiency. To do so, they need to become more innovative to increase total
productivity.

This leads to the second constraint: China is farther behind the frontier economies and potentially more exposed to becoming locked into the
so-called middle-income trap than many imagine. Whether the trap is
real or not, the concept captures the dilemma of middle-income economies like China that have escaped poverty but have not become rich. They
are caught in the middle. Lesser developed countries can out-compete
them in world markets because their wage-skill combination is cheaper
and richer countries at the production frontier can out-compete them on
novel-product innovations, quality and productivity.

Fear of the middle-income trap was particularly motivating of Chinese
leadership thinking around the time of the publication of a joint World
Bank and China's National Development Research Centre study of the
middle-income trap (World Bank 2013). Figures 3.3 to 3.5 show clearly
how far China has to go to catch up with the advanced economies of the
world. By 2015, the per capita GDP (PPP 2011 dollars) of China was about
23 per cent of the United States. Were China to sustain recent reported
rates of growth, and assuming a real growth rate of 2 per cent a year in the
United States, China will be about 45 per cent of the US level by 2030, 57
per cent in 2040 and attain the per capita income of the EU by 2046. Such
a growth scenario in 2020 looked highly optimistic because of the "trade
war" with the United States and the impact of the coronavirus, which had
shrunk the world economy and disrupted global supply chains to China's
disadvantage. Although China's economy came out of 2020 healthier than
any other major economy, economic growth rates look likely to trend far
below recent levels by the mid-2020s (IMF 2020; World Bank 2021).

Escaping the middle-income trap to catch up and even overtake the advanced economies is no simple task. China has used policies, incentives and investment in "national champion" state firms and poured money into S&T and R&D programmes (Applebaum *et al.* 2018). We will look at these efforts below, but no amount of money in the short term will make up for a huge L-related constraint on China raising its productivity. The average level of schooling of the workforce is well behind that of the advanced economies, which is the third constraint. Overall, the education level reported in the 2010 census of 8.8 years of schooling is roughly equivalent to Japan and Europe in 1960 (see Table 5.4). The 2015 intra-censual estimates show that only 15 per cent of the Chinese population has attained a tertiary qualification and another 18 per cent had completed to year 12 of high school (Naughton 2018: 225). In other words, about 67 per cent of the population were high school dropouts. Massive investment in education since 2000 is delivering impressive results, with nearly half of 16–24-year olds having completed high school or post-secondary education (Figure 5.4), but the quality is uneven and in poor provinces and especially their rural areas the level of education attainment remains poor on average.

These data on education underscore the challenge facing China to raise the productivity of its workforce. In fact, once we take into account the quality of education, the challenge is even greater. China is nevertheless investing heavily in initiatives to foster innovation and creativity; in industries that create and use more knowledge-intensive outputs; and in retraining workers from industry to services, although much of recent growth in services employment is low skill (for example, delivery services). When thinking through innovation processes, we can envisage three pathways: top-down government directed; bottom-up firm or individual directed; and horizontal networks and exchange within and across borders (Shambaugh 2016: 47). China has a lot of the first: it is the dominant mode of the party-state in directing S&T and industrial policy; a little of the second and lot less of the third than it needs.

Top-down is the preferred state option. There is a long history of picking winners in China. Gross investment on R&D in China is over 2 per cent of GDP, greater than the EU and second only to the United States. It has risen steadily from a low of 0.5 per cent of GDP in the mid-1990s. China also has a huge army of R&D people in state-run agencies, institutes and universities and the number of patents is soaring. Domestic patent applications between 2000 and 2018 increased 25-fold from 170,682 to 4.3 million (CSY 2019: table 20.17). Many applications, however, were for low-quality utility patents rather than invention patents, which accounted for 48 per cent and 36 per cent respectively of applications (the remainder were design patents). Chinese applications for international patents in the US, Japan and elsewhere numbered 176,340 or just 4.1 per cent of domestic patents (CSY 2019: table 20.19). However, the Chinese rate of international patenting has increased rapidly during the 2010s. Between 2010 and 2017, the quality-adjusted rate of international patenting increased from about 4.4 per cent of US international patents to 7.1 per cent, overtaking France and just shy of the UK (Jiang *et al.* 2019). Patent applications are also driven a lot by government incentives that reward registration without regard for quality, and many of those granted soon lapse. And importantly, R&D spending and patent applications are inputs to innovation when what matters for productivity is raising output per unit of input. This is a big topic and space does not allow more exploration (see Appelbaum *et al.* 2018).

Bottom-up is more of a challenge. Most Chinese firms rely on imported core technologies. That has been recently underscored by the US action against leading technology companies, Huawei and ZTE, which restricted their access to technologies and even components made using US-designed software. Although China became the leading exporter of manufactured high-tech products in the early 2000s, the value added is typically between 15 and 25 per cent, while for Apple products, China added only 1.8–2.5 per cent for the original Apple iPhone and 3.4 per cent or less for the iPad (Taylor 2016: 57; Applebaum *et al.* 2018: 86). China ran a trade deficit in intellectual property (licenses, fees and so on) that was estimated around $10 billion in 2009 (Applebaum *et al.* 2018: 87). A recent study shows that when the value of trade in intangibles such as licence fees are joined with the trade in tangible goods, the US trade deficit with China for 2016 was halved (Fu & Ghauri 2020). These data underscore China's role as an assembler of high-tech products, which took off when leading contract manufacturers shifted their production to China in 2002 after its admission to the WTO. As shown in Figure 6.5, China overtook the United States in 2005 and by 2012 its high-tech exports exceeded those of the United States, Germany, Japan, Taiwan, Korea and Singapore combined. These were designed elsewhere, the components were mostly imported and "the spillover into indigenous technological capabilities were modest" (Naughton 2018: 377). China is still not a major producer of IP.

Figure 6.5 China becomes global leader of hi-tech exports in the mid-2000s

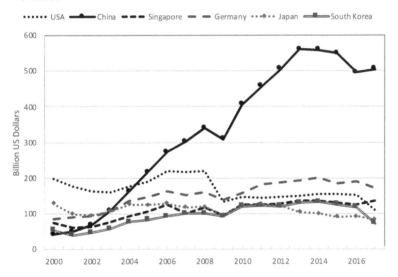

Note: Errors in the WDI data for Singapore and the US for 2004–06 were corrected using the CEIC and Indexmundi databases, although all three supposedly rely on the same original sources.

Sources: World Bank, WDI database, 2019 June update; CEIC database (https://www.ceicdata.com/en/singapore/technology/sg-hightechnology-exports); Indexmundi (https://www.indexmundi.com/facts/singapore/indicator/TX.VAL.TECH.CD).

Chinese firms have successfully translated foreign-invented technologies into products, produced and delivered at lower manufacturing cost than anywhere else in the world. This was the way Huawei grew, making second-best knockoffs of Cisco routers (switches), which power the Internet. But it subsequently developed its own routers, smart phones and notebook computers that are world-class. Often the core chips in these devices are still foreign and that clouds its future as the United States imposes controls on selling high-technology components and software to China. For the most part the products that Chinese firms produced whatever their world standing are not local innovations. The high-speed rail is an excellent example. Over time, however, China has indigenized imported technologies and that is innovation of a sort. China is a minor player relative to the world's leading innovation nations, and its innovations are "typified by short-term, low-risk improvements to production or distribution processes, or incremental improvements to foreign products" (Taylor 2016: 57).

These examples beg the question of what is innovation? China has been successful in making incremental improvements, in developing sophisticated manufacturing and in absorbing advance management know-how to give its industry world-class competencies. That is a major reason, among others such as transport logistics, that has made China the country of choice for outsourcing final assembly. These innovations, however, are not novel-product innovations, which is the common yardstick for measuring innovative capacity. Still, as Breznitz and Murphree (2011) argue, these sorts of second-order innovations have been hugely important in allowing China to run faster and faster, to keep up with the frontier economies even if not overtaking them. In time novel-product innovations will come they argue and for the China's party-state to overly focus on these types of innovations could risk China's future growth.

As for the third pathway for innovations, the horizontal networks that facilitate collaboration, there are two challenges. The first is the degree of openness permitted in China that will allow for information flow and scientific and technical collaboration, and the second is the geopolitical perception of China as a strategic cooperation partner in S&T. The nationalist impulse to indigenize innovation and to control information flows along with the party-state's pervasive inclination to secrecy risks frustrating initiatives for cooperation. This is not new. The control on FDI in the automobile industry, which was designed to force foreign car makers to transfer technology and build an indigenous China car, completely failed, unlike in industries with few controls where innovation has taken place (Brandt & Thun 2016). But the extent to which China seeks supremacy in technological know-how since the mid-2010s is a completely different order. For Xi Jinping, capturing technology is a geopolitical powerplay at the heart of his vision to make China wealthy and powerful (Xi 2014: 135–6).

From the late 1970s to the 2000s there was a shift from mission-push technological autarky of the planned economy, which often had a defence orientation, to an openness in technological development that favoured civilian use and developing a broader technical base. Until the early 2000s there were considerable technology flows. This was often facilitated through foreign investment as well as scientific and technical collaboration. Of course, MNEs were often worried about the weak intellectual property rights such that they transferred their second-best technologies, to the chagrin of their China partners and the party-state. The renewed nationalist impulse to capture benefits to the exclusion of others in a race to technological supremacy in some sectors is increasingly making the exchanges one-sided, with an international consensus that China takes more than it shares in innovation. Another worrying dimension for Western scientific and industrial collaborators is the "military-civil fusion" (*junmin ronghe*) and the explicit dual-use of new technologies in China's planning.

A cursory glance at Xi Jinping's statements makes this drive for world mastery of technology obvious. In a speech to the Chinese Academy of Sciences in 2014 (Xi 2014: 131–42), he said the realization of the China Dream required the implementation of an "innovation-driven strategy" in which "scientific and technological innovation is pivotal to improving social productivity and the comprehensive national strength, so it must be put in a core position in our overall national development" (*ibid.* 131). Global advancement in knowledge had intensified competition and "makes innovative strategic competition more important in the competition for comprehensive national strength" (*ibid.* 132). China had made big advances over the past three decades, he said, and in some fields, it is no longer a follower but had become a "forerunner" or "parallel runner" (*ibid.* 134). Still, China's innovation foundation was "not solid" and it was overly dependent on others for core technologies: "Only by holding key technologies in our own hands can we really take the initiative in competition and development, and ensure our economic security, national security and security in other areas" (*ibid.* 135). And strengthening indigenous innovation capabilities is not just about competing or national strength, but about China having the global standing in emerging industries not only to play in the playground of frontier economies, but also "so that we can make rules for new games" and no longer play according to the rules set by others (*ibid.* 135–6).

Voice was first given to this line of thinking in a major shift in China's techno-industrial strategy that occurred from 2006 with new policies marking greater government intervention to target specific industries (Naughton 2018: 379–83). These stressed creating independent technological capabilities in China. The first was the 2006 Medium-Long Range Plan for Science and Technology (MLP) which identified 16 megaprojects. It was envisaged that spillover effects from these would diffuse through the economy. The next was the Strategic Emerging Industries (2010) policies, which were partly in response to the GFC and partly to move ahead MLP projects. Comprising 20 projects – some linked to the MLP – the programme was an explicit industrial policy with market instruments to induce business to invest and government funding to seed initiatives. Seven industries were flagged: energy conservation, next generation information technology, biotechnology, precision machinery, new energy (wind, solar), new materials and new energy vehicles.

The third set of policies was the "Made in China 2025" (MIC) and

"Internet Plus" rolled out in 2015, which put into policy Xi's vision for technology supremacy. The MIC policies aim to ensure China remains a leading manufacturing nation despite its disadvantages in land, labour and environmental costs. It is envisaged as a three-stage process: by 2025, China will join the ranks of manufacturing powers, with established MNEs with international competitiveness in the global value chains; by 2035, it will attain "the middle level of the world's manufacturing powers"; and by 2049, it will be at "forefront of the world's manufacturing powers" and possess "a world-leading technology system and industrial system" (State Council 2015). The nationalist thrust was naked in not just an emphasis on "indigenous innovation" (*zhizhu chuangxin*), but also aggressive policies to buy overseas firms and technologies. The plan aspired to move whole supply chains for selected high-tech goods into China. The growing international awareness of this aggressive policy produced a backlash and motivated President Donald Trump's "trade war". His trade war with China was not about trade but actually technology. According to Naughton (2018: 383), "Promotion of high-technology industry is arguably the central economic development policy of the Chinese government today". The MIC unifies the various threads of not only contemporary economic policy, but also strategic positioning globally, as was clear in Xi's 2014 speech above.

Techno-industrial policies such as MIC, support for developing "high level talents" in S&T and investment in R&D has advanced China's capabilities in sciences and engineering. The ambition involves not just invention and patents but also setting global standards for new products. China looks set to succeed in creating new global technical standards for many products. It is a leader in 5G mobile technologies based on total patents obtained by firms such as Huawei and ZTE, and in ultra-high-voltage long-distance electricity transmission. Its firms outproduce the world in electrical vehicles as well as steel, concrete, computers, and many other products. Some products are leading edge, but many are "good enough" cheaper substitutes for those from leading Western brands. Adaptation and improvement of advanced technologies invented elsewhere has driven past growth and delivered impressive benefits for China, such as the high-speed rail network, which it now seeks to export. China could well continue to grow doing more of the same. Not that such is good enough for the economic nationalists in Beijing. They want China to catch up and become an advanced economy. This drive for global leadership powerfully motivates the industry policies and the S&T policies. But this policy planning focuses on institutional change within S&T and manufacturing, and rarely if ever explicitly acknowledges another constraint: the politics of innovation: who makes decisions, who benefits and who loses.

In fact, the political aspect of innovation and technological catch-up is largely missed in the academic literature (Taylor 2016). Analyses of China's future widely agree innovation is imperative, but the wider interconnections between S&T, economics and politics is lacking. Sociologists, political scientists and others who study S&T and R&D focus on policies and enabling institutions. They look at the inputs to innovation and less at the outputs. Another group, mostly economists, focus on performance and productivity. They look to the outputs and give too little weight to how potential gains are shaped by policies and institutions. Neither group pays sufficient attention to the politics of who wins or loses from a particular technological choice or path. For this reason, I put politics at the centre of a model to understand how the above identified constraints on the potential for innovation and future economic growth come together.

Any model of the constraints on innovation in contemporary China must be able to account for the past failure as well as account for recent successes. Long-run historical, institutional and cultural factors are at play in shaping economic development in China. A model that can only explain the phenomenal transformation in recent decades but not the past failures must be lacking in one or more components and will as a consequence be blind-sided when it seeks to account for plausible pathways for future change. The model needs to take account of demographic, economic, political and technological factors. I propose a simple parsimonious model that has three spheres of interest or locus of activity, each interdependent. The ultimate operative factor which will influence these spheres will be the political institutions and coalition of elite interest groups who govern the sharing of the benefits from economic development. Figure 6.6 shows the basic relationships.

Figure 6.6 Model of China's innovation dilemma

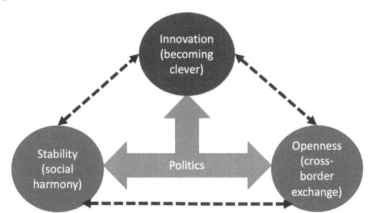

Note: A similar analytic framework but without the integrating dimension of political action was presented by Simon (2018).

The three spheres are linked in a triangular relationship: innovation (becoming clever), openness (international exchange) and social stability (growth with order). Each interacts with the other. Politics is at the centre of the triangle of spheres because it determines which sphere or element is ascendant. The evolution of each sphere is a product of the political institutions that set the rules governing them. As North (1990) noted, elite politics will shape economic structures and opportunities. Political institutions and their agents define what is permissible in a general way and the actions of agents what is permissible in a specific area of interest. Other societal actors must submit to the authority of the political elites or exit the nation-state domain. This is the choice put before the Chinese private sector in September 2020 when the CPC issued instructions to improve party control over the private sector and entrepreneurs and help them pursue "the goal and mission to realize the great rejuvenation of the Chinese nation" (CPC General Office, 15 September 2020). Acting contrarily will not be good for business.

Historically, the politics of innovation was starkly clear in comparing the experience of Europe and China between the sixteenth and nineteenth centuries. Europe was politically highly fragmented, whereas China was a unified empire (excluding the disorder of the Ming–Qing transition). Intellectuals, scientists and clerics who incurred the displeasure of rulers in one state in Europe could move to another (Mokyr 2017). Many European rulers and elites competed with one another to become the patrons of artists, musicians and scientists. Hosting these men of letters (and most were men) brought prestige to the court as well as discomfort at times. In China, the state likewise supported scholarship and inquiry. But with a difference. There was no escape to another realm for the dissident or contrarian voice except into exile or seclusion or execution. In the eighteenth century, the Qing control was tantamount to an inquisition of scholarly views contrarian to the accepted neo-Confucian interpretations and beliefs (Wu 2012; Xue & Koyama 2018). Elsewhere I have argued that this stymied the potential for innovation at the time that may have been a significant contributor to the Great Divergence, the rise of Europe and the decline of China and the rest of the world. Garnaut (2017) argues the practice of elite politics of imperial China is rooted in the behaviour and ideological outlook of the CPC and party-state, which explains the increasing ruthlessness of the suppression of dissent within the party or wider Chinese society under Xi Jinping.

The three spheres are a shorthand for complex economic, institutional and social processes. Before exploring these in more detail and their interactions, what does each sphere entail?

- Innovation: the processes of becoming clever, which encompasses invention, new ways of thinking and new ways of doing. It is about translating scientific knowledge into "useful knowledge", turning propositional knowledge (theory) into

240

technological knowledge (application), to use Mokyr's descriptors (Mokyr 2002, 2017).

- Openness: the processes of engaging in international exchange of ideas and people, and allowing the movement of capital, people, resources and technologies across political borders without distorting limits.
- Social stability: the processes that support the absence of political and social strife, peacefulness if you prefer, which in contemporary China is presented as growth with order, or in party-state speak, a stable and harmonious society.

Each sphere will vary in their importance in explaining the constraints on innovation depending on the perspective of the observer. A set of spheres joined in an equilateral triangle immediately allows us to conceive of them rotating, none having priority over the other. Once we begin to rotate the spheres, to move each sequentially to the apex of the triangle, which prioritizes one sphere over the others in our mental geography, we begin to realize that different questions arise. Not just different questions, but different societal and political actors will be favoured.

Innovation at the apex is in an abstract sense the focus of Xi Jinping in his drive to make China wealthy and strong, but not so in a practical political sense. When innovation is at the apex we ask: how is China to become a clever country, an ingenious country, one that will produce novel technologies of the future? What is needed to sustain economic growth that is innovative, pushing forward the frontier of productivity and raising incomes? These are questions central to China's future economic development. But they are also apolitical and technical questions. And they fail to recognize the boundaries imposed on the possible by political institutions and their actors. Politics is ignored.

Next, rotate the triangle to bring openness to the fore. Cross-border exchange of people, capital and technology has been a huge part of China's success story over the past four decades. That is recognized if sometimes not clearly by the party-state elite. Without engagement with economists from the West and Eastern Europe in the 1980s, Chinese reformers would not have resolved how to adapt market economics to grow the economy in a way that preserved the power for the communist party (Gewirtz 2017). The cross border flows have allowed incremental innovations and absorption of managerial know-how, among other transfers, that has enabled China to run faster and faster (Breznitz & Murphree 2011). This perspective, however, is associated with outsiders. Openness is what multinational enterprises, Western governments and international bodies want from China. It presumed – and for many implied – that China will change to a Western likeness. Open science is championed: neutral exchange, which subordinates the national interest and dismisses the indigenous. Nationalism is rejected. This view is ultimately politically naïve.

Scientific knowledge and technologies are challenging for authoritarian leaders, whether secular or religious. Rubin (2017) showed this in his study of the Ottoman ban on printing in Arabic. Printing would make more accessible the Koran unmediated by trained religious teachers, which threatened their interpretation and devalued their mastering of Koranic laws. These same teachers provided the ideological legitimacy of the Ottoman emperor, his state and clientele elite supporters, so he bowed to the imam's fear and blocked the presses rolling in Arabic for three centuries. In contradistinction, printing had spurred diffusion of literacy in Europe and helped the spread of Luther's ideas and the Reformation, changing the religious, political and economic landscape of Europe (Johnson & Koyama 2019).

Now rotate the triangle to put stability at the apex. This is ultimately what the party-state wants and believes it needs in order to survive. Since 1989 social stability has been the litmus test of policy for the party. The focus here shifts to regime survival and its legitimacy, which ultimately trump all else for Xi and the party. It has been central to Xi's thinking about governance and the future of China. Early in his tenure as party general secretary, Xi Jinping told the Politburo in December 2012: "Stability is a prerequisite for reform and development … Only with social stability can reform and development have a solid foundation" (Xi 2014: 68).

Time and again this theme appears in his speeches, to justify controls over the internet, to deepen the training of local party secretaries, to improve supervision of the financial system and to strengthen the party within the private sector (Xi 2014: 84; 2017: 160; *Financial Times* 2020s, 2021d).

The focus on stability, however, sits uneasily in tension with Xi's promotion of the internationalization of China's economy, science and technology. Innovation based on openness puts at risk the survival of the autocrat and the elite coalition whose co-option is secured through a privileged share of the economic cake (the inner party elite and those in state organization bound to them through patronage networks). Openness increases unpredictability for the party, allows in ideas, people and ways of thinking that may question the underpinning values that inform the legitimacy of the ruling elite and their political regime. Openness is ultimately hostile to authoritarianism and to the survival of the autocrat and the coalition of vested interests.

Anxiety about openness is not new in China. We saw in Chapter 2 that the *ti-yong* debate focused on how to preserve Qing China in the nineteenth century through limited adoption of Western technologies. Similarly, Deng Xiaoping argued in the early 1980s socialist China could borrow from the West selectively without letting in their social (and political) evils. How open China would be to the world and the extent to which it would take on board Western economics to reform the economy was at the centre of ideological debates in the first 15 years of the reform period (Gewirtz 2017). In both historical periods far reaching intellectual and social change accompanied the arrival of new (Western) technologies and ideas. Xi Jinping wants to steer innovation that requires engagement with the world yet simultaneously keep the country cloistered from regime-undermining ideas and ensure the survival of the party.[6]

The CPC's challenge is how to manage institutional and political change to enable innovation to drive the increase in productivity while retaining absolute control. Promoting innovation and productivity is different to becoming a world-leading manufacturing exporter. Success in hard skills is one component, but as alluded to above there is much more, the need for an environment that allows and encourages the exchange of divergent ideas: a marketplace for ideas. Reconciling innovation and political orthodoxy is deeply contradictory. These are apparent in the speeches of Xi. In a speech to the Chinese Academy of Sciences in May 2016 he said innovation – the growing use of science and technology – is crucial to the 2049 goal. "Innovation holds the key to the development of our country", he told the scientists (Xi 2017: 267). At the National Party Congress in October 2017 Xi said that making China a country of innovation, a culture of innovation and openness, was vital for its future. But in a speech on 10 September 2018 to mark Teacher's Day he said researchers and universities must adhere above all else to the leadership and values of the party. We need brilliant and innovative people, Xi Jinping is saying, but we need them to be subservient to the leadership of the CPC.

An unrecognized side effect of the quashing of contrarian discourse is that it ill prepares Chinese citizens and officials to grasp the challenges the country faces. Uniform thinking might be good for party control and legitimacy, but it creates a frog-in-the-well syndrome: the wider world and China's past are invisible and not well understood. It produces ignorance, coupled with hubris and nationalist pride, among officials and the Chinese public alike that blinds them to the gigantic task for China in taking what might seem to them small steps to close the gap with advanced economies but are in fact large strides. There are exceptions, like Liu Yadong, editor-in-chief of *Science and Technology Daily*, run by the Ministry of Science and Technology. In 2018 he told a conference the party leadership had been hoodwinked by overblown claims of the nation's capabilities and achievements: "The large gap in science and technology between China and developed countries in the West, including the US, should be common knowledge, and not a problem. But it became problematic when the people who hype [China's achievements] … fooled the leadership, the public and even themselves." Among the hype he cited was the "four new great inventions" – high-speed rail, electronic payments, bike sharing and online shopping – alluding to those of the past, paper, gun powder, printing and the compass. None of the new are Chinese inventions, he said (SCMP 2018a).

CONCLUSION

China's 1.4 billion people look to a future of rising living standards. Their implicit pact with the party-state after the 1989 Tiananmen Square Incident was that they would stay off the streets in return for increasing prosperity. Delivering that is the basis of the legitimacy of the CPC. So far, the party-state has been successful beyond its wildest dreams. To continue to deliver into the future, China must become more innovative for its cities to be liveable, to contain energy use and improve the environment, and to raise the quality of life in general.

The challenge of innovation, as Xi Jinping makes clear in his speeches, is big and vital to China becoming rich and powerful by 2049. He argues forcefully China must "make innovation the foundation of our development" as the means to "providing care for an ageing population, eliminating poverty, improving health, … to build a beautiful China with blue skies, green vegetation and clean water", and to face "pressures related to energy, food, cyberspace, ecology, biology and national defence, and … to ensure national security" (Xi 2017: 297). But as I have argued in this chapter, becoming an innovative and technologically advanced economy is a very different challenge to that of becoming the world's leading manufacturing exporter these past four decades. It is not a matter of better or more scientific and technological progress; there is a more complex cultural and political dynamic at play. Innovation requires a better educated workforce than China has; a cultural, political and social milieu that nurtures openness, contrarian ideas, innovative thinking and risk taking; the protection of intellectual property; and the rewarding of inventiveness and entrepreneurialism. All are lacking in some measure in China. Innovation is inevitably chaotic, uncertain and always disruptive of the established economic and political interests. Ask, from where will the next smart product come? From where will emerge the next Bill Gates, Steve Jobs, Jeff Bezos or Jack Ma? These are unknown – and unknowable. Cultivating innovativeness does not lend itself to the top-down direction of the authoritarian party-state. That is why much of the current investment in S&T is likely to miss the target, under deliver, and make the 2049 China Dream a faded fantasy.

7

Conclusion: present and future

At the start of 2020 China looked set to deliver the first of the centennial goals its leader Xi Jinping had promised. By 2021, the centenary of the founding of the CPC, China would be a "moderately well off" society and poverty would have been all but vanquished based on the current definition of the poverty line. It had become the second-largest economy in 2010 and an upper-middle-income country. Sure, there were worrying matters, not least the friction between China and the United States over trade, investment and technology. Economic growth had slowed in the 2010s compared with the first three decades after reform began in 1978, but that was to be expected, even though at around 6 per cent a year growth was impressive for such a large economy. Moreover, China had gained an international voice that was stronger than before, some would even say bellicose, as it projected its vision of the future global order through such grandiose schemes as the Belt and Road Initiative.

Less than two months into the year a lot had begun to unravel. A novel coronavirus had taken hold in the central megacity of Wuhan, which led the government to lockdown the country in the third week of January. Rapid spread beyond China soon led to a world pandemic, infecting at least 90 million people with more than two million deaths by early 2021.[1] China's economy massively slid in the early months of the year. China reported its first quarterly GDP contraction of the reform period and the government abandoned in May 2020 predicting the GDP growth rate, which has been the metric by which it and its officials have measured their performance for many years. While the country's success in heading off the virus domestically allowed the economy to begin to recover from late March, the deepening pandemic disrupted the global markets with many economies falling into recession. Of the world's major economies, the IMF (2020) mid-year outlook predicted that only China would record positive growth in 2020 – a paltry 1 per cent – while the United States would grow −8.0 per cent, the EU −10.2 per cent and Japan −5.8 per cent. The year turned out better than most would imagine for the world's economies. As Figure 7.1 shows, the slump in economic growth may be less than first forecast while China has managed a stronger recovery, with a forecast of 2 per cent growth for the year and a bounce to 7.9 per cent in 2021, before falling back to 5.2 per cent in 2022 (World Bank 2021).

Figure 7.1 Covid-19 hits growth of world's major economies (real GDP % change)

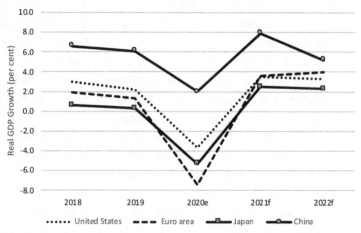

Note: For 2020–22, e = estimates; f = forecasts.　　*Source*: World Bank (2021).

More worrying for China is the disruption of global supply chains in which China is a central node, with MNEs and governments around the world planning diversification away from China. There is talk of "decoupling" from China in trade, technology and wider cooperation (*Financial Times* 2020j, 2020n). Some of this is assuredly protectionist and anti-China rhetoric and some reflects frustration with how China appropriates advanced technology from others and yet is unwilling to share where it has developed leadership. The world most certainly is likely to be quite different after the trauma of the 2020 pandemic and China's role in the global economy perhaps far less than the past. In terms of trade that began several years ago as China became increasingly expensive for low-end manufacturing. Foreign firms have shifted production to Southeast and South Asia, or back home, and even some Chinese manufacturers have followed too (*Financial Times* 2021c). Yet, China's position in the world economy today is different from the not too distant past too. And, far more complex and intertwined. It is now a major exporter of capital with FDI spread around the world and an aggressive buyer of advanced technology companies, which is worrying many governments about its techno-strategic ambitions, as well as a buyer of energy, raw materials and food. The combination of still cheapish technical skills and high-tech manufacturing hubs in Shenzhen and the Lower Yangzi cities centred on Shanghai nevertheless makes China an attractive location for many firms, while its increasingly richer consumers are an enticing market. Decoupling of China would unravel globalization potentially in ways similar to the decades between the First and Second World Wars in the twentieth century, which had tragic consequences with the rise of fascism in the 1930s and war. China's increasing willingness to flex its muscles in regions where it has interests makes the world a lot less safe than it has been since the end of the Cold War and the collapse of the former Soviet Union.

Domestically the size of China's economy will allow it to ride out some of the short-term effects of the global pandemic. Its size enables Chinese companies to experiment, to innovate and to grow their businesses. The impact of the shutdown has affected Chinese incomes. Many of those in the lower 20 per cent of the income distribution have been pushed down and even into poverty, as indeed has happened globally, with a forecast increase in the world's "new poor" of 88–116 million compared with the estimated 2020-baseline (World Bank 2020b). Despite expectations that China would miss its target to eliminate extreme poverty by end-2020, the government declared the goal achieved (Xinhua 2020). After the first quarter of negative growth, the economy bounced back due to capital formation (investment and factory production) and in the third quarter consumption contributed again to growth as consumers began to spend, albeit weakly. Although many Chinese undoubtedly have been adversely affected by the Covid-19 pandemic, China is by any reckoning a relatively well-off middle-income economy. The past four decades has seen a near miraculous escape from poverty. Let us not forget that by world comparative measures 80–90 per cent of the Chinese in 1980 were living in poverty. The Chinese today are richer, healthier and all round better off on average than they have ever been.

The once-in-a-century event of a global pandemic in 2020 will reshape the global economy and world affairs for years to come; it has wrecked forecasts for China's catchup to the United States. Not until at least 2022 will data on global realignments permit plausible projections, but the pre-pandemic predictions are likely to be way off the mark however strongly the growth rebounds. The rebound is anything but certain in view of the recurring pandemic waves, the supply and roll out of vaccines, and fractious international relations, of which those between China, the United States, the EU and India make the world look much less friendly to economic growth. China's narrative about the origin of Covid-19 and its record in controlling the spread has not been helped by a reluctance to allow entry of a WHO investigation team until early 2021 (WSJ 2021).

Sino-American relations hit lows in 2020 not seen since 1989. President Trump doubled down on Chinese technology companies, tightened controls on the export of technologies, and issued an executive order to ban investment in firms with links to the Chinese military. The three state-owned telecommunications companies were delisted from NYSE in early 2021, while Congress enacted laws to delist PRC firms that do not allow US authorities to audit (*Financial Times* 2021a). China in turn threatened to prosecute PRC firms that complied. Meanwhile, the party-state's anxieties about social stability and national security have led to the incarceration of up to 2 million Uighurs in Xinjiang and forced many to work on state-owned cotton farms or in factories, while in Hong Kong a national security law has stifled pro-democracy dissent and led to imprisonment of activists (BBC 2021; *The Economist* 2020c; Zenz 2020; *Financial Times* 2021b). Britain has threatened to fine UK firms that use Chinese "slave labour" from Xinjiang (*Financial Times* 2021e).

Party-state concerns about stability – and especially financial stability – were underscored in several dramatic ways for business. The former chairman of one of China's top four state asset managers, Lai Xiaomin, was sentenced to death in early January for accepting ¥1.79 billion ($277 million) in bribes (SCMP 2021). The authorities at the eleventh hour halted the initial public offering in Shanghai and Hong Kong in November 2020 of Jack Ma's fintech Ant Group, which would have been the world's largest IPO valued at around $37 billion (*The Economist* 2020b; *Financial Times* 2020k, 2020l). Ma had angered the party when he told a conference in late October that state banks had a pawnshop mentality and were unable to innovate; hours earlier Wang Qishan, one of Xi Jinping's most-trusted associates, had told the same conference that stability of the financial system was uppermost in any innovation (*Financial Times* 2020p, 2020q). The party's subsequent targeting of Jack Ma and the monopolistic private-sector empires of others in China is probably long overdue, and in part reflects the growing concern about the unfettered sway of Big Tech in the rest of the world too (*The Economist* 2021; *Financial Times* 2020s, 2021d).[2] And, much as it might be described as an attack on the private sector, the move has been in the works for a while. The party in 2012 began to press ahead to strengthen party branches in private firms after years of neglect and Xi Jinping has stated many times that private firms and the financial sector in particular must adhere to the leadership of the communist party (*The Economist* 2012a; Xi 2017: 304–8).

China as a whole has re-emerged economically over the past four decades to become again a major global economy that it was until as late as the early nineteenth century when it still counted for nearly one-third of world GDP (Maddison 2001). It is some distance from coming out on top again and might well not, but the roller coaster ride of its quest for modernization over the last 150 years began to deliver results in the 1980s. Economic reform unleashed market incentives and loosened the controls of the state over the economy, which delivered China from the hands of state planners to its present standing as an upper-middle-income economy. That is no mean achievement. Capitalism of a kind returned to China, although one perplexingly overseen by the world's largest communist party that reconciled the ideological conundrum with the term "socialist market economy", recognised as the official description of the economic system with its insertion into the PRC constitution in 1993.

Early reform growth was a real muddle. There was little in the way of a blueprint, despite latter-day party ideologues dressing up the success as a triumph of CPC's leadership.[3] Peasant farmers and others launched a private economy from below, which was illegal at the time, and the private sector grew rapidly to now account for the major share of China's economic output and employment. The once dominant state sector declined – it now employs a little above one-tenth of the urban workforce – although the state held tightly to its control of large SOEs that dominate strategic industries. Moreover, the state sector then and now for the party is the core of the Chinese economy whatever its gross inefficiencies (State Council 2018; Lardy 2019). All the while, for Deng Xiaoping, the goal of reform was not to abandon socialism but to find a way forward. In 1979, he said:

> [W]e do not want capitalism, but neither do we want to be poor under socialism. What we want is socialism in which the productive forces are developed, and the country is prosperous and powerful. … It is wrong to maintain that a market economy exists only in capitalist society … Developing a market economy does not mean practicing capitalism (cited in Gewirtz 2017: 61).

We should keep in mind Deng's remarks and the goals of the party in those early years when we puzzle over the nature of the contemporary economy, which many now label "state capitalism" (*The Economist* 2020a), and the trajectory of the PRC under the leadership of Xi Jinping. In reasserting the authority of the party and the primacy of the state in the economy Xi is not so much abandoning the reform goals of the 1980s as reasserting the primary goal laid out by Deng; China will remain socialist, led by the communist party, and become rich and powerful through appropriate use of markets; China will retain socialism, as the party so defines it, having its share of the world's economic cake, if not more; and, China will demand its voice and interests are heeded as befits its economic size and status, rejuvenated as a global power and freed of the humiliations inflicted in the nineteenth century. Xi positions himself within the party as the heir and guardian of the historical mission of Deng and before him Mao Zedong to make China strong again, and to guide the latest twist in the Sinification of Marxism and Leninism. Rhetoric aside, however, Xi Jinping is certainly no heir to the iconoclastic tradition of the Chinese youth of the May Fourth Movement such as Deng and Mao who wanted to remake China anew, in economy, ideology, and personal and social relations, striking hard at Chinese traditions. Instead, Xi Jinping is far more fittingly cast as a successor to a long line of patriarchal autocrats. He might claim to walk in the footsteps of Deng and Mao, but his model of leadership seemingly fits better the eighteenth-century emperor Qianlong, a stout defender of Confucian orthodoxy and warring expansionist who crushed dissent mercilessly and extended the boundaries of the Chinese empire to their farthest reach.

China's combination of a market economy and political authoritarianism has delivered impressive growth in the recent past. There is no quibble about that. But the innovation and creativity required to build China's future I have argued are unlikely to flourish under the controls on information and free speech, which seek to impose ideological uniformity and quell opposition to the party. These controls have increased hugely since 2010. Critical voices have been stifled and many incarcerated: civil society activists, feminists, human rights lawyers, underground church adherents along with ethnic minorities in Tibet and Xinjiang. A more open society will be needed for China to realize its goal of becoming an advance economy. That is not the same as arguing democracy is inevitable, although there is no reason a democracy could not emerge. Taiwan demonstrates democracy and economic growth can thrive together in a Han Chinese society, and other East Asian countries that were once authoritarian – such as South Korea – embraced democracy in their escape from the middle-income status to become advanced economies.

Increased openness is needed if China is to foster creativity and innovation that will produce solutions to the many problems it faces in building liveable cities, improving energy efficiency and reducing pollution, and raising the standard of living and the quality of life for all. Sustained innovation is necessary to unlock productivity of the increasingly smaller and ageing workforce, spur growth and raise incomes in order to escape the middle-income trap and enter the ranks of high-income economies by the 2040s. No middle-income country in the past has made that transition without far-reaching institutional change and political liberalization that makes for a more inclusive society and one that fosters a market for ideas, knowledge exchange and innovation (World Bank 2013). These historical preconditions that enabled previous former middle-income economies to become innovative and rich are not on the CPC's political agenda.

The implication of my argument is that China will be trapped in the middle and not realize the goal of Xi Jinping for the rejuvenation (*fuxing*) of China as a wealthy and strong global power by 2049, his second centennial goal. China however has proved many pundits wrong in the past. It might well again. Who imagined in 1980 that a communist party would steer China into a market-oriented modern economy second only to the United States in size? So, the intriguing and disturbing scenario is that China will carve a new path to becoming an advanced technological superpower by the middle of the twenty-first century and remain, all the while, an authoritarian state with pervasive control over personal liberties inside its borders and even beyond. What would that mean for the global order, human rights and the democracies of the world?

Notes

1. INTRODUCTION: PAST AND PRESENT

1. World Bank World Development Indicators, online database: databank. worldbank.org. Comparisons of the GDP (gross domestic product) of countries is typically reported in local currency converted to US dollars at the prevailing exchange rates. PPP reflects how much an international dollar will buy in different countries. In less developed countries, labour is typically cheap and capital expensive, and the opposite occurs in developed economies.

2. World Bank (1981), *World Development Indicators* states $260, but the online WDI database states $220.

3. The magnitude of the fall is exaggerated because of Broadberry's high estimate of per capita income in 1700, an artefact of new land brought into cultivation and reduced population during the Ming-Qing transition. Based on estimated late Ming income, the level in 1800 was only 24 per cent below 1600 (see Table 1.1).

4. For an assessment of the differences in the impact of New World silver on Europe, China and India, see Findlay & O'Rourke (2007), 212–26.

5. The literature on economic growth and market integration in the eighteenth century is large and the debates remain controversial: Wang (1992); Pomeranz (2000); Shiue & Keller (2007); Rosenthal & Wong (2011); Bernhofen *et al.* (2015); von Glahn (2016), 331–6, 346–7; Vries 2015; Broadberry *et al.* 2018, among others.

6. The "four big inventions" (*si da faming*) of compass, gunpower, paper and printing are well known. Others include: the stern-post rudder and water-tight haul compartments in ships, stirrups and the trace harness for horses, segmented arch bridges, water screws, driving belts and chains, the wheelbarrow, the decimal place and use of zero, among others (Needham 1969).

7. Urbanization in China was lower than Europe, but the countryside in the core regions was densely populated, so conventional definitions underestimate levels of urbanization.

8. The central role of institutions in economic growth owes much to North (1990) and his co-authors. Acemoglu & Robinson (2011) argue that institutions matter most in explaining the differences between nations. Mokyr (2017) emphasize the role of culture and associated institutions in the creation and diffusion of knowledge necessary for economic growth.

9. Li Bozhong (1998) was a pioneer study in the Great Divergence debate, which with later works challenged past views, such as Elvin (1973) who reckoned China had reached a "high level equilibrium trap", constrained by technology and population, while Huang (1985, 1990) argued population growth had induced an involution process with negative returns to labour. From the 1600s, most Lower Yangzi rural households produced some textiles for the market, as did households in North China and Guangdong in the eighteenth and nineteenth centuries (Pomerantz 2000: 87).

10. Adam Smith (1852 [1776]: 30, 86–7): "The accounts of all travellers, inconsistent in many other respects, agree in the low wages of labour, and in the difficulty which a labourer finds in bringing up a family in China. ... The difference between the money price of labour in China and in Europe, is still greater than that between the money price of subsistence; because the real recompense of labour is higher in Europe than in China, the greater part of Europe being in an improving state, while China seems to be standing still."

11. Research on estimating GDP in Asia before the mid-twentieth century includes, for example, the project on historical national income in Asia at Hitotsubashi University, http://www.ier.hit-u.ac.jp/English/introduction/tables1.html, and the Maddison Project at Groningen University, http://www.ggdc.net/MADDISON/oriindex.htm.

2. CHINA'S "LONG" TWENTIETH CENTURY

1. The opium wars are well rehearsed in all histories of this period, but for a recent account that uses extensive British and Chinese archival sources none is better than Lovell (2011).

2. This sense of economics resembles early modern European writing on economics defined as political economy where the focus was on the public administration of the affairs of the state and the subsistence of a nation's inhabitants.

3. For detailed surveys of the diplomacy and the self-strengthening movement, see Hsu (1990, Part III) and Spence (2013, chapters 9 and 10). My periodization is based on Hsu.

4. Zeng Guofen (1811–72) was a Hunan official best known for raising the Xiang army to defeat the Taiping Rebellion. Li Hongzhang (1823–1901) and Zuo Zongtang (1812–85) were Zeng's protégés. Li was the foremost modernizing official of the late Qing dynasty.

5. The China Merchants Group is a central state enterprise (*yangqi*) under the State-owned Assets Supervision and Administration of the State Council. China Merchants Holding (International) is listed on the Stock Exchange of Hong Kong and runs a raft of subsidiaries. The group also owns China Merchants Bank.

6. Li Hongzhang received permission from the court for the British engineer in charge of the Kaiping mine to build a tramway from the mine to a nearby canal with the wagons drawn by mules. The engineer used standard gauge track and four months later he mounted an old mine boiler on a bogey, which became China's first-made locomotive, the "Rocket of China". The first railway in China, however, was the Wusong narrow-gauge line near Shanghai in 1876–77, which was dismantled and shipped off to Taiwan (Huenemann 1984: 44, 76–7).

7. A tael is a unit of silver, equal to 1.208 English ounce of pure silver.

8. There is a large literature on the early nationalist movement and the Wuhan Uprising. Hsu (1990) and Spence (2013) provide a summary and further reading suggestions.

9. The "Nanjing Decade" was so named because the Nationalist Government under Chiang Kai-shek shifted the capital to Nanjing from Beijing (Peking), which was renamed Beiping (Peiping, or northern peace) in 1928 and remained the capital until the retreat to Chongqing (Chungking) after the outbreak of war with Japan.

10. Chang's study was a pioneering reconstruction of industrial development in China before 1949. He, like Rawski, were indebted to Liu & Yeh (1965).

11. Kirby (1992: 185) reports Nationalist estimates in 1946–47 of wartime losses at more than 55 per cent of industrial and mining assets, 72 per cent of shipping and 96 per cent of railways. Coal production was one-third its pre-war peak, including Manchuria. The Manchurian iron and steel industry could only produce 30,000 tonnes of the pre-war peak of 2.5 million tonnes.

12. The prelude, course and consequences of the Sino-Japanese War and the civil war are covered in Hsu (1990: chapters 24 and 25) and Spence (2013: chapters 17 and 18).

13. Spence (2013: 403–404) reckons by 1938 China was split into 10 separate units: Manchukuo, the Inner Mongolian Federation, northeast China south of the Great Wall, east-central China, occupied Guangzhou in south China and Taiwan, all under Japan to varying degrees, along with the Nationalist regime in southwest China and the Communist base area in the northwest.

In addition, there were areas controlled by local warlords, such as in Shanxi in the northwest.

14. Occupied China was fluid in terms of the reach of Japan, the Nationalists and Communists. The Japanese only controlled the major cities, big towns and the transport corridors between them. The countryside was left to collaborators and quasi-independent local powers and their militia along with contingents of Nationalist troops and Communist guerrilla groups.

15. Unless indicated, details for SGN are from Van Slyke (1986: 632, 635, 658, 684–6).

16. The Nationalist's postwar planners sent about 1,000 engineers, scientists and managers to the United States on two-year internships between 1942 and 1946, and many hundreds of NRC staff and state enterprise personnel spent shorter periods there (Kirby 1992: 201).

17. Mao famously said the Chinese were like a blank piece of paper upon which beautiful calligraphy could be written. Like so many intellectuals and political figures in the past, Mao denied agency to the common Chinese who were deemed to have a "cultural level" (*wenhua shuiping*, meaning education) too low to allow them to participate in governing the country.

18. For a summary, see Riskin (1987: 41–8). The 1952 "five-anti" (*wufan*) campaign investigated 450,000 private sector enterprises for alleged profiteering and "evils" such as bribery, tax evasion, theft of state property and stealing economic information.

19. The PRC modern series of gazetteers for Henan and Anhui provinces have chronologies that report thousands of peasants being trucked across provinces to engage in a frenzy of "rural socialist construction".

20. National and provincial deaths rates are from statistical yearbooks; the subprovincial rates from the modern prefecture and county gazetteers series for Anhui and Henan.

21. For a concise summary of the Cultural Revolution, see Spence (2013: chapter 22).

22. The phrase was reputedly first used by Chen Yun, one of the "eight immortals" of the CPC. Chen emphasized the primacy of planning for socialism and that the market should be contained like "a bird in a cage" lest it sullied the socialist economy. His phrase was embraced to signify a pragmatic approach to economic reform; see Gewirtz (2017: 3).

23. Riskin (1986: 242–8). Two examples show this clearly. China's 1976 nitrogen fertiliser to rice price ratio was 4.4:1. At the time a 28hp "East is Red" tractor was priced at 35.5 tonnes grain equivalent compared with a similar Japanese tractor priced at 5.5 tonnes equivalent. See also Lardy (1983).

24. University students occupied Tiananmen Square in central Beijing from April 1989 to demand greater democratic freedoms and a crackdown on corrupt

officials until they were removed during the night of 3/4 June by the army with the loss of an unknown number of lives. Commemoration or mention of the incident is expunged from any legally published media in China to this day.

25. Naughton (2018: 435–6) argues the official FDI origin data underestimates Western FDI, a lot of which came from subsidiaries in Hong Kong or from offices in tax havens. A lot of Hong Kong FDI is "round-tripping" domestic funds re-entering China as "foreign" (see Chapter 3).

26. Jiang Zeming, report to the Fifteenth National Party Congress, 1997; http:// cpc.people.com.cn/GB/64162/64168/64568/index.html.

27. Brown (2018) develops this dimension of the peculiarity of the party's view of itself and reform in recent years, which is at such stark variance with the view of the rest of the world.

3.   MEASURING THE CHINESE ECONOMY

1. Economic history shows that long-run economic growth is influenced most not by the average rate of growth, but the frequency and depth of periods of negative growth, which wipe out gains of the previous years (Broadberry & Wallis 2017). China has avoided long periods of reported negative growth since 1979, although there were major declines in 1989–90, 2008–09 and again in early 2020 due to the impact of the coronavirus pandemic, from which its economy rebounded strongly to become the only major world economy to record positive growth in 2020 (World Bank 2021).

2. PPP estimates rely on various assumptions and benchmark years. Pushed back into time they can become unreliable not only because of methodological problems with chained index numbers but also because the consumption baskets change over time. Comparability between countries might be problematic because of big differences in governance institutions, which includes how GDP is estimated in a country using local currency.

3. Best known is Japan's Ministry of International Industry and Trade (MITI), which guided Japan to become the world's second-largest economy by 1980 (Johnson 1982). There were similar agencies of competent bureaucrats in Taiwan and South Korea. State-led industrial policy in East Asia outside of China from the late 1950s to the 1990s was distinguished by its market orientation. Among the recommended literature on the "Asian tigers" are Lau & Klein (1990 [1986]), Vestal (1993), Vogel (1991), Amsden (1989), Wade (1990), Yamazawa (1990), Ranis (1992) and World Bank (1993).

4. The UN *World Population Prospects* reports its estimates in the form of low, medium and high growth variants. Projected estimates cited here are the medium variant for all series.

5. The effect of the one-child policy is much researched and hotly debated. Its

human dimensions and tragedies are sometimes overlooked or dismissed as a price for economic growth, a story which is well told by Mei Fong (2017).

6. A shrinking population and static economic growth would statistically raise GDP per capita, but how any individual might experience that is uncertain because aging of the population will increase both the state and private burden for healthcare and pensions, and the politics of the distribution of national income between those who work and those who do not will be fraught (Zhao *et al*. 2018).

7. The Chinese currency was overvalued at the start of the reform period and was adjusted downward slowly such that in US dollar terms Chinese wages in the mid-1990s reached an all-time low. There was barely any difference in effective real wages for foreign investors between 1980 and 1998 (Li *et al*. 2012).

8. The statistical classification "non-private" is anomalous to a Western reader. It includes state-owned and collective enterprises as would be expected, but also includes share-issuing limited companies, Hong Kong, Macau and Taiwan invested companies, and foreign-invested companies. These latter three groups would elsewhere be classified as private or non-state.

9. For most market economies 5 per cent unemployed is considered full employment. Fewer would imply a tight labour market and a strong upward pressure on wages and potential inflation.

10. The trade deficit the United States runs with China is overstated in conventional reporting because it captures merchandise trade, tangible goods, and does not include the trade in intangibles such as as patents, know-how, trademarks, copyrights, brands and trade secrets, of which the US firms have an abundance. For a recent attempt to estimate the difference, see Fu and Ghauri (2020).

11. The SEZs were all in South China: Shenzhen, Zhuhai and Shantou in Guangdong and Xiamen in Fuzhou. They offered a package of incentives including foreigners allowed to run wholly owned ventures, lower tax, duty free import of parts and equipment, exemption from export duties, and remittance abroad of earnings. But at the time the infrastructure was poor. The 14 coastal cities were ironically former nineteenth-century Treaty Ports such as Shanghai, Ningbo, Fuzhou, Qingdao and Tianjin. Hainan was part of Guangdong but became a separate province in 1988. New policies between 1986 and 1990 included FDI encouragement measures such as incentives for technology export-oriented firms and liberalized rules for foreign exchange.

12. During the tour Deng pronounced the need to extend economic reform and coined the idea of a "socialist market economy", which joined the future of socialism to ongoing market-oriented policies. In 1991–92 China also issued new FDI-favourable regulations, including amendments to the Equity Joint

Venture Law, revised income tax rules for foreign firms, and provided more protection of intellectual property.

13. Taiwan and South Korean data for FDI (and trade) in the late 1980s and early 1990s was hidden in accounts for political reasons. For Taiwan, there were differences between the data reported by agencies in Taiwan and in China, and a lot of trade and investment was cycled via Hong Kong. South Korea recognized the PRC in 1992, so earlier trade and investment was unofficial and passed through Hong Kong (Deng 2000; Kim & Ma 2006).

14. The PRC 2020 National Security Law for Hong Kong, which has reduced if not destroyed the autonomy guaranteed under the 1997 handover agreement, looks set to change radically its status. The United States has already reclassified manufactured products from Hong Kong as made in China.

15. Tax havens vary widely from those that are highly secretive and whose only business is tourism and providing tax minimizing offshore domiciles for businesses to those countries that simply have low (and sometimes loose) tax regimes. The latter, which includes countries such as the Benelux Group and Ireland, are excluded from my definition.

16. The investment was to supply iron ore to Baoshan Steel in Shanghai. The mine is operated by Rio Tinto in a joint venture with Sinosteel Corp., which holds 40 per cent. The mine has delivered 250 million tonnes and the contract was renewed for a third time in 2017 (see https://www.riotinto.com/en/news/releases/Channar-JV-Sinosteel-extension).

17. Dalian Wanda, then the largest property company in the world, was one of those targeted. The most spectacular fall was Wu Xiaohui, chairman and CEO of Anbang Insurance, which had acquired such real estate icons as New York's Waldorf Astoria hotel. He was arrested in 2017 and imprisoned in 2018. Anbang was taken over by the state and disappeared from the Fortune Global 500 on which it had appeared for the first time only in 2017 ranked 139 with assets of $430 billion. Collier (2018: 38–46) surveys the rise of Wu and Anbang up to his arrest.

18. Data from the World Bank (2020a) for the amount of annual debt service arising from bilateral loans shows China is the largest creditor for seven of the top eight indebted economies in 2020. Pakistan heads the list with an annual bill of $2.92 billion, followed by Angola $2.36 billion, Kenya $849.4 million, Ethiopia $542.8 million, Myanmar $507.2 million, Laos $412.6 million and Cameroon $398.3 million.

19. Analysis of China's OFDI reported here is based on official statistics reported in the CSY for various years on the destinations of OFDI, supplemented with the statistical bulletins of MofCom on outward investments; http://fec.mofcom.gov.cn/article/fwydyl/tjsj/.

20. Xi Jinping launched the Belt and Road Initiative in speeches in September 2013 in Kazakhstan, where he proposed a "silk road economic belt" (corridor)

through Central Asia and in October in Indonesia, where he proposed joining China, Southeast and South Asia together in a "twenty-first century maritime silk road". At the time the BRI was known as "One Belt, One Road", a literal translation of the Chinese contraction *"yidai yilu"*.

21. Financial repression describes the way the state financial system traps household savings into low-return bank deposits that are then used to supply cheap credit to the state's preferred clients such as SOEs. These investments often have low or even negative returns on the investments.

22. For a detailed account of this institutional and regulatory transformation, see Stent (2017: chapter 4). Naughton (2018: 487–94) and Kroeber (2016: 128–31, 136–40) both provide concise and data-focused surveys.

23. Market capitalization can be volatile, which will change the aggregate level of market capitalization, although the rank order for leading exchanges has changed little in recent years. https://www.statista.com/statistics/270126/largest-stock-exchange-operators-by-market-capitalization-of-listed-companies/ (accessed 15 December 2020).

4. FORM OF THE ECONOMY: BUSINESS AND GOVERNMENT

1. The private sector in China is at best a fluid term. Apart from the smallest firms, few are private in the sense that might be understood in Western countries. Broadly, private means the firms are majority non-state owned. In larger private firms, however, the party and the state have influence via a branch of the party or in holding a minority ownership share.

2. Studies of the CPC are many. This section draws on Saich (2015: chapter 4). For accounts of recent internal power struggles, see Brown (2014, 2017, 2018), Garnaut (2013) and McGregor (2012).

3. The size of the SC of the Politburo is not fixed and has varied between five and nine members. The CPC's website has details on party organizations and senior leaders, including career biographies, and many party documents from its history: http://cpc.people.com.cn/GB/64162/. Leaders who are purged also disappear from the site without trace. The party's view of history at any moment in time is *the* history without challenge.

4. Article 35 guarantees "freedom of speech, of the press, of association ..."; Article 36 "freedom of religion ..."; and Article 37 "freedom of the person ... is inviolable". Few would hold that these are observed in any way congruent with a plain language reading of the constitution. The full text of the 2018 constitution in Chinese is on the State Council website (http://www.gov.cn/) and in English at: https://npcobserver.files.wordpress.com/2018/12/PRC-Constitution-2018.pdf. An official translation of the 2004 version at: http://www.npc.gov.cn/zgrdw/englishnpc/Constitution/node_2825.htm.

5. Before June 1989, the then Premier Zhao Ziyang had wanted to separate party

from government. The political crisis that followed the Tiananmen Square demonstrations and subsequent crackdown saw this rolled back by his successor, Jiang Zeming; see Snape (2019) and Snape & Wang (2020).

6. NPC Observer, Annotated Translation: 2018 Amendment to the P.R.C. Constitution (Version 2.0): https://npcobserver.com/2018/03/11/translation-2018-amendment-to-the-p-r-c-constitution/.

7. The State Council website has details on the ministries and agencies and includes brief career biographies for each member of the State Council; http://english.www.gov.cn/statecouncil.

8. The undoing of Bo Xilai, the party secretary of Chongqing Municipality and erstwhile rival to Xi Jinping to become the CPC general secretary was a spectacular political crash. The best account is Garnaut (2013). For a fun fictional account of the patronage networks at the local level, which are particularly venal and the scourge of peasants and urban communities, see the novel by Ma Jian (2018), *China Dream*, a brutal satire on contemporary authoritarianism.

9. Although Xi appears to have distanced himself during his career, the same cannot be said for his immediate family who have benefited from his rise.

10. Like Xi Jinping, Ren Zhiqiang is a "princeling", the son of an early party leader. His father was a government minister under Mao Zedong. But Ren had become a strident critic of Xi. In March 2020, he scathingly criticized Xi's handling of the coronavirus and his authoritarian rule, writing that Xi was not "an emperor in his 'new clothes' but a naked clown" (*Financial Times* 2020m). Ren's alleged corruption was trifling, a mere one million dollars, compared with the billions of dollars many senior officials have been accused of since 2013.

11. There is a large literature on *guanxi* in general and in business. See the book-length studies by Gold *et al.* (2002) and Luo (2007).

12. The network view of the firm described here draws on a large literature that includes social network analysis (see Kilduff & Tsai 2003, for an overview), the transaction cost view of the firm (Williamson 1981, 1986) and the resource-based view of the firm (Barney 1991). For space reasons the summary has no doubt done injury to the subtleties of this literature that underpins much of this network-related research in strategic management.

13. In Chinese the quantitative description of any noun requires the use of a noun classifier in the form numeral + classifier + noun. Although there is an all-purpose classifier (*ge*), there are many dozens of specific ones for whether the object is flat or block-like, plant or animal (English has equivalents, like a flock of geese), and so on. For example, we would say "*liang jia gongzi*" for "two companies".

14. The Rong family businesses were established by the brothers Rong Zongjing and Rong Desheng who separated from their early partnership in a money

lending business to establish empires in textile and flour milling that made them among the richest in China before 1949. Deng Xiaoping asked Rong Desheng's son to help establish CITIC at the end of the 1970s. The Hong Kong company Li & Fung, which invented paper-encased fireworks in the early twentieth century, is today one of the largest operators of complex supply chains for fashion, toys and other goods. The Fung family bought out the silent partner Li To-ming in the 1940s.

15. The use of vertical to describe networks between firms and government should not be confused with vertical integration where a business integrates upstream activities (say ore extraction), with processing (the ore) and downstream activities (the making and selling of end-use metal products).

16. Wuhan Iron and Steel was merged with Baosteel in 2016 to create the Baowu Group.

17. The China Datang Corporation is also the only SASAC SOE that is directly managed by the CPC CC; see http://www.cccme.org.cn/shop/cccme8991/introduction.aspx.

18. Lenovo was spun off from Legend Holdings, which was founded in 1984 by 11 staff from the Institute of Computing Technology at the Chinese Academy of Sciences (CAS). Up to 2009, CAS owned 65 per cent of Legend, which owned a majority in Lenovo, when CAS holdings were reduced to 35 per cent. In 2019, CAS held 29 per cent of Legend and three investment companies with crossing holdings in Legend subsidiaries, owned another 32 per cent. Legend in turn owned 29.1 per cent of Lenovo and the public owned 64.8 per cent; see https://www.lenovo.com/gb/en/lenovo/our-company/, http://www.legendholdings.com.cn/index_en.aspx and https://investor.lenovo.com/en/ir/shareholding.php.

19. There were seven firms identified as China with their headquarters in Hong Kong in the 2019 list: China Resources (ranked 80), Lenovo Group (212), China Merchants Group (244), Jardine Matheson (280), CK Hutchison Holdings (352), AIA Group (388) and China Taiping Insurance (451). Jardine Matheson, CK Hutchison and the AIA Group are not owned by PRC interests and are excluded from the China count. *Fortune* magazine has only included the Hong Kong firms in the China-designated group in recent years.

20. For example, one of China's largest television makers TCL in 2004 acquired two French firms, the television division of Thomson and the mobile phone maker Alcatel. The Thomson deal lost $719 million in the first two years of the venture and TCL discovered that the Alcatel 3G technologies it sought were owned by Alcatel's JV with Fujitsu, outside of its deal. Besides an alarming failure of strategic thinking and due diligence, Shambaugh (2013: 191–3) reckons the biggest problem was the difference in corporate culture between the Chinese executives and the Europeans managers as well as the Chinese attitude to local employee work practices and compensation.

21. The status of Huawei is a matter of public debate. Huawei claims to be employee owned via the company trade union, but under Chinese law in the event of collapse the residual assets would not go to members but revert upward to the party controlled All China Federation of Trade Unions (Balding & Clark 2019). In addition, Lenovo's holding company was majority state owned until 2001 and Haier was originally a collective urban enterprise and the Qingdao government retained interests and influence (Yang & Morgan 2011).

22. At the time in the late 1990s before reform of state banks and SOEs (see Chapter 3), the risk was that such loans from capital raising could disappear into the revolving door of triangular debt, with firms borrowing from each other to pay creditor firms or banks.

5. RICH CHINA, POOR CHINA:
DISPARITIES AND INEQUALITIES

1. The cities in rank order with the number of billionaires in brackets: Beijing (131), Hong Kong (80), Shenzhen (78), Shanghai (70, ranked equal with London), Hangzhou (38), Guangzhou (37), Taipei in Taiwan (30, ranked equal with Seoul), Foshan (17), Chengdu (15) and Ningbo (15) (Hurun 2018).

2. Li Ka-shing was the 28th richest in the world in 2018 on the Forbes World Billionaires List (Ma is 21st), and the 32nd on the Hurun Global Rich List 2018 (Ma is 26th). Li began his career in the 1950s manufacturing plastic flowers in Hong Kong. In the 1960s he bought real estate, acquired English trading firms in Hong Kong, and in the process created the conglomerate Cheung Kong Holdings with interests in property, ports, shipping, utilities, retail, telecommunications, and oil. He retired in May 2018 as chairman of CK Hutchison Holdings (Forbes World Billionaires; https://www.forbes.com/billionaires/#66621a15251c).

3. There are many biographies of Jack Ma in Chinese and English. A highly readable account by an advisor and confident is Duncan Clark's (2016) biography of Ma and his company. Also see Edward Tse (2015: chapter 3).

4. The relative position of the richest can change quickly with fluctuations in the market value of their companies. Jack Ma's status was overtaken by Pony Ma in the first quarter of 2019 but reversed a few months later. In late 2020, Jack Ma was worth $65.6 billion, followed by Pony Ma at $55.2 billion; many of Chinese richest have been enriched further by the lockdown economy (Forbes China Rich List; https://www.forbes.com/china-billionaires/list/#tab: overall). The government late scuppering of the IPO of the Ant Group, which holds the Alipay app, and investigation of Alibaba for monopolist behaviour is reputed to have pushed Jack Ma down to the fourth richest, although not according to Forbes (*The Economist* 2020b; *Financial Times* 2020p, 2021d).

5. The CHIP survey data are a subset of the NSB national household survey data

compiled as part of a long-running international study with the NSB. It covers a selection of China's provinces. There have been six waves: 1988, 1995, 2002, 2007 and 2013. The CHIP data seeks to correct the major flaws in the official NSB data, such as the lack of imputed rent from owner-occupied housing and neglect of subsidies and transfers.

6. Kanbur *et al.* (2017) estimate the Gini coefficient for 1995–2014 by merging the CHIP data for 1995, 2002 and 2007 with the China Family Panel Series data for 2010, 2012 and 2014, with adjustments to ensure compatibility of the two series.

7. For several years around 2010, the NSB did not publish annual estimates of the Gini coefficient.

8. The poverty line in 1978 was ¥100 per person a year, adjusted to ¥200 in the mid-1980s, ¥1,196 in 2008, and ¥2,300 from 2010, adjusted by the CPI annually, which at the time in PPP terms was $1.65 per day per person. See Luo *et al.* (2018: 6).

9. Provincial income alone is not a good predictor of rates of illiteracy, especially for women. Other factors include local customs that affect gender differences in child rearing and attitudes to schooling, as well as past historical investment in education.

10. Anthropometric measures (height and weight) are used not only in human biology and nutritional fields to assess human growth, but also in economic history and development economics as non-monetary indicators of long-run change in human welfare that is related to economic growth. Height is an historical measure of net nutrition available for the growth of a child from *in utero* to the time of measurement; weight measures the contemporary level of nutrition and may fluctuate due to illness or short-lived nutritional deficits; and the body mass index (BMI, weight in kilograms divided by the height in metres squared, kg/m^2) is a measure of body weight adjusted for height. Change in mean height is sensitive to nutrition and correlated positively with income and negatively with income inequality.

11. For girls, the average height of seven-year-old rural girls increased from 116 cm in 1979 to 124.1 cm in 2014, while their urban counterparts rose from 120.4 cm to 126.1 cm. For 17-year-olds, rural girls increased from 155.7 cm to 159.9 and urban from 158.1 cm to 160.5 cm. The rural–urban gap has also narrowed for all age groups.

12. In a nomalized distribution, where the mean is set to zero, a 1-standard deviation (SD) above the mean is a z-score of 1.0 and one below is −1.0. The z-score is used to compare change in values for a measure that differs greatly between different ages such as height and weight. For example, a 5cm difference in height at seven years is very different relatively to the mean compared with the same change for a 17-year-old. The international reference is the WHO's height-for-age and BMI-for-age guidelines (WHO 2007).

13. From the CPC web site, http://cpc.people.com.cn/GB/64162/414940/index. html.

6. A SUSTAINABLE FUTURE?

1. Population densities in rural eastern China have long been high. Jiangsu province in 1983 had an average density of 598 people per m², which was higher than Beijing (556). In Jiangsu, the density of rural districts around Wuxi and Suzhou was several thousand people per m² and the villages were separated by barely a kilometre of fields (CSY 1984: 84).

2. The resettlement programmes have a mixed record. In some places, local officials have uprooted remote communities to meet government targets to reduce extreme poverty. Although the township amenities are a welcomed improvement, the emotional and psychological shock of shifting to low-to-medium rise apartments from the ancestral villages is not often recognized by the authorities.

3. Alipay began as a secure payment portal for Alibaba and was spun off in 2011 into the Ant Financial Group, controlled by Jack Ma. It is the dominant mobile payment app in China.

4. China is an importer of both thermal and coking coal. Imported thermal coal from Australia is of lower sulphur content, higher thermal efficiency and can be landed at eastern China ports more cheaply than freighting by rail from Shanxi, Shaanxi and Inner Mongolia.

5. A useful introduction to this framework is Nicholas Crafts' (2018) analysis of British economic growth from the industrial revolution to the financial crisis; see especially 3–8, 16–22.

6. The 2013 internal party "Communiqué on the Current State of the Ideological Sphere", widely known as "Document 9", warned of the promotion of seven dangerous Western values: constitutional democracy, universal values, civil society, neoliberalism, independent journalism, historical nihilism (questioning the party's view of history), and questioning the socialist nature of socialism with Chinese characteristics. The journalist who leaked the document was later sentenced to seven years in prison. Translation at: https://www.chinafile.com/document-9-chinafile-translation.

CONCLUSION

1. These are confirmed cases of Covid-19 and confirmed deaths, but the actual number of cases and deaths are much higher because many instances were unrecorded due to inadequate testing. Data are from the Our World in Data Covid-19 database; https://ourworldindata.org/coronavirus.

2. Big Tech concentration in China is far greater than in the United States. For

example, the top-three e-commerce firms – Alibaba, JD.com and Pinduoduo – capture 90 per cent of online sales whereas Amazon, Shopify and eBay account for less than half (*The Economist* 2021).

3. The distortion of the history of the early reform period has increased in recent years. Xi Jinping and the party have revised the narrative to strengthen the party's claim in the present as the sole legitimate agent to guide the future development of the country. Just how uncertain and desperate Deng Xiaoping, Zhao Ziyang and others were to find a path forward between the late 1970s and early 1990s, one that would allow China to remain socialist but not poor, is told in Gewirtz (2017).

Chronology

The chronology identifies important events and increases in detail as it nears the present.

960   Song dynasty founded (Northern Song 960–1127; Southern Song 1127–1279).

1279   Yuan dynasty (Mongol) founded.

1368   Ming dynasty founded.

1405   The first of seven voyages of Admiral Zheng He (1374–1433, born Ma He) to Southeast Asia, South Asia, the Persian Gulf and East Africa.

1557   China agrees to the Portuguese residing on Macau.

1571   Spain establishes Manila. Start of the Pacific galleon trade from Acapulco.

1644   Qing dynasty (Manchu) founded.

1662   Kangxi becomes emperor.

1683   Qing captures Taiwan from Ming-loyalist rebels and incorporates the island as part of Fujian Province.

1722   Yongzheng becomes emperor.

1735   Qianlong becomes emperor.

1755–60   Wars to suppress the Mongol Zunghar and the final conquest of Xinjiang.

1759   Western trade with China restricted to Guangzhou (Canton).

1770s   White Lotus Sect (*bailian jiao*) becomes active in central-northern China.

1796   Qianlong abdicates, Jiaqing becomes emperor.

           White Lotus Rebellion erupts in central China; suppressed in 1804.

1799	Jiaqing becomes emperor in his own right.
1821	Daoguang becomes emperor; the economy declines.
1839	First Opium War. The Nanjing Treaty of 1842 opened five "treaty ports" to trade. Hong Kong Island ceded to Britain.
1851	Xianfeng becomes emperor. Taiping Rebellion in open revolt in Guangxi Province. Lasts until 1864. Nian Rebellion erupts in eastern and central China. Lasts until 1868.
1854	Miao Rebellion in central and southwestern China. Lasts until 1873.
1858–60	Second Opium War. More treaty ports opened, including inland ports; foreign diplomats allowed to reside in Beijing.
1862	Tongzhi becomes emperor.
1875	Guangxu becomes emperor. Muslim revolts in Gansu and Xinjiang. Lasts until 1884.
1894	First Sino-Japanese War. The 1895 Shimonoseki Treaty allows foreigners to set up manufacturing firms. Taiwan ceded to Japan.
1898	The 100 Day Reform advocated by Kang Youwei and Liang Qichao. Emperor Guangxu introduces wide-reaching changes but soon reversed.
1900	Boxer rebels lay siege to foreigners in Beijing. An eight-nation allied force lifts siege and extracts huge indemnity.
1911–12	Fall of the Qing dynasty. The Republic of China established (governed the China Mainland until 1949) and Sun Yat-sen becomes the first president briefly.
1921	4 May. Peking University and other students march to the foreign legation area to protest the Versailles Treaty that granted Japan control over Germany's possessions in China.
1921	The Communist Party of China (CPC) founded.
1923	The Nationalist Party (Guomindang, aka KMT [Kuomintang]) and CPC agree a United Front to wage war against the warlords.
1927	Chiang Kai-shek turns on the CPC, killing thousands; the CPC retreats to rural areas.
1928	Nationalist Government in Nanjing established, led by Chiang Kai-shek. State-led modernization resumes, overseen by the National Resources Commission (NRC).
1931	*September*: Manchurian Incident – Japan seizes control of Northeast China, which is renamed Manchukuo in 1932.
1932	*January–February*: Japan attacks the Chinese areas of Shanghai. The Nationalists lose many of its best-trained military units.
1934–35	The Long March. Mao Zedong and CPC flee the Jiangxi base to Yan'an, Shaanxi, where they establish their base area government.

1935	Mao Zedong becomes the recognized leader of the CPC during the Long March.
1936	Xian Incident. Chiang Kai-shek is kidnapped and agrees an anti-Japan United Front pact with the CPC.
1937	*July*: Marco Polo Bridge Incident and the start of the Second Sino-Japanese War. *December*: Nanjing Massacre.
1938	Nationalist Government sets up in Chongqing, Sichuan.
1945	Defeat of Japan in the Second World War.
1946	Civil war breaks out between the Nationalists and the Communists.
1949	The Nationalists retreat to southwestern China and finally to Taiwan. *October*: People's Republic of China is formally established.
1950–52	Land reform and other campaigns consolidate CPC rule in China. The Korean War (1950–53) leads to the blockade and isolation of China.
1953	*October*: first five-year plan introduced Soviet-style industrialization and planning, leading to the "socialization" of commerce and industry.
1954	First PRC Constitution.
1956	*May*: "Hundred Flowers Campaign" invites criticism of CPC policies.
1957	*June*: "Anti-rightist Campaign" to crush critical voices. *September–October*: Third Plenum of the Eighth Central Committee (CC) adopts measures that launch the Great Leap Forward (GLF).
1958	GLF, people's communes established and mass mobilization for industrialization.
1959–61	Catastrophic food shortages cause widespread famine and deaths of many millions.
1960	*July*: Soviet Union withdraws all technical staff from China; Sino-Soviet split.
1961	China resumes purchases of wheat on international markets.
1961–64	Recovery programme allows some market-oriented activities.
1962	*October–November*: border war with India in the Himalayas.
1966	*May*: "Great Proletarian Cultural Revolution" launched; "Better Red than Expert"; thousands of "red guards" fan out across China causing destruction and death.
1969	*March*: border war with the Soviet Union pushes the PRC to realign to the West.
1971	*September*: Mao Zedong designated successor and military leader Lin Biao dies in a plane crash in Mongolia while fleeing to the Soviet Union. *October*: PRC is admitted to the United Nations, replaces Taiwan as the recognized government of China.

1972   *February*: US President Richard Nixon visits China.
Premier Zhou Enlai launches the Four Modernizations, a plan to develop agriculture, industry, science and technology, and the military.

1974   *April*: Deng Xiaoping reappears to deliver a speech at the UN.

1976   *January*: Premier Zhou Enlai dies, and Hua Guofeng appointed acting Premier.
September: Chairman Mao Zedong dies. The Gang of Four, the core group under Mao held responsible for the worse of the Cultural Revolution, are arrested in October.

1977   *August*: Eleventh CPC Congress ends the Cultural Revolution. Deng Xiaoping side lines Hua Guofeng and begins to overhaul the party and economy.

1978   *December*: Third Plenum of the Eleventh CPC CC shifts focus of the party to economic reform.

1979   *February–March*: China invades Vietnam but is soon forced to withdraw.
March: Deng proposes the "Four Basic Principles".
The Democracy Wall tests the limits of speech. Wei Jingsheng calls for a fifth modernization, democracy, and is arrested and later imprisonment.

1980   One-child policy introduced. Ended in 2016 with a de facto two-child policy.
China rejoins the World Bank.

1981   *January*: trial of the Gang of Four.
CPC issues Resolution on Party History; the Cultural Revolution labelled a mistake.

1982   Third National Census with assistance of the UN reveals the GLF famine losses.
New PRC Constitution approved by the National People's Congress.

1984   *October*: CPC issues proposal for major urban reforms, "The Decision on Reform of Economic Structure".

1986   China applies to rejoin the General Agreement on Tariffs and Trade, the forerunner of the World Trade Organization (WTO).
December: student protests lead to Hu Yaobang being replaced by Zhao Ziyang as CPC General Secretary.

1987   *October*: Thirteenth CPC Congress supports continued economic reform.

1989   *April*: Hu Yaobang dies, and student demonstrations begin that last to June.
June 3–4: Tiananmen Square Incident. Pro-democracy student protesters and their supporters are cleared from Tiananmen Square in

the centre of Beijing by the military with an unknown number of deaths.

June 23–24: Fourth Plenum of the Thirteenth CPC CC formally removes Zhao Ziyang and installs the former Shanghai party boss Jiang Zemin as CPC General Secretary.

China enters a two-year period of economic stagnation and political suppression.

1991   Collapse of the Soviet Union.

1992   *January–February*: Deng tours southern China and restarts economic reform, coins the "socialist market economy" and signals continuation of market reforms.

October: Fourteenth CPC Congress approves renewed market reforms.

1993   *November*: Third Plenum of the Fourteenth CPC CC adopts the document "Establishment of a Socialist Market Economy".

1994   Fiscal reform: the central government regains control of taxation from the provinces.

1997   *February*: Deng Xiaoping dies.

March: National Basic Research Program (973 Program) unveiled.

July: Hong Kong returns to China.

October: At the Fifteenth CPC Congress Jiang Zemin gives speech on corporate reforms and the acceptance of the private sector.

1998   *March*: Premier Zhu Rongji unveils major reform package for state firms and banks.

2001   General Secretary Jiang Zemin welcomes private sector entrepreneurs into the CPC.

December: China joins the World Trade Organization (WTO).

2002   *October*: Sixteenth CPC Congress; Hu Jiantao becomes the CPC General Secretary.

2003   *March*: Hu Jintao appointed President and Wen Jiabao the Premier at the National People's Congress.

SARS epidemic breaks out and spreads globally.

2006   China overtakes the United States as the largest emitter of carbon dioxide.

Medium to Long-term Plan for Science and Technology announced.

2007   October: Seventeenth CPC Congress adopts Hu Jintao's "scientific outlook on development" and a "harmonious society" as the goal for economic development.

2008   Unrest in Tibet crushed, which provoke international protests against the Olympics.

August: Summer Olympics held in Beijing.

2009   Unrest in Xinjiang. This and Tibet in 2008 leads the CPC to turn back political reform and a renewed emphasis on social stability and party control.

2010   *March*: Wen Jiabao proposes increased spending on and redistribution of wealth.
China overtakes Japan to become the world's second-largest economy.
October: Liu Xiaobo, becomes the first mainland recipient of a Nobel Prize (for Peace).

2012   *March*: Bo Xilai is removed from post as party secretary of Chongqing.
October: Eighteenth CPC Congress. Xi Jinping becomes the CPC General Secretary. Mo Yan, awarded Nobel Prize in Literature.

2013   *March*: NPC installs Li Keqiang as the Premier and Xi Jinping as President.
Xi Jinping unleashes anti-corruption campaign.
"Document 9" stridently attacks liberalism, federalism, Western democracy and other ideas seen as posing a risk to the CPC's historical vision and its future.
September: Xi Jinping unveils his "Belt and Road Initiative" in a visit to Kazakhstan.
November: Third Plenum of the CC reform plan for a greater role for the market.

2014   *October*: Fourth Plenum of the CC endorses programme for the rule of law.

2015   SOE reforms announced; the "Made in China 2025" industrial policy unveiled.
Share market meltdown leads to major state intervention; market reforms put on hold.
October: Tu Youyou awarded the Nobel Prize (Medicine).

2017   *January*: Davos, World Economic Forum, Xi Jinping stakes a claim to be the defender of the global trade system against the US President Donald Trump's "America First".
October: Nineteenth CPC Congress. Party Secretary General Xi Jinping declares China has entered a "New Era". His thoughts are included in the CPC Constitution and he begins a second term without any obvious successor, contrary to recent past practices.

2018   *March*: PRC Constitution is amended to remove the presidential two-terms limit.
The "trade war" with the United States escalates and the US applies punishing tariffs to China's exports.

2020   January: coronavirus outbreak in Wuhan leads China to lockdown the country; spreads globally, causing economic contraction in China and worldwide downturn.

Suggestions for further reading

The literature on contemporary China is enormous. Keeping up with the books, research papers and reportage is nigh impossible. That on China's economy ranges from the highly technical data-driven studies to the glib and ill-informed. Here I will point to selected studies and sources readers might find useful to consult and browse as their interest may lead them. A thematic approach loosely following the chapters is used to order the suggestions.

GENERAL HISTORIES

There are many excellent surveys, including Immanuel Hsü, *The Rise of Modern China* (Oxford: Oxford University Press, 1990); Jonathan D. Spence, *The Search for Modern China* (New York: Norton, 2013); and Jeffrey N. Wasserstrom and Maura E. Cunningham, *China in the 21st Century* (Oxford: Oxford University Press, 2010). History is never far from contemporary politics. For the nineteenth century opium wars, see Julia Lovel, *The Opium War* (London: Picador, 2012); the on-going influence of the 1919 May 4th Movement on Chinese history and politics, and the "New China" of the 1920s and 30s, Rana Mitter, *A Bitter Revolution* (Oxford: Oxford University Press, 2004); and for the tragedy of the 1959–61 Great Leap Forward, Frank Dikötter, *Mao's Great Famine* (London: Bloomsbury, 2010) and Jisheng Yang, *Tombstone* (London: Penguin, 2012), first published in Chinese in 2008.

ECONOMIC HISTORIES

An impressive recent survey is Richard von Glahn, *The Economic History of China, from Antiquity to the Nineteenth Century* (Cambridge: Cambridge University Press, 2016). Valuable surveys include Lloyd Eastman, *Family, Fields and Ancestors* (New York: Oxford University Press, 1988) and Philip Richardson, *Economic Change in*

China, c.1800–1950 (Cambridge: Cambridge University Press, 1990). To put China in the context of the world economy in the second millennium, see Ronald Finlay and Kevin H. O'Rourke, *Power and Plenty* (Princeton, NJ: Princeton University Press, 2007). For the Great Divergence debate, begin with Kenneth Pomeranz, *The Great Divergence* (Princeton, NJ: Princeton University Press, 2000), supplemented with Peer Vries, *State, Economy and the Great Divergence* (London: Bloomsbury, 2015), Loren Brandt, Debin Ma and Thomas G. Rawski's critical survey article (2014), and Jean-Laurent Rosenthal and R. Bin Wong, *Before and Beyond Divergence* (Cambridge, MA: Harvard University Press, 2011). Lastly, keep an eye out for the forthcoming two volumes, *The Cambridge Economic History of China* edited by Debin Ma and Richard von Glahn (Cambridge University Press).

CHINA'S ECONOMY

The most comprehensive textbook survey is Barry Naughton, *The Chinese Economy* (Cambridge, MA: MIT Press, 2018 [2007]). A shorter introduction is Arthur Kroeber, *China's Economy: What Everyone Needs to Know* (Oxford: Oxford University Press, 2016). A comprehensive but dated survey covering the first 25 years of the reform period is Loren Brandt and Thomas G. Rawski (eds), *China's Great Economic Transformation* (Cambridge: Cambridge University Press, 2008). On reform of international trade and investment, see the listed references for Nicholas Lardy (1992, 1994, 2002). For the emergence of the private sector, Victor Nee and Sophia Opper, *Capitalism from Below* (Cambridge, MA: Harvard University Press, 2012) and Nicholas Lardy, *Markets over Mao* (Washington, DC: Peterson Institute, 2014). Recent volumes focused on current economic issues include George Magnus, *Red Flags* (New Haven, CT: Yale University Press, 2018), Dinny McMahon, *China's Great Wall of Debt* (New York: Houghton Mifflin Harcourt, 2018) and Nicholas Lardy, *The State Strikes Back* (Washington, DC: Peterson Institute, 2019).

SOURCES OF ECONOMIC AND OTHER DATA

Official Chinese statistics have been published by the National Statistical Bureau (NSB) in Chinese in the annual *China Statistical Yearbook* (*zhongguo tongji nianjian*) since 1981 and online since 1999 (www.stats.gov.cn), including an English website. A CD-ROM version with the tables in Excel has been available since the late 1990s. Excel tables were also posted to the website with a one-year lag until 2016 but are now only uploaded as image files. The NSB website has monthly data, statistical bulletins, economic news, and an interactive interface to graph data in both Chinese and English. Other agencies issue statistical bulletins on their websites, such as the Ministry of Commerce's trade and investments bulletins (fec.mofcom.gov.cn). Each province also publishes statistics online in a similar format to the NSB, often to the county or district level, but most provinces only provide the data in Chinese.

International agencies publish data on China. The World Bank has open data resources (https://data.worldbank.org/) including the *World Development Indicators* to compare China with other countries since the 1980s across many socioeconomic variables. For international financial statistics, the direction of international trade, and so on, the IMF (International Monetary Fund) data site (https://data.imf.org) is invaluable. The agencies of United Nations also report China data, such as the population projections (http://population.un.org/wpp/) and human development (http://hdr.undp.org/en). Although China is not a member of the Organisation for Economic Cooperation and Development, the OECD (http://www.oecd.org/) publishes reports on China. The CIA *World Factbook* (https://www.cia.gov/library/publications/resources/the-world-factbook/) is a quick reference for China with sections on the economy, government and society, including useful up-to-date world rankings of China, for example, in exports or energy use, among others. An independent scholarly resource is Our World in Data (https://ourworldindata.org), which publishes comparative data on Covid-19, food supply, income, poverty, and many more topics.

PARTY, POLITICS AND GOVERNANCE

The cited Kerry Brown books (2014, 2017, 2018) are accessible studies of the post-2010 communist party, ideologies and personalities. David Shambaugh, *China's Future* (Cambridge: Polity, 2016) is a short but absorbing discussion of the future trajectories of the party. An in-depth study of the party is Richard McGregor, *The Party* (London: Penguin, 2012) and for the wider picture of Chinese government, Tony Saich, *Governance and Politics of China* (London: Palgrave Macmillian, 2015). On the historical rise of the communist party, see Arif Dirlik, *The Origins of Chinese Communism* (Oxford: Oxford University Press, 1989) and James Harrison, *The Long March to Power* (London: Macmillan, 1972). For a forensic look at corruption in the party, see Minxin Pei, *China's Crony Capitalism* (Cambridge, MA: Harvard University Press, 2016) and also the previously mentioned Brown, McMahon, Saich and Shambaugh, as well as the novelist Ma Jian, *China Dream* (London: Chatto & Windus, 2018) for a searing dystopian view of this perennial trait of the party. David Shambaugh, *China Goes Global* (Oxford: Oxford University Press, 2013) is a critical analysis of China's growing international prominence over three decades until about 2012.

CHINESE SOCIETY

Novels and reportage reveal China through stories of lives lived in ways more tangible than most academic studies. Among the many to pick, Peter Hessler, *River Town* (London: Harper, 2001), records his observations and interactions while teaching English in a remote town on the upper Yangzi River in the 1990s; Leslie Chang, *Factory Girls* (New York: Spiegel & Grau, 2008) recounts the lives and dreams of migrant girls in the export factories of South China; Evan Osnos, *Age of*

Ambition (New York: Vintage, 2014) tells the stories of post-2000 Chinese striving for a better life; and Mei Fong, *One Child* (Oxford: Oneworld, 2016) for life, love and parenthood in China when birth was limited to one child, as well as Ma Jian, *The Dark Road* (London: Chatto & Windus, 2013), a novel about a rural couple fleeing from the birth-control authorities in order to have a second child. The increase in religious practices and spirituality since the 1980s is chronicled in Ian Johnson, *The Souls of China* (London: Allen Lane, 2017). Disabilities, long hidden in society, are revealed in Sara Dauncey, *Disability in Contemporary China* (Cambridge: Cambridge University Press, 2020). Gender topics have long been a focus of studies and accounts of the decline in equality include Leta Hong Fincher, *Leftover Women* (London: Zed Books, 2014) and *Betraying Big Brother* (London: Verso, 2018). And for translations into English of trends on social media in China today, *What's on Weibo* (https://www.whatsonweibo.com/).

SCIENCE, TECHNOLOGY AND INNOVATION

For those interested in the history and philosophy of science in China, then start with the volumes begun by Joseph Needham of *Science and Civilization in China* (Cambridge: Cambridge University Press, 1954–), although the abridgements by Colin Ronan are far more accessible. An up-to-date overview of China's challenge to the global science and technology system is Richard Appleton *et al.*, *Innovation in China* (Cambridge: Polity, 2018). For a concise economic analysis of research, science, and technology, see chapter 15 of Barry Naughton's *The Chinese Economy* (2018). The OECD, the United Nation agencies such as WIPO (https://www.wipo.int/portal/en/), the World Bank and other international agencies publish reports or statistics related to R&D, S&T, patents, and innovation in China.

WEBSITES AND NEWSLETTERS

There are many online resources for China, some free and others by subscription, of which some are selected below. *China Leadership Monitor* (CLM; https://www.prcleader.org/), edited by Minxin Pei, reports trends in China's leadership politics and in its foreign and domestic policies, including on the economy. The *Supreme People's Court Monitor* (https://supremepeoplescourtmonitor.com/) is a blog on legal matters by long-time observer Susan Finder. *China Law Translate* (https://www.chinalawtranslate.com/en/) is a collaborative platform to source (unofficial) translations of new laws begun by Jeremy Daum at the Yale China Law Center. *Foreign Policy* has a free weekly *China Brief* (https://foreignpolicy.com/category/china-brief/); the *China Digital Times* (https://chinadigitaltimes.net/) is a bilingual independent media that aggregates news from many resources on China, Taiwan and Hong Kong; *China File* (https://www.chinafile.com/) is an online magazine run by the Center on US–China Relations at the Asia Society. For a subscription-based daily service of news and commentary, including links and extracts to the original Chinese, *Sinocism* (https://sinocism.com) is run by veteran China watcher Bill Bishop, who translated for international media organizations in China in 1989. And if you want to follow the who's who of the rich in China, then go to the *Forbes China Rich List* (https://www.forbes.com/china-billionaires/list/#tab:overall).

References

English-language works will be cited in preference to Chinese except where necessary.

ABC (Australian Broadcasting Corporation) 2019. "Tesla CEO Elon Musk's massive gamble on China could be thwarted by local rivals". 18 April. https://www.abc.net.au/news/2019-04-18/elon-musk-tesla-gamble-on-china-but-will-local-rivals-thwart-him/11003118?pfmredir=sm

Acemoglu, D. & J. Robinson 2012. *Why Nations Fail: The Origins of Power, Prosperity, and Poverty.* New York: Random House.

ACFIC (All China Federation of Industry and Commerce). Various years. "Zhongguo minying qiye 500 qiang yanjiu fenxi baogao (Analytical report on China's top-500 private enterprises)". http://www.acfic.org.cn/.

AFR (*Australian Financial Review*) 2015. "Yancoal chairman boasts of removing 'bossy' director James Mackenzie". 28 April.

Allen, J. 2018. "Accelerating awareness and action on corporate governance in China". https://www.bsr.org/en/our-insights/blog-view/china-corporate-governance-jamie-allen-interview.

Allen, R. 2009. "Agricultural productivity and rural incomes in England and the Yangtze Delta, c.1620–c.1820". *Economic History Review* 62(3), 525–50.

Allen, R. 2011. *Global Economic History: A Very Short Introduction.* Oxford: Oxford University Press.

Allen, R., J.-P. Bassino, D. Ma, C. Moll-Murata & J. van Zanden 2011. "Wages, prices, and living standards in China, 1738–1925: in comparison with Europe, Japan and India". *Economic History Review* 64(1), S8–38.

Alesina, A. & P. Giuliano 2015. "Culture and institutions". *Journal of Economic Literature* 53(4), 898–944.

Amsden, A. 1989. *Asia's Next Giant: South Korea and Late Industrialization*. New York: Oxford University Press.

Appelbaum, R., C. Cao, X. Han, R. Parker & D. Simon 2018. *Innovation in China*. Cambridge: Polity.

Ash, R. 2006. "Squeezing the peasants: grain extraction, food consumption and rural living standards in Mao's China". *China Quarterly* 188, 959–98

Bai, Y. & R. Jia 2016. "Elite recruitment and political stability: the impact of the abolition of China's civil service exam". *Econometrica* 84(2), 677–733.

Bai, Y., S. Zhang, L. Wang, R. Dang, C. Abbey & S. Rozelle 2019. "Past successes and future challenges in rural China's human capital". *Journal of Contemporary China* 28 (120), 883–98.

Balding, C. & D. Clarke 2019. "Who owns Huawei?" Available at SSRN (https://ssrn.com/), Paper No. 3372669.

Banister, J. 1984. "An analysis of recent data on the population of China". *Population and Development Review* 10(2), 241–71.

Banister, J. 1987. *China's Changing Population*. Stanford, CA: Stanford University Press.

Barney, J. 1991. "Firm resources and sustained competitive advantage". *Journal of Management* 17(1), 99–120.

Bassino, J.-P., S. Broadberry, K. Fukao, B. Gupta, M. Takashima 2019. "Japan and the Great Divergence, 730–1874". *Explorations in Economic History* 72(1), 1–22.

Baten, J., D. Ma, S. L. Morgan & Q. Wang 2010. "Evolution of living standards and human capital in China in the 18–20th centuries: evidences from real wages, age-heaping, and anthropometrics". *Explorations in Economic History* 47(3), 347–59.

BBC (British Broadcasting Corporation) 2021. "China's pressure and propaganda: the reality of reporting Xinjiang". 15 January. https://www.bbc.co.uk/news/world-asia-china-55666153.

Bernhofen, D., M. Eberhart, J. Li & S. L. Morgan 2015. "Assessing market (dis) integration in early modern China and Europe". CESifo Working Paper Series No. 5580; available at SSRN: https://ssrn.com/abstract=2694443.

Bian, M. 2002. "The Sino-Japanese War and the formation of the state enterprise system in China: a case study of the Dadukou Iron and Steel Works, 1938–1945". *Enterprise & Society* 3 (March), 80–123.

Bian, M. 2005. *The Making of the State Enterprise System in Modern China: The Dynamics of Institutional Change*. Cambridge, MA: Harvard University Press.

Bisio, V. 2020. "China's Banking Sector Risks and Implications for the United States". US-China Economic and Security Review Commission, Research Report. 27 May. https://www.uscc.gov/sites/default/files/2020-05/Chinas_Banking_Sector_Risks_and_Implications_for_US.pdf.

Bloom, D. & J. Williamson 1998. "Demographic transitions and economic miracles in emerging Asia". *World Bank Economic Review* 12(3), 419–55.

BP 2019. *BP Statistical Review of World Energy*. 68th edition, June 2019. Data tables available at http://www.bp.com/statisticalreview.

Brandt, L. & T. G. Rawski (eds) 2008. *China's Great Economic Transformation*. Cambridge: Cambridge University Press.

Brandt, L. & T. G. Rawski 2008. "China's great economic transformation". In Brandt & Rawski (eds), *China's Great Economic Transformation*, 1–26.

Brandt, L. & E. Thun 2016. "Constructing a ladder for growth: policy, markets and industrial upgrading in China". *World Development* 80, 78–95.

Brandt, L., C.-t. Hsieh & X. Zhu 2008. "Growth and structural transformation in China." In Brandt and Rawski (eds), *China's Great Economic Transformation*, 263–78.

Brandt, L., D. Ma & T. G. Rawski 2014. "From divergence to convergence: reevaluating the history behind China's economic boom". *Journal of Economic Literature* 52(1), 45–123.

Brandt, L., D. Ma & T. G. Rawski 2017 "Industrialization in China". In K. O'Rourke & J. Williamson (eds), *The Spread of Modern Industry to the Global Periphery Since 1871*, 197–228. Oxford: Oxford University Press.

Brautigam, D. 2009. *The Dragon's Gift: The Real Story of China in Africa*. Oxford: Oxford University Press.

Breznitz, D. & M. Murphree 2011. *Run of the Red Queen: Government, Innovation, Globalization and Economic Growth in China*. New Haven, CT: Yale University Press.

Broadberry, S. N. & J. Wallis 2017. "Growing, shrinking and long-run economic performance: historical perspectives on economic development". Discussion Paper in Economic and Social History No. 154, University of Oxford; https://www.economics.ox.ac.uk/oxford-economic-and-social-history-working-papers/growing-shrinking-and-long-run-economic-performance-historical-perspectives-on-economic-development.

Broadberry, S. N., H. Guan & D. Li 2018. "Europe, and the Great Divergence: a study in historical national accounting, 980–1850". *Journal of Economic History* 78(4), 955–1000.

Brown, K. 2014. *The New Emperors: Power and the Princelings in China*. London: I. B. Tauris.

Brown, K. 2017. *CEO, China: The Rise of Xi Jinping*. London: I. B. Tauris.

Brown, K. 2018. *China's Dream: The Culture of Chinese Communism and the Secret Sources of its Power*. Cambridge: Polity.

Cai, F. 2016. *China's Economic Growth Prospects: From Demographic Dividend to Reform Dividend*. Cheltenham: Elgar.

Cai, F. & Y. Lu 2013. "The end of China's demographic dividend: the perspective of potential GDP growth". In F. Cai, R. Garnaut & L. Song (eds), *China: A New Model for Growth and Development*, 55–74. Canberra: Australian National University.

Cai, F., A. Park & Y. Zhao 2008. "The Chinese labor market in the reform era". In Brandt & Rawski (eds), *China's Great Economic Transformation*, 167–214.

Cai, R., J. Tang, C. Deng, G. Lü, X. Xu, S. Sylvia & J. Pan 2019. "Violence against health care workers in China, 2013–2016: evidence from the national judgment documents". *Human Resources for Health* 17, 103.

Cai, Y. 2013. "China's new demographic reality: learning from the 2010 census". *Population and Development Review* 39(3), 371–96.

Caixin Global 2020. "Fallen energy conglomerate CEFC declared bankrupt". 24 April; https://www.caixinglobal.com/2020-04-25/fallen-energy-conglomerate-cefc-declared-bankrupt-101547143.html.

Calabrese, L. & X. Tang 2020. "Africa's economic transformation: the role of Chinese investment". DFID-ESRC Growth Research Programme Report, June; https://degrp.odi.org/publication/africas-economic-transformation-the-role-of-chinese-investment/.

CARI (China Africa Research Initiative) 2020. "Loan data". China Africa Research Initiative, School of Advances International Studies, Johns Hopkins University; http://www.sais-cari.org/data.

CBRC (China Bank Regulatory Commission) 2019. *Commercial Banks Major Indicators*. http://www.cbrc.gov.cn/.

Chan, K. Y. 2006. *Business Expansion and Structural Change in Pre-war China: Liu Hongsheng and his Enterprises, 1920–1937*. Hong Kong: Hong Kong University Press.

Chan, K. Y. 2018. *Urbanization with Chinese Characteristics: The Hukou System and Migration*. London: Taylor & Francis.

Chan, K. W. 2019. "China's *hukou* system at 60: continuity and reform", In Yep, Wang & Johnson (eds), *Handbook on Urban Development in China*, 59–79.

Chang, J. K. 1969. *Industrial Development in Pre-Communist China, 1912–1949*. Edinburgh: Edinburgh University Press.

Chen, J. 2015. *A Primer on Corporate Governance: China*. New York: Business Expert Press.

Chen, J. & B. J. Dickson 2008. "Allies of the state: democratic support and regime support among China's private entrepreneurs". *China Quarterly* 196, 780–804.

Chen, M.-J. 2001. *Inside Chinese Business: A Guide for Managers Worldwide*. Cambridge, MA: Harvard University Press.

Chen, S. & M. Ravallion 1999. "When economic reform is faster than statistical reform: measuring and explaining income inequality in rural China". *Oxford Bulletin of Economics and Statistics* 61(1), 33–66.

Chi, W. & B. Li 2008. "Glass ceiling or sticky floor? Examining the gender earnings differential across the earnings distribution in urban China, 1987–2004". *Journal of Comparative Economics* 36(2), 243–63.

Chi, W. & B. Li 2014. "Trends in China's gender employment and pay gap: estimating gender pay gaps with employment selection". *Journal of Comparative Economics* 42(3), 708–25.

China Daily 2015. "Change of leadership at Big Three telecoms". 24 August; http://www.chinadaily.com.cn/business/2015-08/24/content_21686239.htm.

China Daily 2019a. "China passes US on Fortune Global 500 for first time". 22 July; https://www.chinadaily.com.cn/a/201907/22/WS5d3566f4a310d8305640055c.html.

China Daily 2019b. "Huawei heads list of China's top 500 private firms". 22 August; https://www.chinadailyhk.com/articles/22/177/55/1566466905229.html.

China Daily 2020. "CPC membership tops 91 million". 30 June; https://www.chinadaily.com.cn/a/202006/30/WS5efb0400a310834817256354.html.

Chowdhury, A. & I. Islam 1993. *The Newly Industrialising Economies of East Asia*. London: Routledge.

Chung, W. K. & G. G. Hamilton 2001. "Social logic as business logic: Guangxi, trustworthiness, and the embeddedness of Chinese business practices". In R. Appelbaum, W. Felster & V. Gessner (eds), *Rules and Networks: The Legal Culture of Global Business Transactions*, 325–46. Oxford: Hart.

CIA (Central Intelligence Agency). Various years. *CIA World Factbook*. https://www.cia.gov/library/publications/resources/the-world-factbook/.

Clark, D. 2016. *Alibaba: The House that Jack Ma Built*. New York: Harper Collins.

Cochran, S. (ed.) 1999. *Inventing Nanjing Road: Commercial Culture in Shanghai, 1900–1945*. Ithaca, NY: Cornell University Press.

Cochrane, S. 2000. *Encountering Chinese Networks: Western, Japanese and Chinese Corporations in China, 1880–1937*. Berkeley, CA: University of California Press.

Collier, A. 2018. *China Buys the World: Analyzing China's Overseas Investments*. London: Palgrave Pivot.

CPC (Communist Party of China). Official website: http://cpc.people.com.cn for records of the party congresses, membership of committees, etc.

CPC. Various years. Documents and other details of historical meetings of the CPC National Party Congresses: http://cpc.people.com.cn/GB/64162/64168/415039/index.html.

CPC General Office 2013. "Communiqué on the current state of the ideological sphere", known as "Document 9", 22 April 2013. Translation available at: https://www.chinafile.com/document-9-chinafile-translation.

CPC General Office 2020. "Guangyu jiaqiang xinshidai minying jingji tongzhan gongzuo de yijian (Opinion on strengthening United Front work of the private economy in the New Era)". 15 September; http://www.gov.cn/ zhengce/2020-09/15/content_5543685.htm.

Craft, N. 2018. *Forging Ahead, Falling Behind and Fighting Back: British Economic Growth from the Industrial Revolution to the Financial Crisis*. Cambridge: Cambridge University Press.

CSY (*China Statistical Yearbook*). National Bureau of Statistics (NSB). Various years. *Zhongguo tongji nianjian* (*China Statistical Yearbook*). Beijing: Statistical Press. Available since 1999 on the NSB website: http://www.stats.gov.cn/. English version: http://www.stats.gov.cn/english/Statisticaldata/AnnualData/. See also entry NSB.

Dauncey, S. 2020. *Disability in Contemporary China: Citizenship, Identity and Culture*. Cambridge: Cambridge University Press.

de Trenck, C., A. Daswani, C. A. Katz & D. Sakma 1998. *Red Chips: And the Globalization of China's Enterprises*. Seattle, WA: University of Washington Press.

Deng, P. 2000. "Taiwan's restriction of investment in China in the 1990s: a relative gains approach". *Asian Survey* 40(6), 958–80.

Dickson, B. J. 2007. "Integrating wealth and power in China: the Communist Party's embrace of the private sector". *China Quarterly* 192, 827–54.

Dickson, B. J. 2008. *Wealth into Power: The Communist Party's Embrace of China's Private Sector*. Cambridge: Cambridge University Press.

The Diplomat 2014. "No one who bought Alibaba stock actually owns Alibaba". 24 September.

Eastman, L. E. 1988. *Family, Fields, and Ancestors: Constancy and Change in China's Social and Economic History, 1550–1949*. New York: Oxford University Press.

The Economist 2010a. "Made in China". 12 March.

The Economist 2010b. "Keqiang ker-ching: how China's next prime minister keeps tabs on its economy". 9 December.

The Economist 2012a. "Where's the party?". 28 January.

The Economist 2012b. "The end of cheap China". 10 March.

The Economist 2015. "Still made in China". 10 September.

The Economist 2017. "A legal vulnerability at the heart of China's big internet firms". 16 September.

The Economist 2020a. "Blooming for the glory of the state". 15 August.

The Economist 2020b. "Ant's jumbo IPO". 10 October.

The Economist 2020c. "Torment of the Uyghurs and the global crisis in human rights". 17 October.

The Economist 2021. "The great mall of China". 2 January.

Economy, E. 2004. *The River Runs Black: The Environmental Challenge to China's Future*. Ithaca, NY: Cornell University Press.

Economy, E. 2018. *The Third Revolution: Xi Jinping and the New Chinese State*. New York: Oxford University Press.

Economy, E. & M. Levi 2018. *By All Means Necessary: How China's Resource Quest is Changing the World*. New York: Oxford University Press.

Elman, B. A. 2000. *A Cultural History of Civil Examinations in Late Imperial China*. Berkeley, CA: University of California Press.

Elman, B. A. 2005. *On Their Own Terms: Science in China, 1550–1900*. Cambridge, MA: Harvard University Press.

Elliot, M. C. 2001. *The Manchu Way: The Eight Banners and Ethnic Identity in Late Imperial China*. Stanford, CA: Stanford University Press.

Elliott, M. C. 2009. *Emperor Qianlong: Son of Heaven, Man of the World*. New York: Pearson.

Elvin, M. 1973. *The Pattern of the Chinese Past*. Stanford, CA: Stanford University Press.

Elvin, M. 2004. *The Retreat of the Elephants: An Environmental History of China*. New Haven, CT: Yale University Press.

EVvolume.com 2020. The Electric Vehicles World Sales Database. http://www.ev-volumes.com/.

Feuerwerker, A. 1958. *China's Early Industrialization, Shen Hsuan-huai (1844–1916) and Mandarin Enterprise*. Cambridge, MA: Harvard University Press.

Financial Times 2014. "Alibaba IPO shows foreign investors able to skirt restrictions". 7 May.

Financial Times 2019. "Shares on China tech exchange surge in trading debut". 22 July.

Financial Times 2020a. "Luckin Coffee ousts chief executive over accounts scandal". 12 May.

Financial Times 2020b. "US Senate passes bill that puts some Chinese listings at risk". 20 May.

Financial Times 2020c. "Global investors prepare to brave China's green bond minefield". 5 June.

Financial Times 2020d. "The mystery document holding up the sale of Anbang hotels". 11 June.

Financial Times 2020e. "Bankers hunt for NY-listed Chinese companies to bring 'home' to Hong Kong". 19 June.

Financial Times 2020f. "Luckin Coffee investors oust founder". 6 July.

Financial Times 2020g. "China allows first commercial bank to go bankrupt in nearly 20 years". 7 July.

Financial Times 2020h. "Chinese state seizes control of 9 insurers, trusts and brokers". 17 July.

Financial Times 2020i. "Rogue tycoon shareholders spur China's financial sector cleanup". 23 July.

Financial Times 2020j. "China's share of global exports fall in supply chain rethink". 17 August.

Financial Times 2020k. "Ant Group: Jack the giant-maker". 25 August.

Financial Times 2020l. "Ant Group files for dual listing". 25 August.

Financial Times 2020m. "Xi Jinping critic sentenced to 18 years in prison". 22 September.

Financial Times 2020n. "The great uncoupling: one supply chain for China, one for everywhere else". 6 October.

Financial Times 2020o. "African debt to China: 'a major drain on the poorest countries'". 26 October.

Financial Times 2020p. "Alibaba's shares tumbled after $37bn Ant IPO halted at eleventh hour". 4 November.

Financial Times 2020q. "How Jack Ma lost his spot at China's top business table". 7 November.

Financial Times 2020r. "China's industrial production rises at fastest rate this year". 15 December.

Financial Times 2020s. "China rethinks the Jack Ma model". 18 December.

Financial Times 2021a. "NYSE reverses plan to delist Chinese telecoms groups". 5 January.

Financial Times 2021b. "'They threatened to storm in': Hong Kong's dawn raids on activists". 8 January.

Financial Times 2021c. "Taiwan manufacturers quit China over trade tensions and rising costs". 11 January.

Financial Times 2021d. "Jack Ma vs Xi Jinping: the future of private business in China". 12 January.

Financial Times 2021e. "UK companies face fines over 'slave labour' China suppliers". 12 January.

Findlay, R. & K. J. O'Rourke 2007. *Power and Plenty: Trade, War, and the World Economy in the Second Millennium*. Princeton, NJ: Princeton University Press.

Floud, R., R. W. Fogel, B. Harris & S. C. Hong 2011. *The Changing Body: Health, Nutrition, and Human Development in the Western World since 1700*. New York: Cambridge University Press.

Fong, M. 2016. *One Child: Life, Love and Parenthood in Modern China*. London: Oneworld.

Forbes Magazine. Various years. "Forbes China Rich List". https://www.forbes.com/china-billionaires/list/.

Forbes Magazine. Various years. "Forbes World Billionaires List". https://www.forbes.com/billionaires/.

Fortune Magazine. Various years. "Fortune Global 500 List". www.fortune.com/global500.

Francks, P. 2016. *Japan and the Great Divergence: A Short Guide*. London: Palgrave Macmillan.

French, H. 2014. *China's Second Continent: How a Million Migrants are Building a New Empire in Africa*. New York: Knopf.

French, P. 2010. *Fat China: How Expanding Waistlines are Changing a Nation*. London: Anthem Press.

Fu, X. & P. Ghauri 2020. "Trade in intangibles and the global trade imbalance". *World Economy*.(in press: DOI: 10.1111/twec.13038).

Fuller, D. B. 2016. "China's political economy: prospects for technological innovation-based growth". In Lewin, Kenny & Murman (eds), *China's Innovation Challenge*, 121–51.

Gao, P. 2015. "Risen from chaos: the development of modern education in China, 1905–1948". PhD dissertation, Department of Economic History, London School of Economics.

Garnaut, J. 2012. *The Rise and Fall of the House of Bo*. Melbourne: Penguin.

Garnaut, J. 2017. "Engineers of the soul: ideology in Xi Jinping's China". An internal Australian government seminar held in August 2017, reproduced in the Sinocism Newsletter, January 2019; https://sinocism.com/p/engineers-of-the-soul-ideology-in.

Gerlach, M. L. 1992. *Alliance Capitalism: The Social Organization of Japanese Business*. Berkeley, CA: University of California Press.

Gewirtz, J. 2017. *Unlikely Partners: Chinese Reformers, Western Economists, and the Making of Global China*. Cambridge, MA: Harvard University Press.

Global Times 2016. "Xi vows to reinforce traditional family values". 14 December; https://www.globaltimes.cn/content/1023566.shtml.

Gold, T., D. Guthrie & D. Wank (eds) 2002. *Social Connections in China: Institutions, Culture, and the Changing Nature of Guanxi*. Cambridge: Cambridge University Press.

Green, S. 2004. *The Development of China's Stock Market, 1984–2002*. London: Routledge Curzon.

Griffin, K. & R. Zhao (eds) 1993. *The Distribution of Income in China*. New York: St Martin's Press.

Gulati, R., N. Nohria & A. Zaheer 2000. "Strategic networks". *Strategic Management Journal* 21, 203–15.

Gustafsson, B. & S. Li 2003. "The ethnic minority–majority income gap in rural China during transition". *Economic Development and Cultural Change* 51(4), 805–22.

Gustafsson, B. & S. Ding 2014. "Why is there no income gap between the Hui Muslim minority and the Han majority in rural Ningxia, China?" *China Quarterly* 220, 968–87.

Guthrie, D. 1999. *Dragon in A Three-Piece Suit: The Emergence of Capitalism in China*. Princeton, NJ: Princeton University Press.

Haggard, S. 1990. *Pathways from the Periphery: The Politics of Growth in the Newly Industrializing Countries*. Ithaca, NY: Cornell University Press.

Haggard, S. & Y. Huang 2008. "The political economy of private sector development in China". In Brandt & Rawski (eds), *China's Great Economic Transformation*, 337–74.

Han, J., Q. Zhao & M. Zhang 2016. "China's income inequality in the global context". *Perspectives in Science* 7, 24–9.

Han, S., R. Green & M. Y. Wang (eds) 2015. *Towards Low Carbon Cities in China: Urban Form and Greenhouse Gas Emissions*. Abingdon: Routledge.

Harrell, S. (ed.) 1995. *Cultural Encounters on China's Ethnic Frontiers*. Seattle, WA: University of Washington Press.

Hatch, W. & K. Yamamura 1996. *Asia in Japan's Embrace: Building Regional Production Networks*. Cambridge: Cambridge University Press.

Heckman, J. J. 2005. "China's human capital investment." *China Economic Review* 16, 50–70.

Heckman, J. J. & J. Yi 2012. "Human capital, economic growth and inequality in China". NBER Working Paper No. 18100. Cambridge: National Bureau of Economic Research.

Helvestona, J. P., Y. Wang, V. Karplus, E. Fuchs 2019. "Institutional complementarities: the origins of experimentation in China's plug-in electric vehicle industry". *Research Policy* 48, 206–22.

Hershatter, G. 1986. *The Workers of Tianjin, 1900–1949*. Stanford, CA: Stanford University Press.

Holtz, C. 2014. "Can we trust the numbers?" *China Economic Quarterly* (March), 43–50.

Hong Fincher, L. 2014. *Leftover Women: The Resurgence of Gender Inequality in China*. London: Zed Books.

Hong Fincher, L. 2018. *Betraying Big Brother: The Feminist Awakening in China*. London: Verso.

Honig, E. 1986. *Sisters and Strangers: Women in the Shanghai Cotton Mills, 1919–1949*. Stanford, CA: Stanford University Press.

Hsü, I. C. Y. 1990. *The Rise of Modern China*. Fourth edition. New York: Oxford University Press.

Hu, A. G. Z., P. Zhang & L. Zhao 2017. "China as number one? Evidence from China's most recent patenting surge". *Journal of Development Economics* 124, 107–19.

Huang, J., K. Otsuka & S. Rozelle 2008. "Agriculture in China's development: past disappointments, recent success, and future challenges". In Brandt & Rawski (eds), *China's Great Economic Transformation*, 467–505.

Huang, P. C. C. 1985. *The Peasant Economy and Social Change in North China*. Stanford, CA: Stanford University Press.

Huang, P. C. C. 1990. *The Peasant Family and Rural Development in the Yangzi Delta, 1350–1988*. Stanford, CA: Stanford University Press.

Huenemann, R. W. 1984. *The Dragon and the Iron Horse: The Economics of Railroads in China, 1876–1937*. Cambridge, MA: Harvard University Press.

Hurun Research Institute. Various years. Hurun Global Rich List. http://www.hurun.net/EN/Article/Details?num=2B1B8F33F9C0.

Hurun Research Institute 2020. "Hurun China 500 most valuable private companies 2019". https://www.hurun.net/EN/Article/Details?num=3E542F6FBA3D.

IMF (International Monetary Fund). Various years. *Direction of Trade Statistics*. Online version. http://data.imf.org.

IMF 2020. "World Economic Outlook Update, June 2020". https://www.imf.org/en/Publications/WEO/Issues/2020/06/24/WEOUpdateJune2020.

Jacobs, J. 1984. *Cities and the Wealth Nations: Principles of Economic Life*. New York: Random House.

Jamison, D. T. 1986. "Child malnutrition and school performance in China". *Journal of Development Economics* 20, 299–309.

Ji, C. & T. O. Cheng 2008. "Prevalence and geographic distribution of childhood obesity in China in 2005". *International Journal of Cardiology* 131(1), 1–8.

Ji, C. & T. O. Cheng 2009. "Epidemic increase in overweight and obesity in Chinese children from 1985 to 2005". *International Journal of Cardiology* 132(1), 1–10.

Ji, Y., X. Wu, S. Sun & G. He 2017. "Unequal care, unequal work: toward a more comprehensive understanding of gender inequality in post-reform urban China". *Sex Roles* 77, 765–78.

Jia, R. 2013. "Weather shocks, sweet potatoes and peasant revolts in historical China". *Economic Journal* 124, 92–118.

Jiang, K. 2017. "Technological progress in developing renewable energies". *Australian Economic Review* 50(4), 469–77.

Jiang, R., H. Shi & G. H. Jefferson 2020. "Measuring China's international technology catchup". *Journal of Contemporary China* 29(124), 519–43.

Jin, S. & W. Xu 1986. *Zhongguo tielu fazhan shi (1876–1949)* [A History of the Development of Chinese Railways (1876–1949)]. Beijing: Zhongguo tiedao.

Johnson, C. 1982. *MITI and the Japanese Miracle: The Growth of Industrial Policy*. Stanford, CA: Stanford University Press.

Johnson, N. D. & M. Koyama 2019. *Persecution and Toleration: The Long Road to Religious Freedom*. New York: Cambridge University Press.

Jones, E. L. 1987. *The European Miracle: Environments, Economics and Geopolitics in the History of Europe and Asia*. Second edition. Cambridge: Cambridge University Press.

Khan, M. & S. Zheng 2016. *Blue Skies Over Beijing: Economic Growth and the Environment in China*. Princeton, NJ: Princeton University Press.

Kanbur, R., Y. Wang, X. Zhang 2017. "The great Chinese inequality turnaround". CEPR Discussion Paper No. 11892; https://cepr.org/active/publications/discussion_papers/dp.php?dpno=11892.

Khor, N., L. Pang, C. Liu, F. Chang, D. Mo, P. Loyalka & S. Rozelle 2016 "China's looming human capital crisis: upper secondary educational attainment rates and the middle-income trap". *China Quarterly* 228, 905–26.

Kilduff, M. & W. Tsai 2003. *Social Networks and Organizations*. London: Sage.

Kim, E. M. & J. S. Ma 2006. "Patterns of South Korea's foreign direct investment flows into China". *Asian Survey* 46(6), 881–97.

Kirby, W. C. 1990. "Continuity and change in modern China: economic planning on the mainland and Taiwan, 1943–1958". *Australian Journal of Chinese Affairs* 24, 121–41.

Kirby, W. C. 1992. "The Chinese war economy". In J. Hsiung & S. Levine (eds), *China's Bitter Victory: The War with Japan 1937–1945*, 185–212. New York: M. E. Sharpe.

Kishimoto, M 2010 [1997]. *Qing dai zhongguo de wujia yu jingji bodong* [Qing China prices and economic fluctuations]. Trans. Liu Diyu. Beijing: Social Sciences Press.

Kroeber, A. R. 2016. *China's Economy: What Everyone Needs to Know*. New York: Oxford University Press.

Kuznets, S. 1955. "Economic growth and income inequality". *American Economic Review* 45(1), 1–28.

The Lancet 2020. Editorial "Protecting Chinese doctors". *The Lancet* 395 (10218), 90, 11 January.

Landa, J. T. 1994. *Trust, Ethnicity, and Identity: Beyond the New Institutional Economics of Ethnic Trading Networks, Contract Law, and Gift-Exchange*. Ann Arbor, MI: University of Michigan Press.

Landes, D. S. 1969. *The Unbound Prometheus*. Cambridge: Cambridge University Press.

Landes, D. S. 1998. *The Wealth and Poverty of Nations: Why Some Are So Rich and Some So Poor*. New York. Norton.

Lau, L. J. & L. R. Klein 1990 [1986]. *Models of Development: A Comparative Study of Economic Growth in South Korea and Taiwan*. San Francisco: ICS Press.

Lardy, N. R. 1983. *Agriculture in China's Modern Economic Development*. New York: Cambridge University Press.

Lardy, N. R. 1992. *Foreign Trade and Economic Reform in China*. Washington, DC: Institute for International Economics.

Lardy, N. R. 1994. *China in the World Economy*. Washington, DC: Institute for International Economics.

Lardy, N. R. 2002. *Integrating China into the Global Economy*. Washington, DC: Brookings Institution Press.

Lardy, N. R. 2014. *Markets over Mao: The Rise of Private Business in China*. Washington, DC: Peterson Institute for International Economics.

Lardy, N. R. 2019. *The State Strikes Back: The End of Economic Reform in China?* Washington, DC: Petersen Institute for International Economics.

Leutert, W. 2016. "Challenges ahead in China's reform of state-owned enterprises". *Asia Policy* 21 (January), 83–99.

Levine, S. I. 1992. "Introduction". In J. Hsiung & S. Levine (eds), *China's Bitter Victory: The War with Japan 1937–1945*, xvii–xxv. New York: M. E. Sharpe.

Lewin, A. Y., M. Kenny & J. P. Murman (eds) 2016. *China's Innovation Challenge: Overcoming the Middle-Income Trap*. Cambridge: Cambridge University Press.

Li, H., L. Meng, Q. Wang, L.-A. Zhou 2008. "Political connections, financing and firm performance: evidence from Chinese private firms". *Journal of Development Economics* 76, 283–99.

Li, B. 1998. *Agricultural Development in Jiangnan, 1620–1850*. London: Macmillan Press.

Li, B. & J. van Zanden 2012. "Before the Great Divergence? Comparing the Yangzi Delta and the Netherlands at the beginning of the nineteenth century". *Journal of Economic History* 72(4), 956–89.

Li, C. 2016. "Holding 'China Inc.' together: the CCP and the rise of China's *Yangqi*". *China Quarterly* 228: 927–49.

Li, Q., S. Li & H. Wan 2020. "Top incomes in China: data collection and the impact on income inequality". *China Economic Review* 62; https://doi.org/10.1016/j.chieco.2020.101495.

Li, S., T. Sicular & F. Tarp 2018. "Inequality in China: development, transition and policy". WIDER Working Paper 2018/174. United Nations World Institute for Development Economics Research.

Li, S. & H. Wan 2015. "Evolution of wealth inequality in China". *China Economic Journal* 8(3), 264–87.

Lin, J. Y. F. 1995. "The Needham puzzle: why the industrial revolution did not originate in China". *Economic Development and Cultural Change* 43(2), 269–92.

Lin, L.-W. 2017. "Reforming China's state-owned enterprises: from structure to people". *China Quarterly* 229, 1–23.

Lin, L.-W. & C. J. Milhaupt 2013. "We are the (national) champions: understanding the mechanisms of state capitalism in China". *Stanford Law Review* 65, 697–759.

Li, Y., C. Zhan, M. de Jong & Z. Lukszo 2016. "Business innovation and government regulation for the promotion of electric vehicle use: lessons from Shenzhen, China". *Journal of Cleaner Production* 134 (Part A), 371–83.

Liu, T.-c. & K.-c. Yeh 1965. *The Economy of the Chinese Mainland: National Income and Economic Development, 1933–1959*. Princeton, NJ: Princeton University Press.

Liu, W. G. 2015. *The Chinese Market Economy, 1000–1500*. Albany, NY: SUNY Press.

Liu, G., W. Dow, A. Fu, J. Akin, P. Lance 2008. "Income productivity in China: on the role of health". *Journal of Health Economics* 27(1), 27–44.

Lo, K. & M. Y. Wang 2015. "Low carbon policies and programs in China". In Han, Green & Wang (eds), 21–50.

Lo, Kevin, M. Y. Wang, B. Qin and S. H. Han. 2015. "Low carbon city development in China." In Han, Green and Wang, (eds) *Towards Low Carbon Cities in China*, 51–75.

Lovell, J. 2012. *The Opium War: Drugs, Dreams and the Making of China*. London: Picador.

Lü, X. & E. J. Perry (eds) 1997. *Danwei: The Changing Chinese Workplace in Historical and Comparative Perspective*. New York: M. E. Sharpe.

Luo, C., S. Li & T. Sicular 2018. "The long-term evolution of income inequality and poverty in China". WIDER Working Paper 2018/153. United Nations World Institute for Development Economics Research.

Luo, Y. 2003. "Industrial dynamics and managerial networking in an emerging market: the case of China". *Strategic Management Journal* 24: 1315–27.

Luo, Y. 2007. *Guanxi and Business*. Singapore: World Scientific.

Ma, D. 2008. "Economic growth in the lower Yangzi region of China in 1911–1937: a quantitative and historical analysis". *Journal of Economic History* 68(2), 355–92.

Ma, J. 2017. *The Economics of Air Pollution in China: Achieving Better and Cleaner Growth*. Trans. B. Cleary. New York: Columbia University Press. Originally published in Chinese in 2014.

Ma, J. 2018. *China Dream*. Trans. Flora Drew. London: Chatto & Windus.

Maddison, A. 2001. *The World Economy: A Millennial Perspective*. Paris: OECD.

Maddison, A. 2007. *Contours of the World Economy 1–2030 AD: Essays in Macro-Economic History.* Oxford: Oxford University Press.

Maddison, A. 2010. "Statistics on world population, GDP and per capita GDP, 1–2008 AD". Groningen Growth and Development Centre; http://www.ggdc.net/MADDISON/oriindex.htm.

Magnus, G. 2018. *Red Flags: Why Xi's China is in Jeopardy.* New Haven, CT: Yale University Press.

McGregor, R. 2012. *The Party: The Secret World of China's Communist Rulers.* Revised edition. London: Penguin.

McMahon, D. 2018. *China's Great Wall of Debt: Shadow Banks, Ghost Cities, Massive Loans, and the End of the Chinese Miracle.* Boston, MA: Houghton Mifflin Harcourt.

Miles, L. 2006. "The application of Anglo-American corporate practices in societies influenced by Confucian values". *Business and Society Review* 111(3), 305–21.

Millward, J. 1998. *Beyond the Pass: Economy, Ethnicity, and Empire in Qing Central Asia.* Stanford, CA: Stanford University Press.

Minami, R. 1986. *The Economic Development of Japan: A Quantitative Study.* Basingstoke: Macmillan.

Minzer, C. 2018. *End of an Era: How China's Authoritarian Revival is Undermining its Rise.* New York: Oxford University Press.

MofCom (Ministry of Commerce – Foreign Investment and Economic Cooperation). Various years. *Statistical Bulletin.* http://fec.mofcom.gov.cn/article/tjsj/tjgb/.

Mohan, G., B. Lampert, M. Tan-Mullins & D. Chang 2014. *Chinese Migrants and Africa's Development: New Imperialists or Agents of Change?* London: Zed Books.

Morgan, S. L. 1994. "The impact of the growth of township enterprises on rural-urban transformation in China, 1978–1991". In A. Dutt, F. Costa, S. Aggarwal & A. Nobel (eds), *Asian City: Processes of Development, Characteristics and Planning*, 213–36. Dordrecht: Kluwer Academic.

Morgan, S. L. 2000. "Richer and taller – stature and the standard of living in China, 1979–1995". *China Journal* 44, 1–39.

Morgan, S. L. 2004a. "Economic growth and the biological standard of living in China, 1880–1930". *Economics and Human Biology* 2(2), 197–218.

Morgan, S. L. 2004b. "Professional associations and the diffusion of new management ideas in Shanghai, 1920–30s – a research agenda". *Business and Economic History Online* 2; http://www.thebhc.org/publications.

Morgan, S. L. 2006. "Transfer of Taylorism to China, 1910s–1930s". *Journal of Management History* 12(4), 408–24.

Morgan, S. L. & S. Liu 2007. "Was Japanese colonialism good for the welfare of the Taiwanese? Stature and the standard of living". *China Quarterly* 192, 990–1017.

Morgan, S. L. 2009a. "Stature and economic development in South China, 1810–1880". *Explorations in Economic History* 46(1), 53–69.

Morgan, S. L. 2009b. "Selling Chinese dreams: fashion, culture and discourse in advertising in China between the two world wars". Available at SSRN: https://ssrn.com/abstract=1524855 or http://dx.doi.org/10.2139/ssrn.1524855.

Morgan, S. L. & F. Su 2011. "Regional inequalities in China – a non-monetary view". In S. Yao, B. Wu, S. Morgan & D. Sutherland (eds), *Sustainable Reform and Development in Post-Olympic China*, 38–59. London: Routledge.

Morgan, S. L. 2014. "Growing fat on reform: obesity and nutritional disparities among Chinese children, 1979–2005". *China Quarterly* 220, 1033–68.

Morgan, S. L. 2018. "Ethnic, regional and nutritional disparities in China, 1985–2014". World Economic History Congress, Boston, 3 August, Session #030220.

Morrisson, C. & F. Murtin 2009. "The century of education". *Journal of Human Capital* 3(1), 1–42.

Mokyr, J. 2002. *The Gifts of Athena: Historical Origins of the Knowledge Economy*. Princeton, NJ: Princeton University Press.

Mokyr, J. 2017. *Culture of Growth: The Origins of the Modern Economy*. Princeton, NJ: Princeton University Press.

Mullaney, T. 2010. *Coming to Terms with the Nation: Ethnic Classification in Modern China*. Berkeley, CA: University of California Press.

Naquin, S. & E. S. Rawski 1987. *Chinese Society in the Eighteenth Century*. New Haven, CT: Yale University Press.

NSB (National Statistics Bureau of China). Bilingual website: www.stats.gov.cn.

NSB (formerly State Statistical Bureau). 1981–present. *Zhongguo tongji nianjian* (*Chinese Statistical Yearbook*). Beijing: Statistical Press. In the text abbreviated as "CSY year".

NSB 2020a. "Households' income and consumption expenditure in 2019". 19 January; http://www.stats.gov.cn/english/PressRelease/202001/t20200119_1723719.html.

NSB 2020b. "Statistical Communiqué of the People's Republic of China on the 2019 National Economic and Social Development". 28 February; http://www.stats.gov.cn/english/PressRelease/202002/t20200228_1728917.html.

NSB 2020c. "Announcement of the National Bureau of Statistics on the Final Verification of GDP in 2019". 30 December; http://www.stats.gov.cn/english/PressRelease/202012/t20201231_1811928.html.

Naughton, B. 1988. "The third front: defence industrialisation in the Chinese interior". *China Quarterly* 115, 351–86.

Naughton, B. 1995. *Growing Out of the Plan: Chinese Economic Reform 1978–1993*. Cambridge: Cambridge University Press.

Naughton, B. 2008. "A political economy of China's economic transition". In Brandt & Rawski (eds), *China's Great Economic Transformation*, 91–135.

Naughton, B. 2018. *The Chinese Economy*. Second edition. Cambridge, MA: MIT Press.

Nee, V. & S. Opper, 2012. *Capitalism from Below: Markets and Institutional Change in China*. Cambridge, MA: Harvard University Press.

Needham, J. 1969. *The Grand Titration: Science and Society in East and West*. London: Allen & Unwin.

Nikkei Asian Review 2020. "Calls for 'China exit' mounts as Japan reviews economic security". 12 May; https://asia.nikkei.com/Politics/Inside-Japanese-politics/Calls-for-China-exit-mount-as-Japan-reviews-economic-security.

North, D. C. 1990. *Institutions, Institutional Change and Economic Performance*. Cambridge: Cambridge University Press.

OECD 2018. *Education at a Glance 2018: OECD Indicators*. Paris: OECD. http://dx.doi.org/10.1787/eag-2018-en.

OECD 2019. "PISA [Programme for International Student Assessment] 2018 Results". https://www.oecd.org/pisa/publications/pisa-2018-results.htm.

Park, S. & Y. Luo 2001. "Guanxi and organizational dynamics: organizational networking in Chinese firms". *Strategic Management Journal* 22(5), 455–77.

Pei, M. 2016. *China's Crony Capitalism: The Dynamics of Regime Decay*. Cambridge, MA: Harvard University Press.

Peng, M. & Y. Luo 2000. "Managerial ties and firm performance in a transition economy: the nature of a micro-macro link". *Academy of Management Journal* 43(3), 486–501.

Peng, M. W. & J. Zhou 2005. "How network strategies and institutional transitions evolve in Asia". *Asia Pacific Journal of Management* 22, 321–36.

Penn World Tables, version 9.0. Groningen Growth and Development Centre, Faculty of Economics and Business, University of Groningen. https://www.rug.nl/ggdc/productivity/pwt/.

Perdue, P. C. 2005. *China Marches West: The Qing Conquest of Central Eurasia*. Cambridge, MA: Harvard University Press.

Pettis, M. 2019. "What is GDP in China?" *China Financial Markets*. Carnegie Endowment. https://carnegieendowment.org/chinafinancialmarkets/78138.

Pomeranz, K. 2000. *The Great Divergence: China, Europe, and the Making of the Modern World Economy*. Princeton, NJ: Princeton University Press.

Ranis, G. (ed.) 1992. *Taiwan, From Developing to Mature Economy*. London: Routledge.

Rawski, T. G. 1989. *Economic Growth in Prewar China*. Berkeley, CA: University of California Press.

Rawski, T. G. 2001a. "What's happening to China's GDP statistics?" *China Economic Review* 12(4), 347–54.

Rawski, T. G. 2001b. "China by the numbers: how reform has affected China's economic statistics" *China Perspectives* 33, 25–34.

Redding, S. G. 1990. *The Spirit of Chinese Capitalism*. Berlin: de Gruyter.

Reuters 2015. "China's state-owned telecoms firms shuffle top executives". 24 August; https://www.reuters.com/article/china-mobile-managementchanges/update-1-chinas-state-owned-telecoms-firms-shuffle-top-executives-idUSL4N10Z20520150824.

Reuters 2018. "China's CEFC chairman investigated for suspected economic crimes: source". 1 March; https://www.reuters.com/article/us-china-cefc-probe-idUSKCN1GD3O9.

Richardson, P. 1999. *Economic Change in China c.1800–1950*. Cambridge: Cambridge University Press.

Riskin, C. 1987. *China's Political Economy: The Quest for Development since 1949*. New York: Oxford University Press.

Riskin, C., R. Zhao & S. Li (eds) 2001. *China's Retreat from Equality: Income Distribution and Economic Transition*. New York: M. E. Sharpe.

Roberts, D. 2020. *The Myth of Chinese Capitalism: The Worker, the Factory, and the Future of the World*. New York: St Martin's Press.

Rock, M. T. & M. A. Toman 2015. *China's Technological Catch-up Strategy: Industrial Development, Energy Efficiency, and CO2 Emissions*. New York: Oxford University Press.

Rosenthal, J.-L. & R. Wong 2011. *Before and Beyond Divergence: The Politics of Economic Change in China and Europe*. Cambridge, MA: Harvard University Press.

Rowe, W. T. 1984. *Hankow: Commerce and Society in a Chinese City, 1796–1889*. Stanford, CA: Stanford University Press.

Rozman, G. 1974. *Urban Networks in Ch'ing China and Tokugawa Japan*. Princeton, NJ: Princeton University Press.

Rubin, J. 2017. *Rulers, Religion, and Riches: Why the West Got Rich and the Middle East Did Not*. New York: Cambridge University Press.

Saich, T. 2015. *Governance and Politics of China*. Fourth edition. London: Palgrave Macmillan.

Sanderson, H. & M. Forsythe 2013. *China's Superbank: Debt, Oil and Influence – How China Development Bank is Rewriting the Rules of Finance*. Singapore: Wiley.

SASAC (State-own Assets Supervision and Administration of the State Council). Chinese website: http://www.sasac.gov.cn/; English website: http://en.sasac.gov.cn/.

SCMP (*South China Morning Post*) 2015a. "Xu Caihou: the general who rose up the ranks but fell from grace". 17 March; https://www.scmp.com/news/china/article/1739577/xu-caihou-general-who-rose-ranks-fell-grace.

SCMP (*South China Morning Post*) 2015b. "Ex-PLA chief Guo Boxiong to be prosecuted for allegedly accepting bribes for promotions". 30 July; https://www.scmp.com/news/china/policies-politics/article/1845230/ex-pla-chief-guo-boxiong-be-prosecuted-allegedly.

SCMP (*South China Morning Post*) 2015c. "China's disgraced PLA general Gu Junshan given suspended death sentence for corruption". 10 August; https://www.scmp.com/news/china/policies-politics/article/1848264/chinas-disgraced-pla-general-gu-junshan-given-suspended.

SCMP (*South China Morning Post*) 2018a. "China must stop fooling itself it is a world leader in science and technology, magazine editor says". 26 June; http://www.scmp.com/news/china/society/article/2152617/china-must-stop-fooling-itself-it-world-leader-science-and.

SCMP (*South China Morning Post*) 2018b. "China detains oil entrepreneur, wiping US$153 million off stocks". 1 March; https://www.scmp.com/business/companies/article/2135238/china-detain-cefc-founder-ye-jianming-stocks.

SCMP (*South China Morning Post*) 2020a. "Is China rich or poor? Nation's wealth debate muddied by conflicting government data". 29 May; https://www.scmp.com/economy/china-economy/article/3086678/china-rich-or-poor-nations-wealth-debate-muddied-conflicting.

SCMP (*South China Morning Post*) 2020b. "Is China rich enough to claim a 'well-off society'? One ex-official says grand economic goal can wait". 28 July; https://www.scmp.com/economy/china-economy/article/3095038/china-rich-enough-claim-well-society-one-ex-official-says.

SCMP (*South China Morning Post*) 2020c. "Obesity rises in China as unhealthy lifestyles take toll". 24 December; https://www.scmp.com/news/china/science/article/3115151/obesity-rises-china-unhealthy-lifestyles-take-toll.

SCMP (*South China Morning Post*) 2021. "Ex-chairman of China Huarong Asset Management sentenced to death for bribery". 5 January; https://www.scmp.com/news/china/politics/article/3116534/ex-chairman-china-huarong-asset-management-sentenced-death.

Shambaugh, D. 2013. *China Goes Global: The Partial Power*. New York: Oxford University Press.

Shambaugh, D. 2016. *China's Future?* Cambridge: Polity.

Shiue, C. H. & W. Keller 2007. "Markets in China and Europe on the eve of the industrial revolution". *American Economic Review* 97(4), 1189–216.

Shleifer, A. & R. Vishny 1997. "A survey of corporate governance". *Journal of Finance* 52(2), 737–83.

Simon, D. 2018. "China's international S&T relations: collaboration, cooperation and competition". UNNC, 7 March 2018.

Skinner, G. W. (ed.) 1977. *The City in Late Imperial China*. Stanford, CA: Stanford University Press.

Skinner, G. W. 1987. "Sichuan's population in the nineteenth century: lessons from disaggregated data". *Late Imperial China* 8(1), 1–79.

Smith, A. [1776] 1852. *An Inquiry into the Nature and Causes of Wealth of Nations*. London: Nelson.

Snape, H. 2019. "Social management or social governance: a review of party and government discourse and why it matters in understanding Chinese politics". *Journal of Chinese Political Science* 24, 687–99.

Snape, H. & W. Wang 2020 "Finding a place for the Party: debunking the "party-state" and rethinking the state-society relationship in China's one-party system". *Journal of Chinese Governance*. DOI: 10.1080/23812346.2020.1796411.

Spence, J. D. 2013. *The Search for Modern China*. Third edition. New York: Norton.

Stanton, E. A. 2011. "Greenhouse gases and human well-being: China in a global perspective". In F. Gang *et al.* (eds), *The Economics of Climate Change in China: Towards a Low-Carbon Economy*. 105–22. London: Earthscan.

State Council, PRC. Official website: www.gov.cn. English: http://english.www.gov.cn/statecouncil.

State Council 2012. "State Council circular on energy saving and new energy vehicle industry development plans (2012–2020)" (in Chinese). http://www.gov.cn/zwgk/2012-07/09/content_2179032.htm.

State Council 2015. "State Council circular on 'Made in China 2025'" (in Chinese). http://www.gov.cn/zhengce/content/2015-05/19/content_9784.htm.

State Council 2018. The State Council website, "China's National Status (*guoqing*)"; http://www.gov.cn/guoqing/index.htm. The constitution (*xianfa*), March 2018 (in Chinese); http://www.gov.cn/guoqing/2018-03/22/content_5276318.htm. English official translation of the 2004 version at http://english.www.gov.cn/archive.

Steidlmeirer, P. 1999. "Gift giving, bribery and corruption: Ethical management of business in China". *Journal of Business Ethics* 20, 121–31.

Student Survey 1979. Zhongguo kexue jishu qingbao yanjiuzuo (China scientific-technical intelligence research institute) (eds), *Kexue jishu chengguo baogao: Zhongguo qingshaonian ertong shenti xingtai, jineng yu shuzhide yanjiu* (*Scientific-technical report: Research on the physique, functions and quality of Chinese youth and children*). Beijing: Kexue jishu wenxian chubanshe, 1982.

Student Survey 1985. Zhongguo xuesheng tizhi yu jiankang yanjiuzu (Chinese student physique and health research group) (eds), *Zhongguo xuesheng tizhi yu jiankang yanjiu* (*Research on the physique and health of Chinese students*). Beijing: Renmin jiaoyu chubanshe, 1988.

Student Survey 2014. Zhongguo xuesheng tizhi yu jiankang diaoyanzu (eds),

2014 nian Zhongguo xuesheng tizhi yu jiankang diaoyan baogao (Report on the Physical Fitness and Health Surveillance of Chinese School Students, 2014). Beijing: Gaodeng jiaoyu chubanshe, 2016.

Tang, J. & A. Ward 2003. *The Changing Face of Chinese Management.* London: Routledge.

Taylor, M. Z. 2016. *The Politics of Innovation: Why Some Countries are Better than Others at Science and Technology.* New York: Oxford University Press.

Timmer, M. P., A. E. Erumban, B. Los, R. Stehrer & G. J. de Vries 2014. "Slicing up global value chains". *Journal of Economic Perspectives* 28(2), 99–118.

Tse, E. 2015. *China's Disruptors: How Alibaba, Xiaomi, Tencent and Other Companies are Changing the Rules of Business.* London: Portfolio Penguin.

United Nations, Department of Economic and Social Affairs, Population Division (2019). *World Population Prospects 2019*, online edition; http://www.un.org/en/development/desa/population/.

Van Slyke, L. 1986. "The Chinese communist movement during the Sino-Japanese War 1937–1945". In J. Fairbank & A. Feuerwerker (eds), *The Cambridge History of China, Vol. 13: Republican China 1912–1949, Part 2*, 609–722. Cambridge: Cambridge University Press.

Vestal, J. 1993. *Planning for Change: Industrial Policy and Japanese Economic Development, 1945–1990.* Oxford: Clarendon Press.

Vogel, E. 1991. *The Four Little Dragons: The Spread of Industrialization in East Asia.* Cambridge, MA: Harvard University Press.

von Glahn, R. 1996. *Fountain of Fortune: Money and Monetary Policy in China, 1000–1700.* Berkeley, CA: University of California Press.

von Glahn, R. 2016. *The Economic History of China: From Antiquity to the Nineteenth Century.* Cambridge: Cambridge University Press.

Vries, P. 2015. *State, Economy and the Great Divergence: Great Britain and China, 1680s–1850s.* London: Bloomsbury.

Wade, R. 1990. *Governing the Market: Economic Theory and the Role of Government in East Asian Industrialisation.* Princeton, NJ: Princeton University Press.

Wang, F. 2005. "Can China afford to continue its one-child policy?" *Asia Pacific Issues* 77 (March). Honolulu: East-West Center; www.eastwestcenter.org/publications/can-china-afford-continue-its-one-child-policy.

Wang, L., M. Li, C. Abbey & S. Rozelle 2018. "Human capital and the middle income trap: how many of China's youth are going to high school?" *Developing Economies* 56(2), 82–103.

Wang, Y.-c. 1992. "The secular trend of rice prices in the Yangzi Delta, 1638–1935". In T. Rawski & L. Li (eds), *Chinese History in Economic Perspective*, 35–68. Berkeley, CA: University of California Press.

Wang, Y.-c. 2003. *Qingdai jingjishi lunwenji* [*Essays on the Economic History of the Qing Dynasty*]. Taipei: Daoxiang Press.

Weidenbaum, M. L. & S. Hughes 1996. *The Bamboo Network: How Expatriate Chinese Entrepreneurs Are Creating a New Economic Superpower in Asia*. New York: Free Press.

Williamson, O. E. 1981. "The economics of organization: the transaction cost approach". *American Journal of Sociology* 87(3), 548–77.

Williamson, O. 1986. *The Economic Institutions of Capitalism*. London: Macmillan.

Wong, R. 1997. *China Transformed: Historical Change and the Limits of European Experience*. Ithaca, NY: Cornell University Press.

Wong, S.-l. 1985. "The Chinese family firm: a model". *British Journal of Sociology* XXXVI(1), 58–72.

WHO (World Health Organisation), Expert Consultation Group 2004. "Appropriate body-mass index for Asian populations and its implications for policy and intervention strategies". *Lancet* 363, 157–63.

WHO 2007a. "The WHO Child Growth Standards". http://www.who.int/childgrowth/en/.

WHO 2007b. "Growth reference data for 5–19 years". http://www.who.int/growthref/en/.

World Bank. Various years. *World Development Report* [Includes the World Development Indicators]. New York: Oxford University Press.

World Bank. "World Development Indicators Database". Online, revision accessed is shown in the table or figure. http://databank.worldbank.org.

World Bank 1993. *The East Asian Miracle: Economic Growth and Public Policy*. New York: Oxford University Press.

World Bank 2013 [2012]. *China 2030: Building a Modern, Harmonious, and Creative Society*. Washington, DC: World Bank. Prepared in collaboration with the National Development Research Center of the State Council, PRC. The February 2012 report released in Beijing is now available as the "final edition", published in March 2013;https://www.worldbank.org/en/news/feature/2012/02/27/china-2030-executive-summary

World Bank 2020a. "2021 International Debt Statistics". https://datatopics.worldbank.org/debt/ids/. December.

World Bank 2020b. "2020 Year in Review: The impact of COVID-19 in 12 charts". 14 December; https://blogs.worldbank.org/voices/2020-year-review-impact-covid-19-12-charts.

World Bank 2021. *Global Economic Prospects*. 5 January; https://www.worldbank.org/en/publication/global-economic-prospects.

WSC (World Shipping Council) 2019. "Top 50 world container ports".

http://www.worldshipping.org/about-the-industry/global-trade/top-50-world-container-ports.

WSJ (*Wall Street Journal*) 2020. "Africa's first pandemic default tests new effort to ease debt from China". 18 November.

WSJ (*Wall Street Journal*) 2021. "China allows WHO experts in to investigate Covid-19 origins". 11 January.

Wu, C. [1999] 2012. "Jingji fazhan, zhidu bianqian he shehui yu sixiang bianqian de guanxi" [The relationship between ideological evolution and economic development, institution change and society]. In C. Wu (ed.), *Jingjishi Lilun yu Shizheng* [*Economic History Theory and Empirics*], 289–92. Zhejiang University Press.

Wu, F. 2015. *Planning for Growth: Urban and Regional Planning in China*. New York: Routledge.

Wu, H. X. 2014. "China's growth and productivity debate revisited: accounting for China's sources of growth with a new data set". The Conference Board Economic Programme Working Paper Series #14-01, January.

Xi, J. 2014. *Governance of China*. Beijing: Foreign Language Press.

Xi, J 2017. *Governance of China, II*. Beijing: Foreign Language Press.

Xin, K. & J. L. Pearce 1996. "Guanxi: connections as substitutes for formal institutional support". *Academy of Management Journal* 39(6), 1641–58.

Xinhua 2020. "Xi announces major victory in poverty alleviation". 4 December; http://www.xinhuanet.com/english/2020-12/04/c_139561739.htm.

Xu, D. & C. Wu [1985] 2007. *Zhongguo zibenzhuyi fazhan shi, yi, Zhongguo zibenzhuyi de mengya* [*Development of Chinese Capitalism, Vol. 1, The Sprouts of Capitalism*]. Beijing: China Academy of Social Sciences Press.

Xue, M. M. & M. Koyama 2018. "Autocratic rule and social capital: evidence from imperial China". Available at SSRN: https://ssrn.com/abstract=2856803.

Yancoal Australia. Website: https://www.yancoal.com.au/.

Yang, H. & S. L. Morgan 2011. *Business Strategy and Corporate Governance in the Chinese Consumer Electronics Sector*. Oxford: Chandos Publishing.

Yang, M. 1994. *Gifts, Favors, and Banquets: The Art of Social Relationships in China*. Ithaca, NY: Cornell University Press.

Yamazawa, I. 1990. *Economic Development and International Trade: The Japanese Model*. Honolulu: East-West Centre.

Yeh, W.-h. 1995. "Corporate space, communal time: everyday life in Shanghai's Bank of China". *American Historical Review* 100(1), 97–122.

Yep, R., J. Wang & T. Johnson (eds) 2019. *Handbook on Urban Development in China*. Cheltenham: Elgar.

Yue, A., Y. Shi, R. Luo, J. Chen; J. Garth; J. Zhang; A. Medina, S. Kotb & S. Rozelle

2017. "China's invisible crisis: cognitive delays among rural toddlers and the absence of modern parenting". *China Journal* 78, 50–80.

Yip, G. & B. McKern 2016. *China's Next Strategic Advantage: From Imitation to Innovation*. Cambridge, MA: MIT Press.

Zenz, A. 2020. "Coercive labor in Xinjiang: labor transfer and the mobilization of ethnic minorities to pick cotton". Center for Global Policy, 14 December; https://cgpolicy.org/briefs/coercive-labor-in-xinjiang-labor-transfer-and-the-mobilization-of-ethnic-minorities-to-pick-cotton/.

Zhang, J. 2017. "The evolution of China's one-child policy and its effects on family outcomes". *Journal of Economic Perspectives* 31(1), 141–59.

Zhang, L., R. LeGates & M. Zhao 2016. *Understanding China's Urbanization: The Great Demographic, Spatial, Economic and Social Transformation*. Cheltenham: Elgar.

Zhang, X. & R. Kanbur 2005. "Spatial inequality in education and health care in China". *China Economic Review* 16, 189–204.

Zhang, X. 2019. "Transformation of Chinese cities and city regions in the era of globalisation". In Yep *et al.* (eds), *Handbook on Urban Development in China*, 137–54.

Zhang, X., H. Wasserman & W. Mano (eds) 2016. *China's Media and Soft Power in Africa*. London: Palgrave Macmillan.

Zhao, R. 2001. "Increasing income inequality and its causes in China". In Riskin, Zhao & Li (eds), 25–43.

Zhao, S. & S. L. Morgan 2016. "Business to government networks in resource acquisition: the case of Chinese private enterprises". In J. Nolan, C. Rowley & M. Warner (eds), *Business Networks in East Asian Capitalisms: Enduring Trends, Emerging Patterns*, 69–91. Kidlington: Elsevier.

Zhao, S. & S. L. Morgan 2019. "Political strategies of Chinese private entrepreneurs: managing party-state networks". Available from ResearchGate.

Zhao, Z., A. Hayes & D. Goodkind 2018. *Routledge Handbook of Asian Demography*. New York: Routledge.

Zhou, K. 1996. *How the Farmers Changed China: Power of the People*. Boulder, CO: Westview.

Index

Note: *italic* page numbers indicate figures; **bold** page numbers indicate tables; numbers in brackets preceded by *n* refer to notes.